Awakening Africa's Sleeping Giant

Awakening Africa's Sleeping Giant

Prospects for Commercial Agriculture in the Guinea Savannah Zone and Beyond

THE WORLD BANK
Washington, DC, USA

FAO
Rome, Italy

World Bank
ISBN: 978-0-8213-7941-7
eISBN: 978-0-8213-7942-4
DOI: 10.1596/978-0-8213-7941-7

FAO
ISBN: 978-92-5-106304-0

Cover photo: © FAO / Alessandra Benedetti.

Cataloging-in-Publication data for this title is available from the Library of Congress.

Contents

Boxes

Figures

Tables

Acknowledgments

This report is one of several outputs of the study on Competitive Commercial Agriculture for Africa (CCAA). The CCAA study was a collaborative effort involving researchers from many organizations, working under the guidance of a team made up of staff from the Sustainable Development Network (SDN) of the World Bank and the Investment Center (TCIS) of the United Nations (UN) Food and Agriculture Organization (FAO). Funding for the study was provided by the government of Italy, Ministry of Foreign Affairs, Directorate General for Development Cooperation (through the Italian Special Contribution to the FAO Trust Fund for Food Security and Food Safety); the World Bank; FAO; the United Kingdom (U.K.) Department for International Development (DFID); and the Canadian International Development Association (CIDA).

The World Bank staff who contributed to the overall CCAA study included Michael Morris (Task Team Leader), Hans Binswanger, Sergio Margulis, Loraine Ronchi, Chris Jackson, Derek Byerlee, Paula Savanti, Rob Townsend, Malick Antoine, Paavo Eliste, Eduardo da Souza, Pedro Arlindo, Lucas Akapa, Azra Lodi, Hawanty Page, and Patrice Sade. The FAO staff included Turi Fileccia, Claudio Gregorio, Guy Evers, Merritt Cluff, Holger Matthey, Jennifer Nyberg, Adam Prakash, Nancy Morgan, Gregoire Tallard, Abdolreza Abbassian, Conception Calpe, Peter Thoenes, and Marianne El Metni.

This synthesis report draws extensively on about 30 background papers and notes prepared by the following authors: John Keyser (Consultant, Lusaka, Zambia); Rudy van Gent (Agridev, Lusaka, Zambia); Colin Poulton, Geoff Tyler, Andrew Dorward, Peter Hazell, Jonathan Kydd, and Mike Stockbridge (Centre for Development, Environment and Policy, School of Oriental and African Studies, University of London); Pasquale De Muro, Elisabetta Martone, Lucia Lombardo, Lucia Russo, Sara Gorgoni, and Laura Silici Riccardo Bocci (Roma Tre University, Rome); Benchaphun Ekasingh, Chapika Sangkapitux, Jirawan Kitchaicharoen, and Pornsiri Suebpongsang (Chiang Mai University, Chiang Mai, Thailand); Geraldo Sant'Ana de Camargo Barros, Lucilio Rogério Aparecido Alves, Humberto Francisco Spolador, Mauro Osaki, Daniela Bacchi Bartholomeu, Andreia Cristina De Oliveira Adami, Simone Fioritti Silva, Guilherme Bellotti de Melo, and Matheus Henrique Scaglica P. de Almeida (University of São Paulo, Brazil); Aderibigbe Olomola (Nigeria Institute of Social and Economic Research, Ibadan); and Peter Coughlin (AgriConsultants, Maputo, Mozambique).

Jeff Lecksell of the World Bank Map Design Unit prepared the maps, based on information provided by Zhe Guo and Stanley Wood of the International Food Policy Research Institute (IFPRI).

Preparation of this CCAA synthesis report was coordinated by a small team comprising Michael Morris, Hans Binswanger, Derek Byerlee, and Paula Savanti (World Bank) and John Staatz (Michigan State University).

Abbreviations

AET	Agricultural education and training
ALRO	Agricultural Land Reform Office (Thailand)
BAAC	Bank for Agriculture and Agricultural Cooperatives (Thailand)
CAADP	Comprehensive Africa Agricultural Development Programme
CCAA	Competitive Commercial Agriculture for Africa
CDC	Commonwealth Development Corporation
CIAT	Centro Internacional de Agricultura Tropical (International Center for Tropical Agriculture)
CIMMYT	Centro Internacional de Mejoramiento de Maís y Trigo (International Maize and Wheat Improvement Center)
DFID	Department for International Development (United Kingdom)
DoAE	Department of Agricultural Extension (Thailand)
DRC	Domestic resource cost
ECF	Emerging commercial farms
EMBRAPA	Empresa Brasileira de Pesquisa Agropequária (Brazilian Agricultural Research Corporation)
EU	European Union
FAM	Family farms

FAO   Food and Agriculture Organization (of the United Nations)
FAOSTAT   FAO Statistical Database
FCRC   Field Crops Research Center (Rayong, Thailand)
GCI   Global Competitiveness Index
GDP   Gross domestic product
HIV/AIDS   Human immunodeficiency virus/acquired
            immunodeficiency syndrome
IITA   International Institute of Tropical Agriculture
IFPRI   International Food Policy Research Institute
LCF   Large commercial farms
LTP   Land Titling Program (Nigeria)
LUA   Land Use Act (Nigeria)
NARS   National Agricultural Research Service
NEPAD   New Partnership for Africa's Development
NERICA   New Rice for Africa
NGO   Nongovernmental organization
OECD   Organisation for European Co-operation and Development
R&D   Research and development
RID   Royal Irrigation Department (Thailand)
SDN   Sustainable Development Network (World Bank)
SV   Shipment value
T&V   Training and visit
TCIS   FAO Investment Center
U.K.   United Kingdom
USAID   United States Agency for International Development
WARDA   Africa Rice Center
WDR   *World Development Report*

Executive Summary

For the foreseeable future, reducing poverty in Africa will depend largely on stimulating agricultural growth. Within agriculture, a powerful driver of growth is commercial agriculture. Commercial agriculture can develop along a number of pathways, yet many developing regions have not progressed very far along any of these. African agriculture continues to lag, as reflected in the erosion during the past 30 years in the international competitiveness of many traditional African export crops, as well as in the competitiveness of some food crops for which import dependence has increased. In contrast, over the same period two relatively backward and landlocked agricultural regions in the developing world—the Cerrado region of Brazil and the Northeast Region of Thailand—have developed at a rapid pace and conquered important world markets. Their success defied the predictions of many skeptics, who had asserted that the two regions' challenging agroecological characteristics, remote locations, and high levels of poverty would prove impossible to overcome.

Perceptions similar to those that fueled pessimism 30 years ago in Brazil and Thailand also fueled pessimism in Africa up until recently. However, two recent developments have led to a change in thinking about the potential of African agriculture.

First, during the past decade, strong agricultural growth has been recorded in many African countries, suggesting that the sector can indeed be a driver of growth when the conditions are right.

Second, the steep rise in prices of food and agricultural commodities that occurred in 2008 has led to a realization that new opportunities may be opening for countries that are endowed with the land, labor, and other resources needed to respond to the growing demand for food and biofuels feedstocks.

This report summarizes the findings of the study on Competitive Commercial Agriculture for Africa (CCAA). The objective of the CCAA study was to explore the feasibility of restoring international competitiveness and growth in African agriculture through the identification of products and production systems that can underpin rapid development of a competitive commercial agriculture. The CCAA study focused on the agricultural potential of Africa's Guinea Savannah zone, which covers about 600 million hectares in Africa, of which about 400 million hectares can be used for agriculture, and of which less than 10 percent are cropped. The African Guinea Savannah is one of the largest underused agricultural land reserves in the world. In terms of its agroclimatic features, the land is similar to that found in the Cerrado region of Brazil and in the Northeast Region of Thailand, with medium-to-high agricultural potential but also significant constraints in the form of infertile soils and variable rainfall.

Based on a careful examination of the factors that contributed to the successes achieved in Brazil and Thailand, as well as comparative analysis of evidence obtained through detailed case studies of three African countries—Mozambique, Nigeria, and Zambia—this report argues that opportunities abound for farmers in Africa to regain international competitiveness, especially in light of projected stronger demand in world markets for agricultural commodities over the long term. This provides reasons for optimism regarding the future prospects for agriculture as a major source of inclusive growth in many parts of Africa. At the same time, the report concludes that success will not be achieved easily. Making African agriculture competitive will depend on getting policies right, strengthening institutions, and increasing and improving investments in the sector. Recent progress observed in a number of African countries, while encouraging, is still very tenuous and could easily be reversed by bad policy choices. The recent global food crisis, while it has created opportunities for African producers, has also engendered calls for quick-fix responses that could undermine competitiveness over the longer term.

The CCAA study included components that were backward looking, seeking to learn lessons from the past, and components that were forward looking, seeking to apply those lessons in the context of the changing economic environment. The backward-looking components included detailed analyses of the Thailand and Brazil "success stories," as well as a broad review of the successes and failures that have resulted from past attempts to introduce commercial agriculture in different parts of Africa. The forward-looking components included analysis of projected global supply and demand trends for six internationally traded commodities of importance to the Guinea Savannah zone: cassava, cotton, maize, soybeans, rice, and sugar. Supply chain analysis was carried out in the three African case study countries to assess their competitiveness in producing one or more of the six target commodities; identify constraints that may be inhibiting competitiveness; and identify areas in which policy reforms, institutional changes, and/or supporting investments can improve future competitiveness. In addition to addressing competitiveness issues, the study also assessed the potential social and environmental impacts of agricultural commercialization in the three African case study countries.

The CCAA study addressed the following main questions:

- To what extent can African countries with agroecological endowments similar to those of Brazil's Cerrado region and the Northeast Region of Thailand become more locally, regionally, and globally competitive in selected agricultural commodities?
- What sorts of investments, policy reforms, institutional changes, and technological innovations would be necessary to replicate in Africa the successes recorded in Brazil and Thailand?
- Can increases in agricultural competitiveness in the African Guinea Savannah, based on expanded commercial agriculture, be achieved in a way that substantially reduces poverty?
- What are the potential environmental and social impacts of expanding commercial agriculture in the African Guinea Savannah?

Looking Backward: The Experiences of Brazil's Cerrado and Northeast Thailand

The agricultural commercialization experiences of the Cerrado region of Brazil and the Northeast Region of Thailand share a number of striking commonalities. Both regions started out with limited agricultural potential and poor infrastructure, and until quite recently both were characterized as economically "backward." Yet they showed remarkable, sustained growth over a 40-year period, allowing them to become highly competitive in world markets. Producers in both regions initially concentrated on commodities that are traded internationally in large quantities and for which quality standards are relatively unimportant. In Brazil, the transformation was led by soybeans, production of which jumped from 250,000 metric tons in 1961 to more than 30 million metric tons in 2000. In the Northeast Region of Thailand, cassava led the export takeoff, with the country's production (heavily concentrated in the Northeast) rising from 1.7 million metric tons in 1961 to 20.7 million metric tons in 1996. Successes were achieved later in other commodities (for example, rice in Brazil, rice and maize in Thailand).

In both cases, international competitiveness was achieved in stages: only after competitiveness had been established in low-value commodities was it also achieved in higher-value commodities, including many that are processed (for example, sugar, soybean oil, cotton lint, cassava starch, and cattle). Brazilian and Thai farmers initially were able to expand production by focusing on specific markets in which they enjoyed de jure or de facto preferential access. Later, when the quantities being produced had increased to such an extent that economies of scale could be captured, they were able to establish themselves as low-cost global producers who could compete in virtually all markets. The Brazilians achieved these market successes by relying on large-scale mechanized production methods, whereas agriculture in the Northeast Region of Thailand was and still is essentially the domain of smallholders.

Supply-side factors as well as demand-side factors contributed to the success in both cases. In the Cerrado, the supply-side factors included (a) improved agricultural technology developed by Empresa Brasileira de Pesquisa Agropequária (Brazilian Agricultural Research Corporation; EMBRAPA); (b) publicly financed infrastructure, rural credit, and business development services; (c) the entrepreneurial know-how of highly skilled farmers from the southern part of the country who migrated to the Cerrado in response to the government's colonization strategy; and (d) a supportive policy environment, brought about by a series of economic and political reforms enacted during the mid-1990s that improved the investment climate and permitted the direct transmission of international market signals to farmers in the Cerrado. These supply-side factors, combined with strong growth in global demand for soybeans and soybean-derived products beginning in the

1970s, resulted in the spectacular transformation of the Cerrado into a leading global supplier of soybeans.

In the Northeast Region of Thailand, the export revolution was similarly driven by a combination of supply-side and demand-side factors. Supply-side factors included (a) improved agricultural technologies; (b) availability of previously uncultivated land, combined with permissive government land policies, that allowed farmers to expand cultivated area rapidly in response to market opportunities; (c) government investment in rail and road infrastructure that reduced costs of market access; and (d) a dynamic private sector that was able to respond quickly to market signals, paving the way for rapid supply response. As in Brazil, these supply-side factors combined with strong export demand, which in Thailand's case resulted from growth in the European Union (EU) of demand for cassava pellets as an inexpensive substitute for cereal-based livestock feed. The resulting spectacular expansion of cassava production in northeast Thailand sparked broader agricultural and economic growth extending throughout the region.

Looking Forward: Factors Affecting Agricultural Competitiveness in the African Guinea Savannah

Value chain analysis helped identify the factors that affect the current and potential future competitiveness of the African CCAA case study countries in six commodities that are well-suited to the Guinea Savannah zone—cassava, cotton, maize, rice, soybeans, and sugar. Six key insights emerged concerning the current and likely future competitiveness of the African case study countries:

Farm-level production costs in Africa are competitive. Farm-level unit production costs in the Guinea Savannah zones of Mozambique, Nigeria, and Zambia generally are comparable to or lower than those in the Brazilian Cerrado and in the Northeast Region of Thailand, even though yields per hectare realized in the African countries are significantly lower. The competitiveness of Africa's producers at the farm level derives mainly from very low returns to labor (reflecting the absence of alternative employment opportunities in rural areas) and limited use of purchased inputs (which results in significant soil nutrient mining). Although the African countries are currently competitive in terms of farm-level production costs, this competitiveness does not represent a sustainable path out of poverty, because at current productivity levels and farm size, agriculture is economically impoverishing and technically unsustainable.

The challenge facing African countries is to invest in developing a more sustainable, productivity-driven base for competitive commercial agriculture over the long run.

Africa's producers are generally competitive in domestic markets. The competitiveness of Africa's producers at the farm level in the production of the targeted commodities makes them generally competitive in domestic markets with imports. For example, Nigerian farmers can produce and deliver soybeans to Ibadan at 62 percent of the cost of imported soybeans, and Zambian farmers can deliver sugar to the market of Nakambala at 55 percent of the cost of imported sugar. High international and domestic logistics costs raise the prices of imported commodities and provide a certain degree of "natural protection" that local producers can exploit. Because domestic markets for many of the targeted commodities are large and growing and because significant imports are already taking place, there is considerable room for expansion of local production to recapture these markets. Prospects are brightest for rice, soybeans, sugar, and maize.

Africa's producers are generally not competitive in global markets. When it comes to exporting the targeted commodities, producers in the African case study countries are generally not competitive. Noteworthy exceptions are cotton, sugar, and maize, which can be exported profitably by some of the case study countries, at least in some years. The same high international and domestic logistics costs that provide natural protection for local producers pose a significant barrier when it comes to exporting, because these costs must be absorbed by African producers if their commodities are to be competitive internationally. For example, Mozambican farmers, who are highly competitive in producing cassava for the domestic market, would have to cut domestic production and logistics costs by more than 80 percent to become competitive exporters of cassava to Europe.

Regional markets appear to offer the most promising opportunities for expansion over the short-to-medium term. The CCAA value chain analysis did not formally analyze competitiveness in regional markets, but given the relatively high logistics costs associated with reaching international markets, it is clear that Africa's producers are favorably positioned to serve regional markets relative to the countries that dominate international trade in the six commodities. Demand in regional markets can be expected to grow rapidly as a result of population growth, income gains, and accelerating urbanization. Exporters in Africa will be able to expand trade not only by exploiting growth in overall demand but also by displacing imports from outside the region, which currently are considerable.

The competitiveness of African case study countries is undermined by inefficiencies in domestic logistics. Domestic logistics costs in the African case study countries are high compared with domestic logistics costs in Brazil and Thailand. The higher logistics costs in the African countries stem from widespread deficiencies in transport, processing, and storage infrastructure; lack of competition in vehicle import and trucking industries; cumbersome and costly transport regulations; and frequent extortion of bribes from truckers at border crossings and police checkpoints.

Smallholders have a critical role to play as a source of competitiveness in the African case study countries. Contrary to expectations, few obvious scale economies were found in the production systems analyzed for the CCAA study. Compared with those of large commercial farms, family farms and emerging commercial farms were typically found to have lower shipment values at the farm level and/or final distribution point (shipment values reflect production and delivery costs). Large commercial farms can play an important strategic role by contributing to the achievement of the critical mass of product needed to attract local and international buyers, but the value chain analysis shows that investments in smallholder agriculture can be an important source of competitiveness in their own right. An additional benefit of smallholder-led agricultural growth is the much higher level of second-round demand effects that occur when income gains are realized by smallholder households, as opposed to large commercial farms.

Potential Social Impacts of Agricultural Commercialization

The CCAA country case studies revealed that the social impacts associated with the expansion of commercial agriculture (including gender impacts) depend critically on the following factors:

- The macroeconomic environment, especially interest and exchange rates (these influence the incentives to mechanize, thus shaping employment opportunities not only in farming but also throughout the value chain)
- The land-tenure system and distribution of land holdings (these determine who benefits directly from increased primary production)
- The divergence between import-parity and export-parity prices (this establishes the degree to which expanded domestic production can reduce domestic food prices—thus increasing the real incomes of the poor)

- The flexibility of domestic marketing systems (this determines how much domestic prices will decline in response to expanded production)
- The extent to which agricultural services (for example, extension, finance, input supply) reach small-scale farmers and women farmers
- The capacity and the willingness of the national and local governments to tap some of the growth from commercial agriculture to finance public investments in health and education
- The degree to which growth contributes to the political and social integration of previously isolated regions within the country.

Conditions in Brazil and Thailand differed with respect to some of these factors, leading to dissimilar social outcomes. In Brazil, land policies that allowed consolidation of vast tracts by individual owners, credit and marketing services that were especially favorable to businesses, and subsidies on agricultural machinery that were channeled through rural credit programs facilitated the emergence of large-scale mechanized agriculture as the dominant mode of production. In Thailand, land policies that facilitated land titling and provided tenure security for small-scale farmers, combined with a generally more smallholder-friendly policy environment, allowed small-scale farming to emerge as the dominant mode of production. In both countries, income gains were mediated through productivity-induced declines in food prices, but the overall poverty-reducing effects were much larger in Thailand because of the dominance of smallholders.

The differences observed between the Brazilian and Thai development pathways raise an obvious question: What is the optimal farm size for driving rapid agricultural commercialization? This question has taken on added urgency with the recent appearance of a growing number of mainly foreign investors who are looking to launch large-scale agribusiness schemes in Africa.

Based on a comprehensive review of the literature, as well as the value chain analysis presented in this report, there is little to suggest that the large-scale farming model is either necessary or even particularly promising for Africa. Although some advocates of large-scale agriculture have pointed to the settler farms of eastern and southern Africa as successful examples, closer examination reveals that in many cases these farms were created by expropriating land from indigenous populations and nurtured with a stream of preferential policies, subsidies, and supporting investments. More recent attempts to foster large-scale farming in Africa, including those pursued by the Commonwealth Development Corporation (CDC), were hardly more encouraging, except in some plantation crops. Background papers on commercial farming in Africa commissioned as part of the CCAA study turned up not a single case where large-scale farms, outside of the settler economies, have ever achieved competitiveness in the export of food crops.

The CCAA value chain analysis suggests that the case in favor of large-scale farming in Africa is strongest in the presence of three particular sets of circumstances:

- When economies of scale are present, as for example in the so-called plantation crops (for example, sugar, oil palm, tea, bananas, and many horticultural crops grown for export). After being harvested, these crops need to be processed very quickly and/or transferred to a cold-storage facility; otherwise, they experience rapid declines in quality and hence value. If the farm operations of planting and harvesting can be successfully coordinated with the off-farm operations of processing and shipping, the economies of scale associated with the processing and/or shipping of these crops are transmitted to the farm level.

- When Africa's producers must compete in overseas export markets that have very stringent quality requirements and demand backward traceability of output all the way to the farm level, and in which contract farming is not feasible (for example, because of poor enforcement of contracts).

- When relatively fertile land must be developed in very low population-density areas (which include vast tracts of Guinea Savannah land). Without a large agricultural population representing a potential labor force, expansion into these areas will necessarily require mechanization. Although mechanization of smallholder agriculture is possible through the use of draft animals or hired machinery services, even if these technologies can be made available, development of relatively unpopulated areas still may require significant in-migration from other areas of higher population density, to which there may be political obstacles. Under such conditions, large-scale mechanized farming may be the best model, even for the production of staple foods.

In all three of these cases in which large-scale farming may be cost-effective, allocation of extensive tracts to farming enterprises is likely to engender land-tenure problems. Because there are virtually no areas that are entirely unused and unclaimed, land-tenure problems will often pose enormous challenges—challenges that may be as difficult to resolve as the political issues surrounding in-migration of farmers and agricultural workers from elsewhere.

That large-scale farming is in most cases unlikely to be the most appropriate avenue for the commercialization of African agriculture does not mean that there are not important investment opportunities waiting in the sector. For the foreseeable future, however, the main opportunities for private investors, domestic or foreign, will remain in seed development, input supply, marketing, and processing. Over the longer term, attractive opportunities for large-scale farming could emerge in plantation crops, including sugarcane and oil palm, which are the most efficient sources of biofuels.

If the Brazilian model of large-scale farming appears to have severe limitations in Africa, what about the Thai model of small-scale farms? Is the smallholder-led commercialization strategy pioneered by Thailand appropriate for African countries? There is no doubt that smallholder agriculture can drive rapid agricultural growth and bring about poverty reduction on a massive scale; this has been amply demonstrated by many Asian and also several African countries. The theoretical and empirical literature show that the increased incentives felt by family farmers to work hard and manage their enterprises efficiently are at the root of the productivity advantage of the family farm. The finding of the CCAA value chain analysis that family farms are often the lowest-cost producers for the six target commodities is consistent with previous studies. This is not to say, however, that smallholder producers are the most efficient producers of all commodities: as discussed earlier, economies of scale are found in the plantation crops and among highly perishable commodities that must be processed and/or shipped quickly.

Yet smallholder-led commercialization strategies can also have downsides. Even when the income earned by smallholder households increases with commercialization, the intrahousehold distribution of income may worsen. Case study evidence shows that the welfare of women and dependents within some households deteriorates when those households switch to producing exportable cash crops. The relationship between the commercialization of agriculture, intrahousehold income distribution, and household nutrition is complex and varies widely, depending on underlying socioeconomic factors. In encouraging smallholder-led commercial agriculture, governments and donors therefore need to pay careful attention to how the key determinants of intrahousehold welfare express themselves in particular local settings.

Potential Environmental Impacts of Agricultural Commercialization

Everywhere in the world, agricultural intensification—including intensification associated with the rise of commercial agriculture—has affected the environment. In the mass media, the impacts tend to be portrayed in negative terms: deforestation and associated biodiversity losses, degradation of soil and water resources, and adverse health effects associated with the use of crop chemicals. At least for the countries analyzed as part of the CCAA study, this portrayal is not always supported by empirical data. A review of the evidence suggested that there is a need to better understand the environmental impacts potentially associated with commercialization of agriculture, as well as the lessons learned from past experiences that might allow negative environmental impacts to be attenuated through improved policies and technologies.

When assessing the likely environmental impacts of commercial agriculture, it is important to consider the counterfactual: the environmental effects that would occur in the absence of commercialization. Localized environmental damage caused by intensive commercial agriculture may be acceptable if the alternative would be even greater environmental damage occurring elsewhere as the result of expansion of low-productivity agriculture into highly vulnerable areas. The likely environmental impacts of commercial agriculture therefore need to be assessed in the context of the environmental problems relating to agriculture more generally, some of which stem from unsustainable practices associated with low-productivity subsistence farming practiced by smallholders forced by population pressure to clear forests, shorten fallows, or move to more fragile areas.

The commercialization experiences of Brazil and Thailand (and those of many other countries) show that the rise of commercial agriculture is associated with significant conversion of forests, woodlands, and savannah to agricultural uses. This brings some risk of environmental problems, including inappropriate use of fertilizers; problems associated with irrigation, such as damage to natural habitats caused by dams, reduction of downstream nutrient flow, and salinization of cropland; release of sequestered carbon into the atmosphere; and pesticide pollution and impacts on human health. Although these problems do not yet apply to much of Africa, where the main environmental problems have more to do with inadequate levels of intensification and insufficient use of modern inputs, clearly there are lessons to be learned from the experiences of Brazil, Thailand, and many other countries about minimizing the costs of environmental problems associated with intensification. Intensification inevitably comes at some environmental cost, but arguably a lower one than might have been incurred with further extensification.

Bright Prospects for Commercial Agriculture in the African Guinea Savannah

The CCAA country case studies carried out in Mozambique, Nigeria, and Zambia suggest that the prospects for commercial agricultural success in these countries today are as good as, or better than, they were in Brazil and Thailand during the period when those two countries were going through their agricultural revolutions. The positive outlook is grounded in five principal factors:

- **Rapid economic growth and strong demand prospects.** Accelerating rates of income growth in Africa (above 3 percent per capita annually in most countries), combined with still-high population growth rates and rapid urbanization, provide diverse and ample opportunities in domestic and regional markets. The substantial and growing reliance of many African countries on food imports presents a large scope for import substitution, both nationally and regionally, and capturing nearby markets is less demanding logistically and in terms of product standards than breaking into international markets. World market prospects also look stronger, driven by growing demand in Asia and expansion of biofuels production.

- **Favorable domestic policy environments.** The macroeconomic environment in many African countries is today not only broadly favorable to agriculture but is also more favorable than was the case in Brazil in the 1960s, when the agricultural revolution began in the Cerrado region. Because of the spread of macroeconomic stability, introduction of market-determined exchange rates, and opening of trade regimes, economic growth rates have sharply accelerated. Net taxation of agriculture has fallen across Africa, and lower inflation and real interest rates favor expanded agricultural investment.

- **Improved business climate.** The business climate has improved markedly in recent years in many African countries—including (to varying degrees) in Mozambique, Nigeria, and Zambia. Investments in basic infrastructure such as roads, electricity, water, and communications are being given priority, and institutional reforms are being implemented to reduce administrative burdens on business and combat corruption. Decentralization initiatives and the development of civil society have improved the ability of rural populations to participate in their own development and defend their interests. This in turn has started to open space for independent producer and business organizations of all kinds. A number of African countries have already reformed (or are in the process of reforming) their land laws, protecting customary rights while at the same time opening opportunities for security of tenure for investors.

- **Increased incentives to invest in agriculture.** Stronger demand, better macro and sector policies, and an improved business climate will lead to higher returns to agriculture in Africa, inducing increased investment from home and abroad. Foreign capital (including repatriated funds that previously fled Africa for safer havens) is beginning to flow into African agriculture and related value chains, as evidenced by recent Chinese acquisition of land leases in Tanzania and the Democratic Republic of Congo, rising interest on the part of European energy firms in securing land concessions for biofuels feedstock production, and surging foreign investment in high-value African agricultural export enterprises.

- **New technologies.** New technologies offer agricultural entrepreneurs in Africa advantages that their Thai and Brazilian counterparts have acquired over the past four decades. Techniques for managing Guinea Savannah soils to make them more productive and sustainable are much more advanced than a generation ago, although research is still needed to adapt technologies developed in other regions to African conditions. The biotechnology revolution offers the potential to tailor solutions more quickly to constraints limiting expansion of cash crops in Africa, but only if the African countries develop the regulatory and research capacity to exploit this potential.

The cell phone revolution is helping to link African farmers and traders quickly and affordably to information about potential sources of demand and supply.

Constraints to Be Overcome

Although clear potential exists for commercial agriculture to take off in Africa, the ability of Africa's entrepreneurs to replicate the successes of the Brazilian Cerrado and Northeast Region of Thailand is constrained by five main factors:

- **Tougher international competition.** Compared with those of Brazilian and Thai producers during earlier decades, Africa's producers today face a more competitive international environment. Product specification requirements have become more exacting than in the past, even for unprocessed bulk commodities, as evidenced by the recent tightening of regulations relating to levels of aflatoxin that may be present in grains and regulations relating to the percentage of genetically modified organisms that may be present in imports into some countries. Organisation for European Co-operation and Development (OECD) agricultural subsidies and protection measures also continue to reduce export and import substitution opportunities.

- **Exogenous shocks: HIV/AIDS, global climate change, and global markets.** Despite the spread of antiretroviral drugs, the human immunodeficiency virus/acquired immunodeficiency syndrome (HIV/AIDS) epidemic continues to exact a heavy toll in Africa, eroding African capacity in agricultural research and extension, among many other areas. Global climate change, which is likely to reduce the level of rainfall in Guinea Savannah zones in West Africa and significantly increase rainfall variability across the continent, will create new challenges in many areas, including research, crop and land management, and financial intermediation. Finally, volatility of global agricultural markets is likely to remain high because of a number of factors, including climate change and the close link between agricultural and oil prices as a result of the growing influence of biofuels production on agricultural markets.

- **Weak national commitment.** In Mozambique, Nigeria, and Zambia, as well as more broadly in Africa, policy makers have made encouraging declarations regarding the importance of agricultural development, in part because of their adoption of the Comprehensive Africa Agricultural Development Programme (CAADP) of the New Partnership for Africa's Development (NEPAD). These declarations, however, have not yet been supported by sustained political commitment, policy reforms, and investments similar to those seen in Brazil and Thailand in earlier decades. Today, African governments invest only 4 percent of the value of agricultural gross domestic product (GDP) in the sector, relative to at least 10 percent in other regions, where agriculture comprises a much smaller share of the economy (World Bank 2007c).

- **Weak donor commitment.** The weak commitment to agriculture seen at the national level is also evident at the level of the donors. Like many African governments, most of the major donors have declared their strong support for agricultural development (including the CAADP/ NEPAD agenda), and in recent years the level of support to agriculture has increased modestly from earlier extremely low levels. Yet as with the African governments, the donors' rhetoric in support of African agriculture has far exceeded their actual funding commitments. In particular, sustained donor commitment to supporting the prime movers of agricultural development (such as research, infrastructure, and human and institutional capital development), such as was seen in Brazil and Thailand, has been absent in Africa over the past 20 years.

- **Lack of social cohesion, political stability, and bureaucratic capacity.** In many parts of Africa, emergence of a successful commercial agriculture is impeded by weak social cohesion, which reduces trust among and between market participants and raises transaction costs. These transaction costs make it more expensive to negotiate between individuals in the private sector and ensure fair adjudication of any subsequent contract disputes, and they also hinder political mobilization of investment in the public goods that are critical to agricultural growth. In contrast to Brazil and Thailand, which benefited from a stable and competent civil service, the capacity of African government bureaucracies to manage and facilitate coordination of different actors in the value chain while maintaining a competitive environment remains underdeveloped, leading to fewer public-private partnerships than accompanied the growth of commercial agriculture in Brazil and Thailand.

Needed Interventions: Policy Reforms, Scaled-Up Investments, and Strengthened Institutions

A number of actions are needed to realize the agricultural potential of Africa's Guinea Savannah zones:

Continuing macro policy reforms. In recent years, there has been marked progress in the overall macroeconomic environments in Mozambique, Nigeria, and Zambia, as well as in many other African countries, favoring agricultural development. Agricultural exports in Africa are still being taxed at higher levels than in other regions, so governments need to continue to move domestic prices toward export parity prices by removing export taxes and replacing them with other less distortionary sources of taxation. Countries also need to urgently focus on implementation of regional integration agreements, including banning of arbitrary export restrictions, streamlining border logistics, and harmonizing standards and regulations that are major impediments to regional trade.

Land policy reforms. The contrasting experiences of Brazil and Thailand show that land policy, legislation, and implementation arrangements, more than any other factors, determine the pattern and distributional consequences of agricultural growth. Providing secure and transferable land rights is critical to protecting the interests of local populations while permitting entrepreneurial farmers to acquire unused land in regions of low population density, allowing land to change hands over time to those who can use it most productively, and providing incentives to invest in increasing land productivity.

The land consolidation that accompanied the growth of commercial agriculture in the Brazilian Cerrado offers a cautionary tale for the African case study countries. Ineffectual land policies and failed settlement programs, combined with subsidized credit and marketing interventions up until the mid-1980s, resulted in a skewed distributional outcome in terms of land ownership and farm income that has not been corrected by the series of land reforms introduced since the 1990s. This contrasts sharply with the systematic land-reform and land-titling policies pursued by Thailand over the past 30 years that maintained or increased equity in land ownership and contributed to rapid and inclusive rural growth.

For the African case study countries, the challenge is whether they can construct sets of institutions and equitable enforcement structures that will enable smallholders to access land and engage successfully in profitable commercial agriculture. Failure to do so can have huge costs, as evidenced by the land-tenure–induced crises witnessed recently in Côte d'Ivoire and Zimbabwe, among other countries. This challenge is likely to increase in importance in future years, given the growing demand for land to be used for commercial farming. The government in Mozambique is already struggling to respond to requests for land concessions for biofuel plantations that exceed the cultivated area of the country (Boughton, pers. comm.).

Progress has been made in a number of African countries in designing good land policies and laws, and also in implementing relatively low-cost mechanisms for the certification of land rights of communities and individuals in communities. To translate the legal provisions into practice, however, strong political commitment to the protection of customary rights is needed, as well as implementation capacity. Recent examples of land rushes in the presence of good legislation in a number of countries add urgency to the need to strengthen implementation capacity. In the absence of such capacity, the risk remains high that rapid commercialization will lead to adverse distributional outcomes.

Scaling up public investments. Development of competitive commercial agriculture in Africa will not be possible without sharply increased levels of public investments. Agricultural development cannot be done on the cheap, ignoring the fundamental pillars of productivity growth in the food system, as governments and donors have tried to do in Africa over the past 20 years.

Particularly damaging to the prospects of African agriculture has been the low level of investment in agricultural research, combined with its fragmentation into many small and underfunded institutions. Brazil's long-term commitment to developing EMBRAPA and the payoffs from that investment in developing the Cerrado are particularly striking. In Africa, the problem of underfunding of research is widespread: about one-half of all African countries have experienced absolute declines in research funding during the past decade. Because many research systems in Africa are small, the need for regional cooperation is much larger than it was in the cases of Brazil and Thailand. Nor has the international agricultural research system filled the gap, with far fewer fundamental breakthroughs from this system than was the case in the Asian and Latin American green revolutions. The reforms of the international system agreed to in late 2008— when implemented—should help focus and coordinate efforts of the system on high-priority problems of African agriculture.

Increased investment is also needed in Africa to strengthen agricultural education at all levels, from the postgraduate level (to replenish Africa's graying agricultural research establishment) to the technical level (to produce the large number of well-trained technicians required by modern agriculture and value chains) to the vocational level (to instill in rural households the basic skills needed to access and master new production technologies). A major and as yet unresolved challenge is to develop cost-effective and demand-driven advisory services through effective partnerships among farmers, public agencies, and civil society.

Massive investment is needed in many African countries to rebuild the aging infrastructure base needed to launch and sustain internationally competitive commercial agriculture. Highest priorities are irrigation, roads, energy, and overall logistics, especially port infrastructure. The experiences of Brazil and Thailand show that investment in road and port infrastructure is critical to competitiveness in international markets, along with policies to improve competition in the transport sector. In Africa, considerable recent progress has been noted in improving main roads and (to a much lesser extent) rural roads, and small-scale irrigation.

Inducing private investment. Given the scope and complexity of the tasks needed to develop agriculture in Africa's Guinea Savannah zones, ranging from farm-level investments to international marketing, the private sector needs to take the lead in many of the critical investments and activities. Continuing efforts to improve the business climate are especially important to commercial agriculture, as they are needed to facilitate the entry of private seed and agriprocessing companies that have played an important role in Latin America and Asia. Creating space for strong farmer organizations and promoting vigorous private-sector and civil society organizations is vital, as the Thai experience illustrates.

Institutional reforms to make markets work better. Almost by definition, successful commercialization of agriculture depends on well-functioning markets. The greatest challenge to commercial agriculture is to put in place the institutions to make markets more efficient and less risky.

Given the weak development of private markets throughout much of Africa, the state needs to offer certain critical services that the private sector currently has few incentives to provide. The needed actions will vary by commodity and country, and experimentation is required to develop appropriate models. A key challenge is knowing when the state should step aside and give greater scope to the private sector as markets for these services mature, because it is easy for the state to overstep and crowd out private initiative.

Development of commodity exchanges using modern electronic communication technology through a public-private partnership (as is being piloted in Ethiopia) is an important step toward more integrated national markets. Commodity exchanges can also help reduce price risks, and some could eventually be developed into full-fledged futures markets at the regional level, a role already played by the South African Futures Exchange for the countries of southern Africa. Commodity exchanges can also include warehouse receipt systems to reduce distress sales after harvest and encourage seasonal storage.

The recent revival of input subsidies in the form of "market-smart" approaches needs to be carefully assessed as a basis for scaling up. Once farmers have gained experience in using a particular input and the volume used of the input has grown enough to allow economies of scale to be realized in manufacturing and distribution, subsidies can be scaled back and eliminated. Yet when subsidy programs are scaled up, as has happened with fertilizer subsidy programs in Malawi, Zambia, and other countries, they risk becoming fiscally unsustainable, and the cost can easily crowd out other key government investments in public goods. In any event, input subsidies need to be complemented by other measures to develop private input suppliers, such as training and financing for input dealers, regulation of input quality, and development of trade associations.

Although it is clear that access to finance is central to successful development of commercial agriculture, there has been very little progress throughout most of Africa in creating self-sustaining rural financial systems with significant outreach to the farm population. Policy makers must continue to seek ways to tie rural savings-and-loan associations more effectively to broader commercial banking systems to provide greater financial intermediation and diversification of risks. Also, many African countries still have poorly performing state banks for agriculture, which begs the question of whether it will be possible to replicate the Thai success through reform of these banks.

Public sector reform and governance. It is clear that the state must play an important facilitating role in the development of a dynamic and equitable commercial agriculture. A major challenge is to develop governance structures and capacities for the state to assume this role. Ministries of agriculture require sharply upgraded capacities and skills in areas such as marketing and business development services, as well as the ability to forge a variety of public-private-civil society partnerships that characterize the new roles of the state. Moreover, these skills must extend well beyond the ministries of agriculture to local governments and to a range of other ministries that have important complementary roles in commercial agriculture.

A major governance challenge to successful commercial agricultural development will be how to coordinate the services and investments of multiple ministries and levels of government and coordinate public and private investments. High-level political leadership is needed to ensure that agricultural development for specific regions is a priority, as seen in both the Brazilian and Thai examples. The importance of these leadership and coordination roles suggests that efforts to foster commercial agriculture should be spatially organized into priority development corridors, with these roles located in the office of the prime minister or president.

Management of social impacts. Commercial agriculture in Africa is unlikely to contribute effectively to national policy objectives of broad-based growth and poverty reduction unless care is taken to ensure that the wealth created by commercial agriculture is shared widely. Although the Brazilian and Thai models can both work well, the smallholder-led agricultural transformation that occurred in Thailand seems generally more compatible with the employment-generation objectives of many African countries than the transformation that occurred in Brazil, which was dominated by wealthy farmers who had the economic and political power needed to secure large areas of land and leverage the capital needed to invest in large-scale, highly mechanized production technologies. A critical challenge in Africa will be reform of customary land policies to allow equitable distribution of land and secure tenancy. Yet broad-based benefits need not derive from farming alone. Experience in Chile, Thailand, and many other countries has shown that given appropriate policies, a vibrant commercial agriculture can generate a large number of jobs in both upstream and downstream portions of the value chain (in input provision and output processing, packaging, and marketing), even if the scale of farm-level production increases over time. This consideration is particularly important for Mozambique, Nigeria, and Zambia, where it appears questionable whether, with current technology, very small farms (for example, less than two hectares) can provide rural households with an income high enough to escape poverty if they focus entirely on staple food production.

Management of environmental impacts. Transforming the natural ecosystems found in the Guinea Savannah into vibrant commercial farming systems will not be possible without converting forest and pasture land to more intensive agricultural uses. This will inevitably bring some environmental costs. The low-input extensification of agriculture currently taking place in many areas is exacting especially high environmental costs through deforestation and land degradation, loss of biodiversity, and release of sequestered carbon in soils and trees. A more intensive pattern of land use based on the use of fertilizer and other soil amendments can reduce these costs by reducing land conversion rates. However, more intensive strategies can also bring risks for water resources and negative health impacts from increased use of agrochemicals. Experience from many parts of the world, including Brazil and Thailand, shows that the environmental costs associated with the development of commercial agriculture can be reduced and managed through use of appropriate technologies combined with vigilant monitoring of environmental impacts backed by effective enforcement of environmental rules and regulations.

The Road Ahead

There are good reasons to be optimistic about the prospects for commercial agriculture in the African Guinea Savannah, but it is important to be clear-eyed about the challenges that lie ahead. Although it would be easy to feel overwhelmed by the list of constraints facing African farmers, Brazil and Thailand provide important lessons about how these constraints can be overcome. Arguably the most important lesson of all relates to the role of the state. In Brazil and Thailand, successive governments played a vital role by establishing a conducive enabling environment characterized by favorable macroeconomic policies, adequate infrastructure, a strong human capital base, competent government administration, and political stability. This conducive enabling environment was a critical factor that allowed the private sector to mobilize its creativity, drive, and resources in ways that served broader social goals, as well as private interests. Rather than relying solely on heavy state management and investment, central and local governments of Brazil and Thailand were able to engage effectively with private investors, farmers' organizations, rural communities, and civil society organizations. After decades of state domination, many initiatives currently underway in the African countries are beginning to use similar approaches.

One advantage that African policy makers have today is the knowledge from the Thai and Brazilian experiences that there are multiple paths to agricultural commercialization. Modern commercial agriculture need not be synonymous with large, highly mechanized farms. Although the Thai and Brazilian experiences show that agricultural revolutions can be driven by either smallholders or large-scale commercial farmers, on balance the weight of the evidence suggests that the fruits of those revolutions are more widely shared when smallholders participate. Second-round employment and poverty-alleviation effects are likely to be much larger with the smallholder-led model, because of the consumption linkages associated with growth in smallholder income, which tend to generate more demand for locally produced nontradables. In the case of low-value staples, however, it is unlikely that land-constrained households farming 1–2 hectares or less will be able to earn sufficient income to exit poverty. The emerging pattern of commercial agriculture in the African Guinea Savannah therefore must provide diversification opportunities for producers of low-value staples.

Further grounds for encouragement come from the knowledge that if the development of smallholder-based commercial agriculture begins solidly, the process can be self-reinforcing. As the Thai experience illustrates, those who initially gain in the process (for example, commercial farmers, farmer organizations, and agribusiness firms) will be motivated to lobby for policies and investments that can sustain the commercialization process, while at the same time generating some of the needed financial resources. As commercialization broadens and deepens, larger private sector actors will have increasing incentives to invest in infrastructure and supporting services for value-chain coordination, thereby reducing the burden on government while generating expanded off-farm employment. At the same time, political leaders must continue to play an active role by providing the vision, strategy, consistent implementation, and long-term commitment needed to make the promise of agricultural transformation a reality.

CHAPTER 1

Introduction and Objectives

For the foreseeable future, reducing poverty in Africa will depend largely on stimulating agricultural growth (World Bank 2007c).[1] Within agriculture, a powerful driver of growth is often commercial agriculture. Commercial agriculture can develop along a number of pathways, yet many developing regions have not progressed far along any of these. African agriculture has actually lost ground, as reflected in the steady erosion during the past 30 years in the international competitiveness of traditional African export crops such as coffee, oil palm, rubber, and groundnuts, as well as the many food crops for which import dependence has increased. In contrast, over the same period two relatively backward and landlocked agricultural regions in the developing world—the Cerrado region of Brazil and the Northeast Region of Thailand—have developed at a rapid pace and conquered important world markets. Their success defied the predictions of many skeptics, who had asserted that the two regions' challenging agroecological characteristics, remote locations, and high levels of poverty would prove impossible to overcome.

Perceptions similar to those that fueled pessimism 30 years ago in Brazil and Thailand also fueled pessimism in Africa up until recently.

However, two recent developments have led to a change in thinking about the potential of African agriculture.

First, during the past decade, stronger agricultural growth has been recorded in many African countries, suggesting that the sector can indeed be a driver of growth when the conditions are right.

Second, the dramatic rise in global food prices that occurred in 2008 led to a realization that new opportunities may be opening for countries that are endowed with the land, labor, and other resources needed to respond to the accelerating demand for food and biofuels feedstocks.

Based on a careful examination of the factors that contributed to the successes achieved in Brazil and Thailand, as well as comparative analysis of evidence obtained through detailed case studies of three African countries—Mozambique, Nigeria, and Zambia—this report argues that opportunities abound for agriculture in a major agroecological region of Africa, the Guinea Savannah, to regain international competitiveness, especially in light of projected stronger demand in world markets for agricultural commodities over the long term. This provides reasons for optimism regarding the future prospects for African agriculture as a major source of pro-poor growth.

Study Objectives

This report summarizes the main findings and conclusions of the study on Competitive Commercial Agriculture for Africa (CCAA). The principal objective of the CCAA study was to explore the feasibility of revitalizing agricultural competitiveness and growth in African agriculture through the identification of key products and production systems that could underpin a rapid development of competitive commercial agriculture. Comparability between the three African countries on the one hand and northwest Brazil and northeast Thailand on the other was enabled by focusing on a single, but very large, agroecological zone that is recognized as significantly underutilized, the Guinea Savannah (see box 1.1). The extent of the Guinea Savannah zone is shown in figure 1.1. Although the report contains significant lessons for all agroclimate zones of Africa, the commodities and farming systems analyzed in detail are specific to the Guinea Savannah, so the findings and recommendations are especially relevant for that zone. The Guinea Savannah, which is characterized by medium-to-high agricultural potential, extends across more than 700 million hectares in Africa. Much of this area is sparsely populated, with only 6 percent under cultivation, providing huge scope for expansion of

Box 1.1

Characteristics of Africa's Guinea Savannah Zone

The Guinea Savannah zone of Africa features a warm tropical climate with 800–1,200 millimeters of rainfall annually, allowing for a growing period of 150–210 days. Rainfall, however, varies considerably from year to year, affecting agricultural activities. Soils are typically low-activity clays and high-base-saturation loams (lixisols), as well as more acid soils with lower base saturation in more humid areas (acrisols) and acid sandy soils (arenosols) in drier regions. Arenosols are easy to work, but nutrient-deficient, and they do not retain moisture well. Acrisols have low natural fertility and require lime and phosphate applications to increase yields. The variable annual rainfall and poor soil quality make this a challenging agroecological environment.

The Guinea Savannah zone supports three main farming systems: (a) the root crop farming system, (b) the mixed cereal-root crop farming system, and (c) the maize mixed farming system. All have potential for increasing agricultural production. The Guinea Savannah zone is one of the major underutilized resources in Africa. It accounts for about one-third of the land area in Sub-Saharan Africa and underpins the livelihoods of more than one-quarter of all African farmers. The extent of the Guinea Savannah zone is summarized in the following table:

Extent of the Guinea Savannah Zone, Case Study Countries, and All Africa

	Country land area		Guinea Savannah area		Guinea Savannah area that is cropped	
				As % of total land area	As % of total Guinea Savannah area	As % of total cropped area in country
	Km^2	Km^2	As % of total land area	Km^2		
Mozambique	793,980	541,215	68.2	21,242	3.9	63.5
Nigeria	913,388	581,620	63.7	176,000	30.3	64.9
Zambia	753,941	598,981	79.4	6,676	1.1	60.4
All Sub-Saharan Africa	20,626,624	7,072,281	34.3	481,338	6.8	40.2

Source: Calculated by the authors based on data provided by the International Food Policy Research Institute (IFPRI).

(continued)

Box 1.1 *(Continued)*

The *cereal-root crop mixed farming system* accounts for 13 percent of the agricultural area of Sub-Saharan Africa and supports 15 percent of the region's agricultural population. Several characteristics set this farming system apart from other farming systems: low altitude, high temperatures, low population density, abundant cultivatable land, and poor transport and communications infrastructure. Historically, development of this farming system was constrained by two major diseases, one affecting humans *(onchocerciasis)* and one affecting animals *(trypanosomosis)*. *Onchocerciasis* (river blindness) control efforts have freed an estimated 25 million hectares of cultivatable land for agricultural development. Crops grown on this land include maize and sorghum, millet (in the drier parts), cotton, cassava, soybeans, cowpeas, yams (especially near the border of the root crop zone), and wetland rice (in parts of the river plains and valley areas). In areas less affected by *trypanosomosis*, livestock are prevalent, and the region as a whole sustains about 42 million head. In the 1980s and early 1990s, smallholder maize and cotton expanded rapidly at the expense of sorghum and root crops, especially in the more northern, drier part of the Guinea Savannah, as a result of the diffusion of improved early-maturing maize varieties facilitated by fertilizer subsidies and production credit.

The *root crop farming system* accounts for around 11 percent of the land area in Africa and employs 11 percent of the agricultural population. Rainfall is either bimodal or nearly continuous, and risk of crop failure is low. The system also supports 17 million cattle. This zone has many of the same characteristics as the cereal-root crop mixed system, although oil palm is a major crop with considerable potential for expansion.

The *maize mixed farming system* is the most important food production system in eastern and southern Africa, extending across plateau and highland areas at altitudes of 800 to 1,500 meters. It accounts for 10 percent of the land area and 19 percent of the cultivated area and employs 15 percent of the regional population. Since the early 1990s, input use in this system has fallen sharply in many areas, and yields have stagnated as fertilizer subsidies were phased out. However, long-term agricultural growth prospects are good, and the potential for reduction of poverty is high.

Source: Dixon, Gulliver, and Gibbon 2001.

agriculture. Prospects for restoring agricultural competitiveness in the Guinea Savannah depend on a number of factors, including the technical performance of agricultural commodity chains; supply and demand conditions in domestic, regional, and global markets; and the institutional and

Figure 1.1   Extent of the Guinea Savannah Zone in Sub-Saharan Africa

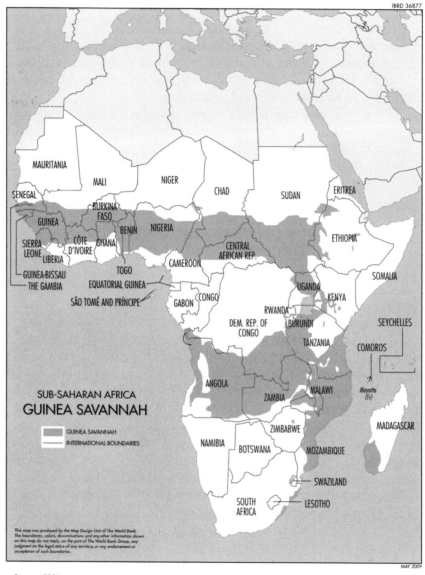

IBRD 36877

MAURITANIA
MALI
NIGER
SENEGAL
CHAD
SUDAN
ERITREA
BURKINA FASO
GUINEA
BENIN
NIGERIA
SIERRA LEONE
CÔTE D'IVOIRE
GHANA
ETHIOPIA
LIBERIA
CENTRAL AFRICAN REP.
GUINEA-BISSAU
TOGO
CAMEROON
SOMALIA
THE GAMBIA
EQUATORIAL GUINEA
SÃO TOMÉ AND PRÍNCIPE
GABON
CONGO
UGANDA
KENYA
RWANDA
DEM. REP. OF CONGO
BURUNDI
SEYCHELLES
TANZANIA
COMOROS
ANGOLA
MALAWI
Mayotte (Fr)
ZAMBIA

SUB-SAHARAN AFRICA
GUINEA SAVANNAH

- GUINEA SAVANNAH
- INTERNATIONAL BOUNDARIES

ZIMBABWE
MADAGASCAR
NAMIBIA
BOTSWANA
MOZAMBIQUE
SWAZILAND
SOUTH AFRICA
LESOTHO

This map was produced by the Map Design Unit of The World Bank. The boundaries, colors, denominations and any other information shown on this map do not imply, on the part of The World Bank Group, any judgment on the legal status of any territory, or any endorsement or acceptance of such boundaries.

MAY 2009

Source: IFPRI.

policy environments. By identifying value chains that have potential to compete effectively in an increasingly globalized world economy, the CCAA study can help inform the design of integrated programs of policy reforms, institutional changes, and supporting investments needed to promote the emergence of successful commercial agriculture in Africa.

The key questions addressed by the CCAA study can be summarized as follows:

- To what extent can African countries with similar agroecological endowments to those of Brazil's Cerrado region and the Northeast Region of Thailand become more locally, regionally, and globally competitive in selected agricultural commodities?
- What sorts of investments, policies, and technological and institutional changes would be necessary to replicate the successes of commercial agriculture in these areas of Brazil and Thailand in areas of Africa with similar natural resource endowments?
- Can increases in agricultural competitiveness in Africa, based on expanded commercial agriculture, be achieved in a way that substantially reduces poverty?
- What are the potential environmental and social impacts of expanding commercial agriculture in Africa?

Consistent with the strategy of drawing lessons from the past and assessing their potential relevance for the future, the CCAA study includes both backward-looking and forward-looking components. The backward-looking components include detailed analyses of the Thai and Brazilian "success stories," as well as a broad review of past attempts to introduce commercial agriculture in Africa. The forward-looking components include analyses of projected global supply and demand trends for six internationally traded commodities important or potentially important to the Guinea Savannah: cassava, cotton, maize, soybeans, rice, and sugar. In addition, detailed competitiveness case studies were carried out in the three African case study countries, using value chain analysis. The objectives of the competitiveness case studies were to assess the current competitiveness of each of the three African countries in producing one or more of the six commodities; to identify constraints that may be inhibiting competitiveness; and to identify opportunities in which policy reforms, institutional changes, and/or supporting investments can improve future competitiveness. (Details of all of these background studies appear in appendix A.)

In addition to addressing competitiveness issues, the CCAA study also assessed the potential social and environmental impacts of agricultural commercialization in the three African case study countries. The potential social and environmental impacts were assessed through a review of past experience with commercial agriculture in Brazil, Thailand, and selected countries of Sub-Saharan Africa, along with formal assessments of the likely social and environmental impacts of the different paths of commercialization in the three African case study countries.

Study Context: The Reemergence of Agriculture in the Development Agenda

Even though support to agriculture in Africa has fallen over the past two decades, the important contribution that agriculture can make to development is no longer subject to debate. Most recently, the *World Development Report 2008: Agriculture for Development (WDR 2008)* (World Bank 2007c) extensively reviewed a large body of evidence and made a convincing case that agriculture can and must be given much higher priority to serve at least four critical development challenges: (a) trigger overall growth in the early stages of development, especially in Africa; (b) act as a powerful engine for poverty reduction; (c) contribute to food security; and (d) help meet the environmental agenda.

Agriculture can be an especially effective trigger for growth in the early stages of development, not only because of its heavy weight in the economy (agriculture contributes more than one-third of gross domestic product [GDP] in most of Sub-Saharan Africa) but also because of the strong growth linkages that are generated in other sectors of the economy when agricultural growth is well distributed. Growth based on increasing productivity of food staples and providing affordable food is vital to overall economic competitiveness. And—very important for this study—agriculture is often the sector where African countries are likely to have comparative advantage in generating foreign exchange, at least for the medium term, until infrastructure, the business climate, and consumer demand allow other sectors to take off. In fact, the evidence over the past 10 years points to the leading role played by agriculture in reviving overall growth in African countries and moving countries from the so-called "first rural world" of agriculture-based economies to the so-called "second rural world" of transforming economies, in which nonagricultural sectors lead overall growth (World Bank 2007c).[2]

WDR 2008 found that growth originating in the agricultural sector is two to four times as effective as growth originating in the nonagricultural sector in increasing incomes of the bottom third of the income distribution. This result derives from the fact that 75 percent of the poor live in rural areas and most of them depend on agriculture for their livelihood. The well-known experiences of China and India illustrate the critical role that agricultural growth—and rural growth more generally—can play in successfully reducing poverty. Additional supporting evidence comes from Africa (for example, Christiaensen and Demery [2007]). However, the strength of the relationship between agricultural growth and poverty reduction is very dependent on the agrarian structure. The relationship is much weaker in countries such as Brazil, where agricultural growth has been mostly driven by large-scale commercial agriculture.

Growth originating in the agricultural sector also promotes increased food security by providing the means for the poor to access food. In many African countries, locally produced food continues to be very important in the food security equation, not only because many locally produced staples are effectively nontradable (because they are not consumed extensively outside Africa) but also because high transaction costs put imported foods beyond the reach of consumers, especially consumers located in inaccessible interior regions. Lack of foreign exchange to import food and high variability in domestic food supplies also contribute to food insecurity in many African countries. For these reasons, raising productivity in staples and stabilizing food supplies remain major priorities for enhancing food security in most African countries.

Agricultural growth is important not only because it contributes directly to poverty reduction and food security but also because agriculture is a major user of land and water. For this reason, it is critical not only that agricultural growth occur but also that it occur in a way that is environmentally friendly. In the context of high population growth and a shrinking land frontier, agricultural growth based on extensification leads to land degradation and deforestation. Sustainable agricultural intensification thus provides the only viable strategy for achieving long-term development objectives.

Today there is a broad consensus that agriculture must be a lead sector for growth and poverty reduction in much of Africa. Unleashing the power of agricultural growth in Africa will require continued policy reforms and more and better investments in the sector guided by a two-pronged strategy aimed at (a) improving smallholder competitiveness in high- and medium-potential areas to generate growth and (b) improving livelihoods, food security, and resilience in remote and risky environments, where returns to investment are more modest. The key elements of a successful agricultural development strategy are described in *WDR 2008*:

- Launching a smallholder-based productivity revolution in agriculture, grounded in better soil and water management practices

- Achieving balanced growth in the production of food staples, traditional bulk exports, and higher-value products (including livestock), but with productivity growth in food staples as a priority in most countries
- Building markets and value chains to secure market demand for increased agricultural production
- Expanding agricultural exports by increasing competitiveness and reducing trade barriers, especially within the region
- Securing the livelihood and food security of subsistence farmers by developing more resilient farming systems based on improved management of their natural resources and community-driven approaches
- Enhancing labor mobility and stimulating rural nonfarm development to provide pathways out of low-paying agricultural activities, especially in marginal areas
- Improving health and education and providing safety nets to protect the assets of the rural poor from drought, disease, and the death of a family member.

In describing the broad investments and policy reforms that will be needed to unlock the transformative power of agricultural growth in Africa, *WDR 2008* (World Bank 2007c) cautions that specific structural features of each country must be taken into account in designing an appropriate policy and investment agenda. In this light, the CCAA study can be seen as extending the conceptual foundation laid by *WDR 2008* (World Bank 2007c): it analyzes the unique structural features of a specific—but very important—agroecological zone with large potential for growth (that is, the Guinea Savannah) and assesses the priority elements of a successful agricultural development agenda for that zone. At the same time, it is important to understand that the CCAA report is intended to be a road map that provides general guidance on the way forward, not a detailed blueprint containing specific operational recommendations tailored to particular countries. Detailed country-specific blueprints will have to be built at the country level, designed by local experts and championed by local policy makers, to ensure successful implementation.

Study Design: A Case Study Approach with Comparability

The analytical approach used for the CCAA study consists of a series of comparative country case studies. The experiences of two areas that have experienced major agricultural successes—the Cerrado region of Brazil and the Northeast Region of Thailand—are compared with those of similar agroecological areas in Mozambique, Nigeria, and Zambia in terms of their ability to competitively produce a given set of agricultural commodities. The set of products chosen for comparison (cassava, cotton, maize, rice, soybeans, and sugar) were those that were most important in the agricultural development of the study regions in Thailand and Brazil. Detailed value chain analyses for these products in the different study areas are used to assess the factors that drove the increased competitiveness of the Cerrado and the Northeast Region and that could contribute to increasing competitiveness in the three African case study countries.

Case studies can provide important country-specific insights—quantitative as well as qualitative—into the key determinants of growth. Case studies easily accommodate country-specific factors (see, for example, Rodrik [2003]), and they provide a relevant method for examining agricultural growth in particular (see, for example, Byerlee, Diao, and Jackson [2005]). Case studies are particularly useful for providing operational conclusions of direct interest to policy makers. At the same time, aggregating across case studies to draw general conclusions of relevance to countries that are not directly under investigation can be problematic. Differences in the questions being asked, in the specific methodology employed, or in the country context tend to make conclusions derived through case studies highly time- and location-specific.

The CCAA study used an approach that was designed to generate the detailed insights achievable through case studies while ensuring comparability of findings across countries. Five detailed country-level case studies were carried out with common terms of reference to establish a robust microeconomic evidence base, while at the same time ensuring the comparability of results across case study countries, with the goal of providing for more general policy-relevant conclusions of potentially wider applicability. Two of the case studies—those focusing on the "success story" countries, Brazil and Thailand—were backward looking, in the sense that they focused primarily on the factors that allowed Brazil and Thailand to become competitive in international markets. Three of the case studies—those focusing on the African countries—were more forward-looking in the sense that they focused on the factors that could allow the African countries to become competitive (or, in some cases, more competitive) in international markets.

With the objective of tapping into a cross-section of regional experience, the three African country case studies were undertaken in Mozambique,

Nigeria, and Zambia. These three countries feature high levels of poverty, depend heavily on agriculture for incomes and employment, and contain extensive tracts of underutilized land in their Guinea Savannah zones. Although all six of the targeted CCAA commodities are not currently being produced on a large scale in all of the countries, at least four of the commodities are being grown in every country, and the commodities that are not being grown are in all cases considered to have good potential.

The common analytical framework selected for the country case studies was value chain analysis. For each of the five case study countries (Brazil, Thailand, Mozambique, Nigeria, Zambia), existing value chain studies were identified and reviewed. Knowledge gaps identified during the literature review were partially filled by additional data gathering. In the African countries, key commodities, production systems, and marketing strategies were identified that could underpin rapid development of competitive commercial agriculture, and the potential social and environmental impacts associated with these promising strategies were assessed. Knowledge of potential social and environmental impacts can help inform the design of agricultural commercialization policies and programs that avoid harming people and the environment.

The fact that the CCAA study focuses on a specific set of target commodities does not imply that these are the commodities in which the African case study countries have the highest comparative advantage. Rather, the set of target commodities was selected for two main reasons:

- **All of the CCAA target commodities are traded internationally in bulk form.** Most low-income countries that have experienced export-led growth have done so initially by exporting bulk commodities, for which natural resource endowments (and transport infrastructure) are more important determinants of comparative advantage than are more sophisticated investments in human capital, research and development (R&D), and logistics (Abbott and Brehdahl 1994).
- **Use of a common set of commodities across all the study zones can provide important insights** into how key investments and institutional changes in Brazil and Thailand were able to create new comparative advantages over time and to examine the scope for similar types of actions to increase competitiveness in the African study countries.

One of the methodological challenges associated with the case study approach is that even though the natural resource endowment of the study regions is similar, other endowments (for example, cultural and political heritage), as well as the external environment, differ across regions and over time (for example, between the period when Brazil and Thailand were experiencing their agricultural successes and today). Therefore, caution must be exercised in deciding to what extent the three African countries will be able to follow a similar path to the one followed by Brazil and Thailand in creating new comparative advantages. In extrapolating from the Brazilian and Thai cases to the African cases, it is important to identify clearly what is similar and what is different among and between the case studies, both spatially and temporally.

Defining Key Concepts: Comparative Advantage and Competitiveness

The CCAA study objectives cannot be addressed without a clear understanding of the relationship between comparative advantage and competitiveness. The long-run competitiveness of a country or region in producing a particular good depends on its comparative advantage, which depends on the opportunity cost to the country of producing the good in terms of forgone production of other goods and services. A country is said to have a comparative advantage in the production of a good if it has a lower opportunity cost of producing the good (in terms of forgone production of other goods and services) than do other countries.

A country is competitive in international markets if it produces at a lower cost than alternative suppliers, in terms of either the prevailing import or export status of a particular good. Competitiveness does not explicitly consider opportunity costs to the country of transfers and subsidies that affect the direct costs of production. In the short run, a country can be competitive in a particular activity if that activity is subsidized with resources drawn from elsewhere in the economy or from donors, but unless those transfers lead to long-run declines in the opportunity cost of carrying out the activity, that competitiveness will not be economically sustainable. Box 1.2 explores in more depth these relationships among competitiveness, comparative advantage, and subsidies.

Comparative advantage in the least developed countries largely derives from their original natural resource endowment (for example, in terms of soil, climate, and geographic location), but as countries develop investments in technology, resource enhancements (for example, education of the labor force) and institutions that structure incentives in the economy increasingly determine these countries' comparative advantage.

Box 1.2

Comparative Advantage, Efficiency, and Competitiveness

A fundamental notion in economics is ***opportunity cost***—the value of the opportunity forgone by taking one action rather than another. For example, the opportunity cost of land devoted to maize production is the forgone value of some other product that could be produced on that land. A nation is better off if it produces those goods for which the opportunity cost is lowest because the country thus gives up the least, in terms of forgone production, for the goods and services it produces. This is the basic notion of ***comparative advantage,*** which was first developed extensively by David Ricardo in the 19th century to explain why trade could be beneficial to a country even if it could produce all goods at a lower absolute cost than its potential trading partners. Ricardo (1821) showed that countries could gain from trade if they specialized in producing goods for which they have lower opportunity costs than other countries and traded for other higher-opportunity-cost goods. A country has a comparative advantage in the production of a good if the country has a lower opportunity cost of produc-ing the good (in terms of forgone production of other goods and services) than do other countries.

Economists speak of the economic and financial costs of producing a good (Gittinger 1982). The ***economic cost*** represents the cost to society as a whole of producing the good, independent of any transfer payments among actors within the economy, such as taxes and subsidies. Such payments simply redistribute ownership claims within the economy, but neither increase nor decrease the total resources available to the economy. Thus, the economic cost of producing a good represents the opportunity cost to the nation as a whole of producing that good. A country that produces goods at their lowest possible economic cost (that is, produces them in an *economically* efficient manner) is thus following its comparative advantage. In this sense, economic efficiency and comparative advantage are equivalent terms.

Financial cost refers to the opportunity cost to a particular actor in the econ-omy of producing a good or service and includes net transfers to or from that actor as a result of ***taxes and subsidies.*** If the transfers to the actor from others in the economy (for example, via subsidies) are high enough, the actor may be able sell the good *competitively* in international markets (that is, at a lower cost than alternative suppliers) even if the opportunity cost to the country as a whole of producing the good is higher than in other competing countries. For the country as a whole, subsidies represent simply a transfer of resources among actors within

(continued)

Box 1.2 *(Continued)*

the country, implying no change in the cost to the country of producing the good and hence no change in comparative advantage. Thus, in the short run, because of transfers and subsidies, a country can have a **competitive advantage** in a market without having a **comparative advantage**. In the long run, however, the subsidy has to be financed through forgone production elsewhere in the economy (or from outside sources, if financed by donors). Thus, the sustainability of this kind of competitive advantage depends on the willingness of those financing the subsidy (other sectors of the economy or outside donors) to continue to pay the bill.

The foregoing analysis is essentially static. Opportunity costs, however, are not static (Abbott and Brehdal 1994). They derive not only from a country's original natural resource endowment (for example, soil particularly well suited to growing cotton relative to other crops), but also from human-created factors as well. In fact, while in the least developed countries, the original natural resource endowment is usually the main source of comparative advantage, the role of resource endowments generally declines over time for three reasons:

- Resource endowments change over time because of population growth and how people manage those resources. For example, increasing population pressure on the land will typically shift comparative advantage more toward labor-intensive agricultural goods and away from land-intensive goods (Boserup 1993).
- Investments and disinvestments in infrastructure and education change the natural and human resource base available, and new technologies change the efficiency with which those resources can be transformed into different products, thus changing relative opportunity costs.
- All costs, including the opportunity costs that define comparative advantage, are in part social constructions, depending on the institutional rules that determine *which* costs and *whose* costs are taken into account in the economic calculus in a particular country (Bromley 1997; Unger 2007). Changes in the rules governing the economy thus influence comparative advantage, as well as the incentives to develop and adopt new technologies. For example, institutions that secure land tenure and property rights provide incentives to private investors.

Michael Porter (1998) has expanded the notion of **competitiveness** to take into account more dynamic factors. His analysis of a country's competitiveness seeks to explain why certain countries become home to firms that consistently

(continued)

Box 1.2 *(Continued)*

earn higher profits than their competitors. Porter identified four key determinants of national competiveness: (a) factor conditions (similar to the notion of original resource endowment, but supplemented by additional investments—for example, through advanced education of the labor force—to develop those resources further); (b) demand conditions (for example, a strong local or regional market can help achieve scale economies, allowing a firm to compete more effectively in international markets); (c) agglomeration economies (fostered by strategic investments in infrastructure); and (d) firm strategy, structure, and rivalry (conditioned by government policies). His definition of national competitiveness therefore is consistent with the dynamic view of comparative advantage used in this report.

The notion that comparative advantage depends on institutional rules, meaning that it can be modified over time through investments in technologies, education, and infrastructure, raises questions about whether government expenditures aimed at increasing the country's comparative advantage *and* competitiveness in a particular product or industry represent investments or subsidies.

If strategic investments by government (which, of course, have to be financed somehow—for example, though taxation, borrowing, or inflation) can lower the relative costs of producing different goods (that is, its comparative advantage), then what is the difference between a subsidy and a public investment, because each involves a transfer from one set of actors to another? Here, we define a **subsidy** as a transfer that reduces the firm's unit cost of production of a product only for as long as the subsidy is in place. A subsidy creates no structural change in the underlying opportunity costs of producing different goods. A successful **public investment**, in contrast, reduces the opportunity cost of production of the targeted good even after the investment has ended. By this definition, the payment by the government of a portion of a farmer's fertilizer costs would be a subsidy if, when the payment ended, the opportunity cost of producing the crop on which the fertilizer was applied remained unchanged. However, if the subsidy allows the farmer to learn about and adopt a new cost-reducing technology (for example, a new fertilizer-responsive variety) or input suppliers to achieve economies of scale in distribution, the government payment would represent an investment because these changes represent permanent changes in the opportunity costs of producing a good. The difficulty in distinguishing between subsidies and investments ex ante leads to much confusion in the debate about subsidies and comparative advantage (Unger 2007).

(continued)

Box 1.2 *(Continued)*

This understanding of the dynamic nature of comparative advantage and competitiveness is fundamental to following the logic underlying the CCAA study. The key question asked by the study is whether the African case study countries can, through strategic investments and policy changes, modify their comparative advantage to become more competitive over time in certain agricultural exports, as did Brazil and Thailand.

The CCAA study is grounded in the notion that not only competitiveness but also underlying comparative advantage are essentially dynamic concepts:

• The study is built around comparative case studies of areas in Brazil, Thailand, Mozambique, Nigeria, and Zambia that are agroecologically similar. Starting with that natural resource endowment, Brazil and Thailand made a series of investments and institutional changes that allowed the Cerrado and the Northeast Region to gain comparative advantage in the international markets for certain commodities. The central analytic question asked by the CCAA study is whether the study areas in Africa, starting with a similar natural endowment, can make a comparable set of investments and institutional changes that will allow them to replicate the success of Brazil and Thailand in the export markets for these commodities. Thus, the focus of the analysis is on the scope for creating new comparative advantages, rather than simply relying on an "inherent" comparative advantage based solely on natural resource endowment.

• The analysis of the social and environmental impacts of Brazil's and Thailand's "agricultural success stories" and the analysis of the potential social and environmental impacts of the African study countries (assuming that they follow a similar developmental path) are based on the notion that comparative advantage depends upon the institutions under which the economy operates. For example, to the extent that the institutional structure does not guarantee the land rights of indigenous people, those people can be displaced at relatively little cost to settlers intent on converting the land to commercial agriculture. The indigenous people's lost livelihoods are not counted as a cost by the economy, and hence the country may have a strong (socially constructed) comparative advantage in production of the good. A similar logic applies to institutional rules that allow actors to ignore environmental impacts of their actions. With a different set of institutional rules that give effective property rights to indigenous populations and/or to those who suffer environmental damages from the expansion of commercial agriculture, the country would have a different (socially constructed) degree of comparative advantage in production of those goods. The notions of competiveness of commercial agriculture (based on comparative advantage) and of commercial agriculture's social and environmental impacts thus are linked and cannot be analyzed independently of one another.[3]

Notes

1. For simplicity, throughout this report the term "Africa" is used to denote "Sub-Saharan Africa."

2. During 1993-2005, agricultural growth at 4.0 percent per annum exceeded nonagricultural growth of 2.9 percent per annum in the agriculture-based countries, most of which are in Sub-Saharan Africa. Significantly too, agricultural growth has consistently accelerated in Sub-Saharan Africa since 1990.

3. Many of the debates surrounding international trade negotiations revolve around the issue of which sets of institutional rules (for example, regarding labor and environmental standards) should be universally applied to all countries versus which fall under the domain of national sovereignty. This debate is ultimately ethical rather than just technical (Singer 2002).

CHAPTER 2

Past Experience: Asia and Latin America vs. Sub-Saharan Africa

History provides a number of examples in which challenging agroecological conditions similar to those facing many African countries today have been overcome, with impressive results in terms of agricultural development, economic growth, and poverty reduction. Two of these examples were examined in some detail as part of the CCAA study and compared with three African case study countries, in the hope that the comparison can provide insights that may be of use in promoting successful agricultural commercialization strategies in Africa.

Brazil and Thailand

Over the past 40 years, two relatively backward and landlocked agricultural regions in the developing world—the Cerrado region of Brazil and the Northeast Region of Thailand—have developed at a rapid pace and conquered important world markets. Their success defied the predictions of many skeptics, who had asserted that the two regions' challenging agroecological characteristics, remote locations, and high levels of poverty would prove impossible to overcome.

The Cerrado Region of Brazil

In terms of climate and natural resource endowments, the Cerrado region of northwest Brazil (figure 2.1) would not appear to be a particularly promising place to give rise to an agricultural revolution.[1] Rain in the Cerrado falls mainly from October to March; from May to September, precipitation is negligible. Most of the soils in the Cerrado are highly weathered Oxisols (46 percent), Ultisols (15 percent), and Entisols (15 percent). These soil types are generally suitable for agriculture, but they are highly permeable, and as a result they tend also to be extremely leached and low in key macro- and micronutrients. Cerrado soils also tend to be very acidic, featuring pH levels ranging from less than 4 to slightly above 5. This reduces their agricultural potential, unless the chemical imbalances can be corrected by application of lime and fertilizer. In addition, given the low water retention capacity of the predominant soil types and the frequent occurrence of intraseasonal dry spells, agriculture in the Cerrado is prone to drought. With regard to topography, the mostly flat terrain makes the Cerrado highly suitable for mechanized agriculture.

Throughout most of the modern history of Brazil, the Cerrado region was a backwater, a remote and sparsely populated expanse that made little direct contribution to the national economy. The expansion of agriculture into the so-called "empty space" of the Cerrado began in the 1930s under the Marcha para o Oeste program.[2] It received further impetus from the 1940 law establishing *colonias-nucleos* (nucleus colonies), which explicitly envisaged the establishment of a small-farm agrarian structure. However, over the next two decades, the impact of these initiatives was limited. The population of the Cerrado increased very little, and most agricultural expansion occurred in other areas that were closer to existing industrialized zones.

Significant changes began after the relocation of the federal capital in 1961. Spurred by rising urban demand for food and facilitated by new roads connecting Brasilia to the rest of the country, policy initiatives were undertaken to increase the colonization[3] of the Cerrado, such as the Programa de Colonizacao Dirigida, which aimed to settle one million families. Special programs for the development of particular states followed, which sought to stimulate migration into sparsely populated areas and to encourage the transformation of land into productive agriculture. Complementary agricultural policies were introduced to support these objectives, including subsidies on agricultural inputs, concessional credit for farmers, and agricultural price supports. However, the support provided to agricultural terms of trade through these sectoral policies was

Figure 2.1   The Cerrado Region of Brazil

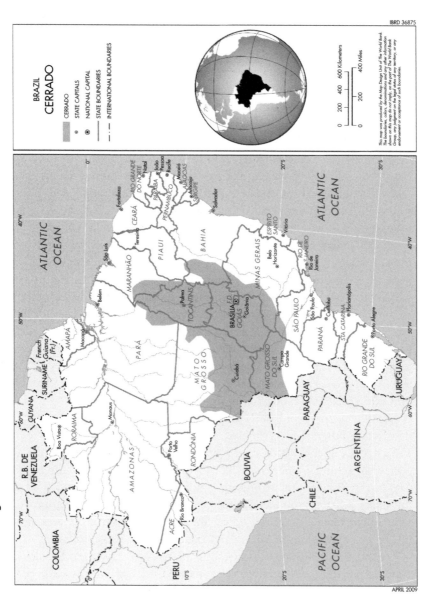

IBRD 36875

BRAZIL
CERRADO

- CERRADO
- ⊕ STATE CAPITALS
- ⊛ NATIONAL CAPITAL
- –·–·– STATE BOUNDARIES
- ––––– INTERNATIONAL BOUNDARIES

0   200   400   600 Kilometers
0   200   400 Miles

This map was produced by the Map Design Unit of The World Bank.
The boundaries, colors, denominations and any other information
shown on this map do not imply, on the part of The World Bank
Group, any judgment on the legal status of any territory, or any
endorsement or acceptance of such boundaries.

APRIL 2009

Source: IFPRI.

43

largely undermined by negative macroeconomic policies (Schiff and Valdés 1998).[4]

During the 1980s and 1990s, progressive liberalization of the economy, coupled with better targeting of agricultural policies, contributed to a major transformation of Brazilian agriculture. Brazil's current highly diversified agricultural sector (including agroindustry) can be cited as one of the most spectacular examples of economic success achieved anywhere in the world in recent decades. Since 1990, grain production has doubled, and livestock production has nearly tripled. During the same period, agricultural exports expanded rapidly, with average export growth rates between 1990 and 2003 ranking second to only those of Mexico. Much of the growth occurred in the Cerrado region, which now accounts for more than one-half of the national soybean crop, one-third of the national maize and cotton crops, and one-quarter of the national rice crop.

Brazil's rise to prominence in international agricultural markets was led by a remarkable transformation of the national soybean subsector. In 2005, 33 percent of the soybeans and soybean-derived products (oil, meal) traded in international markets were sourced from Brazil. Soybean production in Brazil underwent two periods of rapid growth, the first of which was largely led by the government and the second by the private sector. The area planted to soybeans expanded from less than 250,000 hectares in 1961 to almost 9 million hectares in 1980. During the same period, production of soybeans increased from just over 250,000 metric tons per year to more than 15 million metric tons per year. Between 1990 and 2000, production doubled once again, while the area under cultivation saw a relatively modest increase of about 14 percent.

Five key factors drove the transformation of the Cerrado region into an international export powerhouse.

First, the national agricultural research organization EMBRAPA developed the technology necessary to cultivate soybeans successfully in the Cerrado, including a range of high-yielding soybean varieties adapted to the many different production microenvironments, as well as improved crop management practices based on the use of fertilizer and lime (needed to neutralize the natural acidity of many Cerrado soils).

Second, following the relocation of the national capital to Brasilia in 1961, large public investments were made in infrastructure, rural credit, and business development services as the government promoted migration to the previously underdeveloped Cerrado.

Third, the government's policies to promote colonization of the Cerrado attracted many experienced agricultural entrepreneurs from the southern part of the country who provided the investment capital and know-how that stimulated the growth of soybean cultivation.

Fourth, economic and political reforms enacted during the mid-1990s improved the investment climate and permitted the direct transmission of international market signals that served to highlight the cost advantage of Brazilian agriculture. Allowed to compete unencumbered in international markets, the private sector began to drive a development process that previously had been dominated by public agencies and parastatals. Private trading and processing firms made large investments in infrastructure, such as railways and waterways, that drove down freight and port costs and further improved the competitiveness of soybeans.

These four factors—agricultural technology, public investment in infrastructure, entrepreneurial know-how, and a supportive policy environment—affected the supply side.

The fifth and final factor that led to the emergence of the Cerrado region as an agricultural powerhouse was the strong growth in global demand for soybeans and soybean-derived products. This resulted mainly from rapid growth in the use of manufactured livestock feeds, but it was given further impetus by a series of crop failures in traditional soybean-producing countries such as the United States. These crop failures led to historic spikes in international soybean prices during the early 1970s and induced many traditional importers to turn to alternative sources.

Since 1960, the Cerrado region of Brazil has been transformed from a sleepy backwater into a highly productive, globally competitive agricultural exporter. What is striking is that this transformation occurred in a region characterized by the agroecological challenges that are typical of Guinea Savannah zones of Africa today. The experience of the Brazilian Cerrado provides an example of successful agricultural production in difficult agroecological conditions similar to those found in Africa.

The Northeast Region of Thailand

Like the Cerrado region of Brazil, the Northeast Region of Thailand is an unlikely location for an agricultural revolution (figure 2.2). The Northeast Region is blessed by abundant rainfall, but this rainfall is concentrated within a single, relatively short rainy season, and even then its distribution is erratic and unreliable. The region's sandy soils have poor absorption capacity, leaving farmers vulnerable to droughts and floods. The long dry season is very hot. The terrain is relatively level, making it generally suitable for mechanization. Irrigation is possible only in limited areas. About one-third of the total agricultural land (roughly 2.8 million hectares out

Figure 2.2   Extent of the Guinea Savannah Zone Equivalent in Thailand

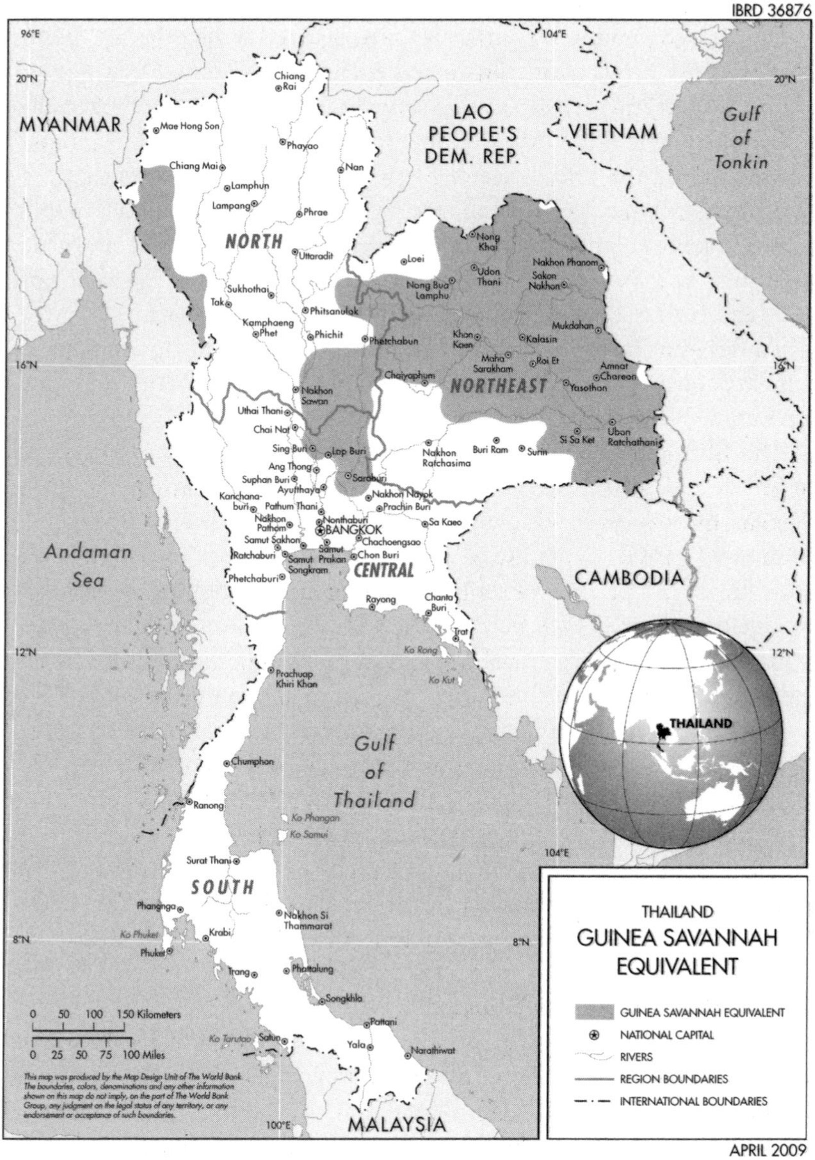

Source: IFPRI.

of 8.6 million hectares) is subject to saline contamination, adversely impacting its suitability for agriculture. Farming is mostly rainfed, but investment in irrigation has increased in recent years, and today about 17 percent of the cropped area is irrigated; however, salinization has emerged as a problem in many irrigated zones, affecting an estimated 10 percent of the irrigated area. The Northeast Region differs from the Cerrado (and from Guinea Savannah environments in general) in that rainfall is abundant, but the problem for agriculture is that the timing is highly unpredictable. Abundance of rainfall also brings its own risks, particularly the risk of flooding, which occurs with some regularity.

The Northeast Region of Thailand was long regarded as "backward," isolated from the country's more dynamic economic hubs, and trapped in a state of perpetual stagnation. Yet despite its modest agroecological potential, the Northeast Region today supports a flourishing agricultural sector that in turn fuels a strong regional economy. Regional economic growth averaged 6.7 percent per year over the past two decades, comparable to the best performances in Latin America and Asia. Between 1988 and 2005, regional GDP more than doubled, and the incidence of poverty fell from 48 percent in 1988 to 17 percent in 2002 (World Bank and NESDB 2005). The thriving regional economy has attracted a considerable amount of immigration. The current population density in the Northeast Region of 129 persons per square kilometer is higher than the national average, marking a significant change for what was once a relatively sparsely populated area.

Public investment in infrastructure played an important role in opening up the Northeast Region of Thailand to agriculture. Spatial dimensions to development planning were absent in early National Plans, and it was not until the Fifth National Plan (1982–86) that rural development received explicit attention. By that time, some rural infrastructure investments were already being made, financed in part by the United States for geostrategic reasons. Rural infrastructure development initially focused on railways, which in addition to their other uses provided a convenient means for transporting locally produced rice to urban centers in the south of the country. During the 1950s and 1960s, attention was increasingly directed to improving rural road access as a way of encouraging more diversified commercial agriculture. The unofficial policy of encouraging commercial agriculture was formally codified in the Sixth National Plan (1987–91), which for the first time targeted "production for sale." Today, the dominant crop grown in the Northeast Region continues to be rice, which is produced partly for home consumption and partly for sale (60 percent of the region's 10 million hectares are planted to rice, and Thailand is the world's largest rice exporter). However, production of crops that are purely cash crops has increased steadily, led initially by cassava, which became important during the 1970s. Responding to relative price movements and other factors, farmers in the Northeast Region regularly alternate between cash crops (including sugar and, to a lesser extent, maize), but cassava remains the dominant cash crop in the region in terms of cultivated area. Thailand is the world's only significant exporter of cassava products.

The development of the cassava subsector in the Northeast Region has been nothing short of spectacular. The Northeast Region accounts for more than 80 percent of national cassava production, so developments in the region have been reflected in national statistics. For Thailand as a whole, production of cassava increased from 1.7 million metric tons in 1961 to 20.7 million metric tons in 1996. This rapid expansion was fueled almost exclusively by growing demand in export markets: approximately 80 percent of the crop is exported (Ratanawaraha, Senanarong, and Suriyaphan 2000).

Five key factors were instrumental in driving the transformation of the Northeast Region into an agricultural success story.

First, Thailand's cassava producers were able to capitalize on a favorable market opportunity, just as the Cerrado soybean farmers had been able to. During the 1970s, trade and agricultural policies in the European Union (EU) drove up the prices of cereals in EU markets; when many European livestock producers turned to cassava as a low-cost feed substitute, international prices for cassava soared (Hershey et al. 2001). Up until 1980, Thai cassava chips and pellets used for feed could be imported into the EU free from tariffs or quotas, and after 1980 they continued to benefit from favorable tariff treatment up to a voluntary export quota limit (Ratanawaraha, Senanarong, and Suriyaphan 2000).

Second, producers in the Northeast Region were able to respond to strengthening demand for cassava and other cash crops by expanding the cultivated area. The expansion was made possible by the availability of uncultivated land in forested areas of the Northeast Region, combined with lax government enforcement of nonencroachment policies (Hershey et al. 2001). That the rise of commercial agriculture in the Northeast Region was made possible through extensification can be seen from the fact that yields for most cash crops have increased only modestly, even as the area planted has expanded.

Third, access to markets (including processing facilities) was already well established by the time commercial agriculture began to take off. As part of its long-standing policy to encourage settlement in the Northeast Region in the face of threatened communist encroachment from Laos, the government had invested heavily in a good road system linking the Northeast Region to urban population centers in the south (Cropper, Griffiths, and Mani 1997; Hershey et al. 2001).

Fourth, a strong research program led by the Rayong Field Crops Research Center (Rayong-FCRC), with important input from the Colombia-based Centro Internacional de Agricultura Tropical (International Center for Tropical Agriculture; CIAT), generated the technologies needed by farmers to respond to changes in growing conditions and in market demand, including appropriate varieties and improved management practices for soil nutrient conservation and erosion control to combat declining soil fertility.

Fifth, a dynamic private sector was able to respond quickly to market signals, paving the way for rapid supply response. The private sector included resourceful local traders capable of organizing plot consolidation among farmers to permit increased mechanization and efficiency in planting and production (Hershey et al. 2001). Land consolidation is an important consideration because the agrarian system in Thailand is dominated by small peasant or family farms, with a very low incidence of large farms and estate farming.

Since 1960, the Northeast Region of Thailand has been transformed from a sleepy backwater into a highly productive, globally competitive agricultural exporter. As in the case of the Cerrado of Brazil, this transformation occurred in a region characterized by the agroecological challenges that are typical of Guinea Savannah zones. The experience of the Northeast Region thus provides a second example of successful agricultural production in difficult agroecological conditions similar to those found in Africa.

Brazil and Thailand: Summary
The agricultural commercialization experiences of the Cerrado region of Brazil and the Northeast Region of Thailand share a number of striking commonalities. Both regions started out with limited agricultural potential, and until quite recently both were characterized as economically backward. In both regions, commercial agriculture initially was concentrated in a small number of commodities that are traded internationally in large quantities and for which quality standards are relatively unimportant. Mostly these were low-value commodities (soybeans and rice in Brazil; cassava, rice, and maize in Thailand). Only after international competitiveness had been established in low-value commodities was competitiveness also established in higher-value commodities, including processed commodities (for example, sugar, soybean oil, cotton lint, cassava starch, and cattle). In both regions, initially producers were able to expand production by focusing on specific markets in which they enjoyed

de jure or de facto preferential access; only later, when the quantities being produced and exported had increased to such an extent that economies of scale could be captured, did Brazilian and Thai farmers establish themselves as low-cost global producers who were able to compete in virtually all markets. In both regions, ample available land, government investment in transport infrastructure, a vibrant private sector, and new agricultural technology were also important factors.

But if the agricultural commercialization experiences of the Brazilian Cerrado and Thailand's Northeast Region were similar in a number of respects, they were also very different in other respects. Most obviously, agricultural production systems in the Cerrado were and continue to be characterized by large-scale mechanized production technologies, whereas agriculture in the Northeast Region was and remains essentially the domain of smallholders.

The Cerrado region of Brazil and the Northeast Region of Thailand both represent examples of rapid agricultural development that led to greater economic prosperity and widespread reductions in poverty. Yet the Brazil and Thailand success stories are not without detractors. Concerns have been raised in both countries over the environmental costs that accompanied economic growth, as well as over the distribution of benefits among different social groups. For this reason, any analysis of lessons learned from Brazil's and Thailand's success stories must include a careful and objective assessment not just of the immediate economic benefits achieved through commercialization but also of the broader developmental consequences that may become apparent only over the longer term.

Sub-Saharan Africa

The successful agricultural commercialization experiences of Brazil and Thailand provide important clues regarding the factors that are likely to determine the future competitiveness of agriculture in many African countries, especially including the three CCAA case study countries that feature large expanses of underutilized Guinea Savannah: Mozambique, Nigeria, and Zambia.

Physical Setting

Physical factors, including land, labor, water, and energy, were key drivers of growth and competitiveness in Brazil and Thailand. The same factors could be drivers of growth and competitiveness in Mozambique, Nigeria, and Zambia.

Mozambique is home to immense tracts of unused forests and sparsely populated savannah land. Nearly one-half (46 percent) of the national land are cultivatable, yet only 10 percent is currently farmed. About 97 percent of the land under cultivation is farmed by smallholders. The average rural household farms only 1.7 hectares, which works out to slightly less than 0.5 hectares per adult equivalent. Annual rainfall averages more than 800 millimeters in most parts of the country. Roughly 541,000 square kilometers can be characterized as Guinea Savannah, representing about 68 percent of the total land surface. Of the Guinea Savannah land, only 21,000 square kilometers are currently cropped (3.9 percent). Most soils found in Mozambique feature moderate-to-low fertility; the only exceptions are a few small pockets of alluvial soils. Many cultivated soils have suffered from moderate-to-high nutrient mining, reflecting the low use of fertilizer. The topography is mostly flat and thus suitable for mechanization. The country is not landlocked, but this advantage has not been translated into a thriving agricultural export sector. Endowed with the best land, the central and northern provinces export agricultural products, while the southern provinces import food and other commodities from the central provinces and from South Africa.

Nigeria features extremely diverse agroecological conditions, ranging from arid and semiarid savannahs in the northern and central parts of the country to subhumid and humid forests in the southern part. Approximately 582,000 square kilometers can be characterized as Guinea Savannah, representing about 64 percent of the national land area. Of the Guinea Savannah land, 176,000 square kilometers are currently cropped (30.3 percent). Rainfall in the Guinea Savannah zone ranges between 700 and 1,100 millimeters per year. Paradoxically, the Guinea Savannah zone has a low population density compared with that of other regions, reflecting the predominance of difficult soils, as well as severe human and animal disease problems. Cropping systems in the Guinea Savannah feature mainly millet, sorghum, and cowpeas, but with the addition of a significant amount of maize, yams, and rice in the more humid areas. Soybeans have emerged as a commercial crop in the past 10–15 years.

Zambia also has considerable agricultural potential, but this potential remains largely unexploited. Of the country's total land area of around 754,000 square kilometers, approximately 79 percent can be characterized as Guinea Savannah. Of the land considered arable, nearly 420,000 square kilometers are classified as having medium-to-high potential for agriculture, but only about 15 percent of the medium-to-high–potential arable land is currently being utilized, and of this, fewer than 7,000 square kilometers lie in the Guinea Savannah. The population density in most of the productive regions is still very low, ranging from 1 to 11 people per square kilometer. Rainfall ranges between 800 and 1,400 millimeters annually, increasing from south to north. The northern regions receive ample rainfall and are quite sparsely populated. The southern regions are much drier and suffer from frequent drought. It is here that livestock production is most prevalent. On the plateaus around Lusaka, Livingstone, Kabwe, and Chipata, soils are generally fertile, and rainfall is sufficient to support production of a wide range of crops. Further north, the soils are naturally less productive, but their lack of fertility could be overcome with small investments in fertilizer and lime.

Institutional Setting

Mozambique, Nigeria, and Zambia, like many other African countries, have considerable untapped agricultural potential, yet this potential is not being realized. Looking back over 40 years of recent history, it is clear that the emergence of a competitive commercial agriculture sector, not only in these three countries but throughout Africa more generally, has been prevented by institutional bottlenecks and policy constraints that have hampered economic growth in general and agricultural growth in particular.

One of the greatest constraints impeding the development of a modern, efficient agriculture in Africa has been a lack of political commitment to supporting the sector. Successful agricultural commercialization requires strong and sustained support from the state in the form of facilitating policies backed by appropriate investments. Such support is likely to emerge only if political leaders perceive that it is in their interests to provide it. For example, they must feel the need to respond to a strong agricultural constituency, or they must believe that agricultural development is instrumental to some broader political priority. This could involve preserving national unity through incorporation of more remote rural areas, promoting broader economic transformation, or attracting increased foreign assistance from donors concerned about rural poverty. In Brazil and Thailand, beginning in the 1950s and 1960s, successive governments made large and sustained commitments to agricultural development because they were motivated by the desire to ensure adequate food supplies for industrialization, to ensure the territorial integrity of the nation, and/or to avoid communist insurgencies (Thailand). In subsequent decades, new sources of political support for such policies emerged, arising from the quest for agrarian reform and democratic consolidation.

In both countries, powerful agribusiness interests also played an increasingly important role in advocating for supportive policies and programs.

The same decades in Africa were dominated by struggles for independence (often led by urban elites), followed by consolidation of new states during the postcolonial period. Extending infrastructure, education, health services, and other social benefits to the population was often the primary concern of policy makers, along with the promotion of rapid industrialization. Frequently, governments were controlled by dominant political parties that did not need to rely on rural voters to stay in power, being more oriented to the concerns of urban consumers and the military.

Three other factors also contributed to policies that discriminated against agriculture in Africa.

First, most urban-based African leaders saw smallholder agriculture as a backward sector unable to contribute to economic transformation, except through the provision of cheap food and labor to the infant industrial sector (which itself was often protected in ways that further discriminated against agriculture).[5]

Second, because of weak physical infrastructure, widespread information asymmetries, and low levels of marketed surplus, agricultural markets generally performed poorly, characterized by high transaction costs and volatile prices resulting from the markets' residual nature. This poor performance, combined with an ideological distrust of markets by many of the postindependence leaders, often led states to assume very strong roles in all spheres of economic activity. The creation and expansion of food and agricultural marketing boards and parastatals, aimed at dealing with the perceived poor performance of food and agricultural markets, did not address the underlying structural problems giving rise to that poor performance, but simply substituted government bureaucracies for private agents, frequently worsening incentives for farmers.

Third, in the absence of administrative capacity to implement less distortionary taxes (for example, on incomes), export agriculture became a major source of government revenue. Government marketing boards extracted much of the locational rents arising from the countries' inherent comparative advantage in production of export crops, and the failure to reinvest any of these revenues in maintaining or expanding agricultural competitiveness bled the sector dry. In the absence of strong agricultural or agribusiness constituencies, and lacking any conviction that agriculture was strategic to reaching broader goals of economic development and political stability, political leaders had few incentives to focus on agriculture until the long-term consequences of its neglect became apparent in periodic food crises or broader economic malaise. Although programs were occasionally launched to support production of food crops in response to these periodic crises, the incentives introduced under agricultural sector-specific policies usually failed to compensate for the adverse effects of exchange rate overvaluation, industrial protection measures, and trade barriers.

More recently, following a long period of neglect, agriculture has reappeared on the radar screen of many African policy makers, for many reasons. Democratization and decentralization have given more voice to rural constituencies, and disillusionment with state-dominated approaches to development has led to acceptance of more market-oriented approaches. Furthermore, there is now greater awareness, based on observation of the experience of the Asian green revolution and the success of export agriculture in Asia and Latin America, that agriculture can play a key role in catalyzing broader economic growth. Under the aegis of the New Partnership for Africa's Development (NEPAD), African heads of state endorsed the Comprehensive Africa Agricultural Development Programme (CAADP) and—in the 2004 Maputo Declaration—formally committed to investing 10 percent of public budgets in support of agriculture. A year later, in 2005 at the G-8 meeting held in Gleneagles, Scotland, the principal development partners reaffirmed their commitment to agricultural development in general (and to the CAADP agenda in particular) and pledged a tripling of support, raising further the potential political payoffs to African leaders of supporting agriculture. Although these pledges by the African heads of state and by the leaders of Organisation for European Co-operation and Development (OECD) countries are still far from being fulfilled, taxation of the sector has been reduced, and public investment in agriculture has picked up in recent years, indicating stronger commitment than in the recent past.

Notes

1. For simplicity, in this report the Cerrado region is sometimes referred to simply as "the Cerrado."

2. In reality, this land was not always empty; often it was populated by indigenous groups.

3. In the Brazilian context, "colonization" refers to a group of migrants from elsewhere in Brazil beginning to live in areas that were considered to be unoccupied. In fact, indigenous groups were already occupying the area, albeit at a very low population density.

4. Schiff and Valdés (1998) report data for Brazil from 1969 to 1983. During this period, agriculture sector-specific policies supported the economy and increased the agricultural terms of trade by about 10 percent (relative to the level that they would have been, absent any policy interventions). However, indirect bias from overvalued currency and other macroeconomic policies actually depressed the agricultural terms of trade by 18 percent, more than offsetting the support provided through sector-specific policies.

5. A notable exception to this view was that of Felix Houphouët-Boigny, Côte d'Ivoire's postindependence leader. As a cocoa planter whose political base lay in the rural areas, Houphouët-Boigny clearly saw agriculture as a powerful engine for the country's economic development. His government implemented policies very favorable to the sector, with the result that agriculture grew much more strongly in Côte d'Ivoire in the 1960s and 1970s than in most other African countries.

CHAPTER 3

Outlook for Commercial Agriculture in Sub-Saharan Africa

Market opportunities for commercial producers in Africa may exist at several levels: national, regional and subregional, and global.[1] National and regional markets are likely to offer the most attractive opportunities in the short run because they are physically closer and hence more easily accessed, but global markets determine overall price trends and volatility, so they are reviewed first.

Global Outlook for the Studied Commodities

Following a long period of relative stability, prices of international agricultural commodities have recently entered a new era characterized by extreme short-term volatility. Before 1988, the index of real international prices for agricultural commodities (measured in terms of industrial country exports) had fallen steadily for approximately 25 years and then leveled off for a further 7 years. Things changed dramatically beginning in 2005, when the index began to rise sharply in response to a combination of factors (for example, exploding demand for feed grains in several large emerging economies, and weather-related supply shocks in several traditional exporting countries). Over the course of just three years, the index more than doubled, peaking in June 2008. Thereafter, international agricultural commodity prices collapsed as a consequence of the global financial crisis, and by the end of 2008, the index had fallen back to approximately 150 percent of its average 1998–2000 level.

Given the continuing uncertainties prevailing in the global economy, projecting the future course of international agricultural commodity prices is risky. Rather than making such risky projections, the CCAA study sought to derive broad perspectives on possible future developments by examining long-term trends in global supply and demand. Three main questions are addressed, the answers to which are likely to affect the future competitiveness of African agriculture: (a) At what level are agricultural commodity prices likely to settle? (b) Will the recent extreme price volatility continue? (c) How will international trade policies play out in affecting price trends and volatility?

Global Trends in Demand

Global demand for agricultural commodities is determined mainly by three factors: population growth, income growth, and urbanization. In Sub-Saharan Africa, population growth projected to average around 2 percent per year for the foreseeable future will continue to be a major driver of demand growth, especially for food staples. In all developing regions, including Sub-Saharan Africa, rapid income growth and increasing urbanization are causing diets to diversify away from food staples toward livestock products (and feed grains), vegetable oils, fruits, and vegetables, with new markets also emerging for biofuels. Urban consumers are also demanding greater amounts of processed and convenience foods.

Models developed by the International Food Policy Research Institute (IFPRI) indicate that global food consumption will increase more slowly in the future. Growth in cereal consumption will slow from 1.9 percent annually in 1969–99 to 0.9 percent per year during 2000–30; growth in meat consumption will also slow from 2.9 percent annually to 1.4 percent per year. The projected slowdown reflects two factors: a slowing of overall population growth to 0.8 percent per year (nearly all future population growth will come in developing countries), and the fact that staple food consumption per capita is already at fairly high levels in some of the most populous developing countries (for example, China).

These projections may not fully account for possible effects from increases in demand for cereals used in the production of biofuels. The recent surge in worldwide interest in biofuels production, spurred by high energy prices and subsidies, has sparked a significant response in Brazil (sugar-based), North America (maize-based), and the EU (rapeseed-based), leading to immediate major impacts on international prices of these commodities. Brazil is the world's largest and most efficient producer of biofuels, based on its low-cost production of sugarcane. Should oil prices average above US$50 per barrel, as projected by most global forecasts, biofuels production will be profitable and will stimulate increased demand for feedstocks: cereals, sugar, and oilseeds. Recent initiatives to scale up production of biofuels using cassava and palm oil, including in Sub-Saharan Africa, could significantly affect global markets for these two commodities as well. Above US$50 per barrel, agricultural prices will likely be increasingly linked to oil prices and also reflect volatility of oil prices (World Bank 2009).

Global Trends in Supply

Global supplies of food and agricultural commodities are likely to tighten, for several reasons.

Land and water constraints. In the more densely populated parts of the world, the land frontier has essentially been exhausted. In Asia, land scarcity has become acute in most countries, and rapid urbanization is reducing the area available for agriculture. In Latin America, there is considerable scope for agricultural land expansion, but further expansion often will have to come at the cost of cutting down subtropical and tropical forests and woodlands. In some parts of Africa, especially the Guinea Savannah zone, there is much potential to bring additional land under cultivation, but this land can be converted to productive agriculture only with large investments in infrastructure, as well as in human and animal disease control measures.

Meanwhile, water needed for irrigated agriculture will become increasingly scarce in most developing countries because of heightened competition from rapidly growing urban populations and industrial users. Irrigated food production in large areas of China, South Asia, and the Middle East and North Africa is already threatened because ground water is being extracted at unsustainable rates. In Africa and Latin America, untapped water resources are still available for agriculture, but large investments will be needed to exploit their potential.

Uncertain effects of climate change. Global climate change has created tremendous uncertainty for agriculture. In recent years, changes in precipitation patterns have made some regions wetter, but parts of southern Africa and South Asia have become drier, with negative effects for agriculture. Climate change will also lead to greater variability in precipitation and temperatures, increasing the frequency and intensity of droughts and floods that will significantly magnify the impacts of climate shocks on agriculture. Africa will be negatively affected by these developments.

High energy prices. Despite the large fluctuations in oil prices witnessed in 2008, there is broad agreement that over the longer term, prices of fossil fuels will be higher than the average prices experienced during the past decade. This will lead to higher agricultural production costs than in the past (through pressure on the cost of fuel and other energy-dependent inputs such as fertilizer), increased demand for biofuels, and upward pressure on agricultural prices. Beyond the farm gate, costs of inputs and long-distance food distribution will also be affected by higher transport and refrigeration costs.

Slowing of technical change. Among the major cereals—rice, wheat, and maize—yield growth has slowed since the 1980s in most developing countries. This suggests that the easy gains that can be achieved by adopting green revolution inputs have already been realized, except in Africa. The slowdown in R&D spending in many countries, combined with the slow pace of uptake of new products of biotechnology because of regulatory weaknesses and consumer backlash, has raised concerns about the pace of future gains. However, rising food prices could easily reverse these trends, and exploitable yield gaps remain high in medium- to high-potential areas of Africa.

The Bottom Line: Rising Prices and More Uncertainty

What will be the combined effect, over the medium-to-long term, of rapidly growing global demand for agricultural commodities and tightening supplies? Under its baseline scenario, the IFPRI IMPACTS model projects a reversal of the long-term decline in agricultural prices observed in recent decades. It predicts prices will settle at higher levels than during the early years of this century. Although recognizing the uncertainty of long-term projections, IFPRI predicts that under a baseline "business as usual" scenario, cereal prices will increase at a rate of 1.0 percent per year through 2050 (Rosegrant et al. 2008). Increased investment in the sector—for example, a ramping up of spending on agricultural R&D—would likely mitigate some of this impact (World Bank 2009).

These global projections mask some substantial supply-demand imbalances that are expected to emerge in developing countries. Net cereal imports by developing countries of Asia, Africa, and Latin America are projected to increase from 85 million tons in 2000 to 285 million tons in 2050, greatly increasing the importance of developing countries in global food markets, both as suppliers and as consumers. In Sub-Saharan Africa, a growing import gap projected at 75 million tons of cereals per year will provide a major opportunity for domestic and regional market development, as discussed below.

Higher food prices are likely to be accompanied by increased price volatility in global markets because of changes in stockholding policies of some large exporters, and domestic production shocks could become more frequent because of climate change. Countries will need to increase their capacity to manage shocks through production risk mitigation (better water control or drought-tolerant varieties), forward markets, trade, and perhaps insurance.

The most recent medium-term projections by OECD and FAO (2008) are consistent with the IFPRI projections. Projected prices for all commodities to 2018 are higher than those experienced over the period 2003–07, but lower than the 2008 peak (figure 3.1). The largest increase is for oilseeds, through a combination of demand for food, feed, and biofuels. These are average estimates—OECD and FAO are also expecting a more uncertain outlook and more volatile prices.

International Trade Policies

Global market prospects for the CCAA target commodities (cassava, cotton, maize, rice, sugar, and soybeans) are greatly influenced by international trade policies. Agricultural trade is governed by a vast and often

Figure 3.1   International Commodity Price Projections, 2005–2018

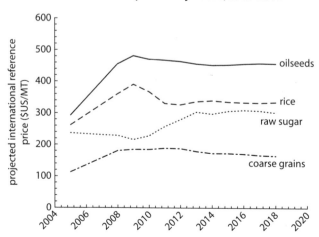

Source: OECD and FAQ 2008.
Note: Data for 2005 are average actual prices for 2003–07. MT = metric ton.

bewildering web of trading rules and regulations that can significantly affect not only the quantities traded but also the prices paid and received.

Trade Policy Distortions and Reform

International trade policies for agriculture are frequently criticized for being distortionary, inequitable, and inefficient. Long-standing policies of OECD countries in particular have been shown to have many negative impacts for developing countries:

- They lower the prices received by farmers in developing countries who produce for the export market. For example, Sumner (2003) estimates that policies implemented by the United States depress world prices of cotton by around 10 percent, significantly reducing returns to cotton producers in many African countries in which cotton is an important export crop.
- They reduce the volume of exports from developing countries. For example, Hassett and Shapiro (2003) estimate that trade barriers enacted in the EU have reduced African meat exports by about 60 percent and African grain exports by more than 40 percent.
- They reduce the cost of imports into developing countries, increasing competition for producers in those countries in domestic and regional markets. For example, in the case of rice—a commodity imported in significant quantities across Africa—international prices are lower by about 4 percent compared with what they would be in the absence of producer support measures and subsidies in OECD countries.

But trade policies enacted by OECD countries are not alone in disadvantaging producers in developing countries. Many developing countries also maintain trade barriers and policies that have significant negative impacts for local producers, especially in oilseeds, sugar, and rice.

Reform of trade-distorting policies has been under discussion in the Doha round of trade negotiations, but the latest round of negotiations has collapsed, largely because of failure to agree on agricultural policy reforms. The reform agenda remains important, however: full trade liberalization would lead to large gains for those developing countries that are already large agricultural exporters, including the two CCAA "success story" countries, Brazil and Thailand. These two countries are already able to compete in global markets, even without subsidies, and despite the adverse international trade environment. With appropriate policies and investments, many African countries could potentially mirror the success of Brazil and Thailand. Diao and Yanoma (2007) estimate that African countries would benefit by US$5 billion annually from full trade reform.

The impacts of trade liberalization would not be positive for all developing countries, however. Countries such as Nigeria that are net food importers would lose from the modest rise in cereal prices expected to follow from trade liberalization (World Bank 2009). Still, it is worth noting that the projected price rises from trade liberalization are quite small relative to recent increases in cereal prices caused by increased food demand, tightening global supplies, and rapidly rising demand for grain for biofuel.

Preferential Trade Policies for Africa

International trade policies have been instrumental in helping a number of African countries achieve footholds in global commodities markets. Preferential market access granted to African countries by the EU and the United States has already created attractive export opportunities for the African case study countries. For example, current sugar exports from Mozambique and Zambia depend critically on preferential access to the EU market.

Preferential trade agreements can help boost exports in the short-to-medium term, but they have an efficiency cost because they shield producers from competitive forces and allow inefficient production methods to persist. History tells us that eventually the inefficiency costs become too expensive to maintain, leading to market liberalization measures that can leave producers noncompetitive. For example, under the renegotiated EU trade preferences regime that will soon come into effect, sugar will become freely importable into the EU, but the price will be lower than in the past because of the changes in the EU sugar regime. Mozambican and Zambian sugar producers may not be able to compete at the new, lower prices.

Nontariff Barriers

In recent years, phytosanitary regulations have emerged as important barriers that have served to slow agricultural and agroindustrial exports from developing countries. The rapid evolution of phytosanitary standards and their increasing stringency are often driven by consumer demand factors, although it must be recognized that phytosanitary standards can also be used by trade regulators in lieu of tariff barriers to protect against imports (World Bank 2005a). If African countries are to avoid being shut out of the international trade arena, they will have little choice but to participate in the standard-setting processes and bodies, while at the same time building capacity in their export sectors to comply with rapidly evolving regulations. Small countries face a particular challenge in this area, because it will be relatively more expensive for them to bear the fixed costs needed to provide the necessary services. Regional collaboration and adoption of common standards will facilitate compliance at an affordable cost.

Domestic and Regional Markets

Although prices of most agricultural commodities are set mainly in global markets, domestic and regional markets are likely to offer the most attractive opportunities for African producers, at least in the short-to-medium term. In this respect, the situation facing African producers today is quite different from the situation facing producers in Brazil and Thailand when their agricultural sectors were commercializing. It is different for two reasons.

First, domestic and regional markets for food staples are not only enormous in Africa, but they are growing rapidly, fueled by population growth and rising incomes. Expressed in value terms, the demand for food staples in Africa was projected to double from US$50 billion in 2005 to US$100 billion in 2015. An increasing share of output will be commercialized as the continent becomes more urbanized (Diao and Yanoma 2007).

Second, capacity to produce food has declined in many countries. Although this trend has recently been reversed in a few countries, the dependence on food imports continues to grow in most African countries, providing a large and assured market for food crops with an import substitution potential.

Market prospects for the three African CCAA countries are summarized in table 3.1. Of the six target commodities, only cotton is produced mainly for export into global markets. Sub-Saharan Africa is a net importer of rice, maize, and soybeans. Sugar represents a special case: Africa exports nearly US$1 billion annually, but it also imports US$825 million annually from outside the region, reflecting the special concessions provided in the EU to African sugar exporters.

Although many of the same food crops are grown throughout large parts of Africa (for example, maize in eastern and southern Africa, roots and tubers in western and central Africa, and sorghum and millet in the Sahelian countries), there are clear differences between countries in patterns of comparative advantage. These differences provide opportunities for regional trade. Diao and Yanoma (2007) used revealed comparative

Table 3.1 Market Prospects for CCAA Target Commodities

	Mozambique		Nigeria		Zambia	
	Average value (2004–06)	Growth rate (1996–2006)	Average value (2004–06)	Growth rate (1996–2006)	Average value (2004–06)	Growth rate (1996–2006)
MAIZE						
Area ('000 ha)	1,494	2.7	4,314	1.1	843	−2.3
Yield (t/ha)	1.1	1.1	1.6	3.5	1.6	1.6
Production ('000 t)	1,607	3.9	7,112	4.7	1,334	−0.8
Net trade ('000 t)	16	—	57	—	182	—
Imports/Cons (%)	7.0	—	0.8	—	0.8	—
Market outlook	Increasing demand for both food and livestock feed. Significant opportunities for regional trade.		Rapid growth for food in the 1980s has slowed, but demand for feed should provide significant potential for growth.		Major food staple, with demand driven by population and income growth. Significant opportunities for growth through regional trade.	
RICE						
Area ('000 ha)	203	1.9	2,410	1.7	13	1.4
Yield (t/ha)	1.0	−0.4	1.6	0.9	1.0	0.8
Production ('000 t)	201	1.5	3,608	2.7	12.0	2.2
Net trade ('000 t)	−372	—	−1,583	—	−21	—
Imports/Cons (%)	71.7	—	41.7	—	72	—
Market outlook	Major potential for import substitution. Expanding market via urbanization.		One of the world's largest importers. Rising demand caused by urbanization provides almost unlimited markets.		Relatively minor crop, but could target regional markets.	

(continued)

Table 3.1 Market Prospects for CCAA Target Commodities *(Continued)*

	Mozambique		Nigeria		Zambia	
	Average value (2004–06)	*Growth rate (1996–2006)*	*Average value (2004–06)*	*Growth rate (1996–2006)*	*Average value (2004–06)*	*Growth rate (1996–2006)*
CASSAVA						
Area ('000 ha)	997	0.8	3,870	2.3	177	1.8
Yield (t/ha)	7.4	2.7	12.1	2.4	5.4	–0.6
Production ('000 t)	7,425	3.5	46,817	4.7	948	1.2
Net trade ('000 t)	0.0	0.0	0.0	0.0	0.0	0.0
Imports/Cons (%)	0.0	0.0	0.0	0.0	0.0	0.0
	Small domestic market. Prospects for regional markets and for developing new local markets (for example, substitution for wheat flour).		Most important food crop, but low income elasticity of demand. Good prospects for animal feed and other uses.		One of the fastest-growing food staples, substituting for maize. Demand depends on maize policies and development of processing sector.	
SOYBEANS						
Area ('000 ha)	—	—	632	1.3	11	–0.1
Yield (t/ha)	—	—	0.7	0.6	1.2	–1.4
Production ('000 t)	—	—	467	2.0	12.5	–1.5
Net trade ('000 t)	—	—	0.0	—	–5.0	—
Imports/Cons (%)	—	—	0.0	—	28.3	—
	Growing demand for livestock feed.		Growing demand for both human and animal feed.		Small but growing market for livestock feed, currently served by the large-scale sector. Potential for regional markets.	

SUGAR

Area ('000 ha)	177	2.9	48	2.1	24	0.0
Yield (t/ha)	14.7	0.0	21.1	0.0	104.2	0.0
Production ('000 t)	2,600	3.0	1,015	2.1	2,500	0.0
Net trade ('000 t)	280	—	60	—	304	—
Imports/Cons (%)	0.0	—	0.0	—	0.0	—
	Could expand to EU markets with sugar policy reforms.		Huge market for import substitution if competitive.		Reform of EU sugar policy will expand market opportunities, but reduce preferential prices. Good prospects for regional markets and possibly biofuels.	

COTTON

Area ('000 ha)	190	-4.7	390	3.1	185	1.7
Yield (t/ha)	0.2	4.1	0.2	0.7	0.2	-1.2
Production ('000 t)	28.7	-0.9	84	3.9	36	0.5
Net trade ('000 t)	29	—	25	—	33	—
Imports/Cons (%)	0.0	—	23.6	—	0.0	—
	International exports are growing and considerable future potential.		Domestic demand depends on revival of textile industry.		Rapidly expanding sector accounting for 40% of agricultural exports. Impacts of textile trade reforms on AGOA may reduce competitiveness.	

Source: FAOSTAT (http://faostat.fao.org/), accessed 12/15/2008.

Note: ha = hectares. — = not available. n.a. = not applicable. t = tons. Cons = Consumption. AGOA = African Growth and Opportunity Act.

advantage to identify 29 food commodities for which there are significant exports and imports within the region and that have the potential for regional trade. Subregional trade could also help to smooth out the impacts of drought on production and prices at country and subregional levels, because of weak correlation between production and rainfall even within a subregion (Badiane and Resnick 2005). Adding to the attractiveness of national and regional markets are the lower quality requirements, compared with those typically prevailing in international markets.

Despite the appeal of regional trade, limited success has been achieved in developing reliable intra-African trade in food crops. Total intraregional trade in food staples is only US$0.8 billion annually, out of a total food import bill of US$6 billion. The major trade flows are outside the region, rather than within. Maize is the only one of the six CCAA commodities for which there is currently significant intraregional trade.

African governments have recognized the importance of regional trade. Freeing trade within the region is one of the major objectives of NEPAD and subregional organizations. But intraregional trade in food crops and associated inputs (for example, seed and fertilizer) continues to be severely constrained by a number of factors:

- The dispersed nature of production, large distances between production and consumption centers, and poor infrastructure, including uncoordinated transport connectivity across countries
- Institutional constraints (for example, the lack of credit, poorly functioning market information systems, differences in food safety requirements, and quality and product standards)
- High border transaction costs associated with bureaucratic procedures and rent-seeking activities
- The unpredictable behavior of governments in imposing export bans whenever they fear food shortages in their own markets. Few governments will be willing to make credible long-term commitments to allow free cross-border trade in staple foods until there is some assurance that food will be readily available within the region in all except the very worst years.

Although domestic and subregional markets for food crops appear to present the most promising opportunities in the short-to-medium run, there are and increasingly will be opportunities for African countries to export into international markets. Still, when considering the prospects for successfully exporting food crops, it is important to note that almost all past cases of African agricultural export success have involved high-value, relatively nonperishable commodities—cocoa, coffee, cotton, tobacco, tea, groundnuts, cashews, oil palm, and rubber. Most of these crops tend to be grown in restricted areas featuring specialized agroclimatic characteristics, which limits global supplies. Many also require large amounts of labor for production or processing, which confers clear advantage to African producers having plentiful, low-cost labor supplies.

In contrast, Africa has yet to record any significant export success with low-value bulk commodities, including cereals, pulses, oilseeds, and roots and tubers. These commodities tend to have less stringent agroclimatic requirements and can therefore be grown in a wide range of locations throughout the world. Also, their production is often amenable to mechanization, making them economically attractive even in places where labor supplies may be constrained. Although quite a few African countries may be able to compete effectively with imports of food commodities, because transport and handling costs often add markedly to the landed cost of these commodities, the same countries usually face a formidable challenge in attempting to cross the threshold from import substitution to competitiveness as international exporters.

Improved competitiveness on the part of African countries in the production of food staples could indirectly improve competitiveness in the production of food and non-food by relaxing the food security constraint—both for governments and for farmers. In the long run, given the more favorable outlook for world markets, the CCAA countries reviewed in this study, with their relatively good land and water resources and low population density, could emerge as major exporters on world markets in commodities such as soybeans, sugar, cotton, and rice.

Note

1. This section draws heavily on World Bank (2007) and Rosegrant et al. (2006).

CHAPTER 4

Commodity-Specific Competitiveness Analysis

Value chain analysis was carried out in the CCAA countries to generate a set of quantitative indicators that can be used to make cross-country comparisons. The method also facilitates identification of specific areas in which cost reductions and/or productivity increases have potential to improve international competitiveness. The analysis was carried out using an original spreadsheet-based methodology designed to provide a practical way of calculating standardized indicators (for details, see Keyser [2006]). In Africa, the value chain analysis was undertaken for Mozambique, Nigeria, and Zambia. To establish international benchmarks, value chain analysis was also carried out for Brazil and Thailand.

Consistent with the overall CCAA study design, the value chain analysis covered six commodities (cassava, cotton, maize, rice, soybeans, and sugar) and three farm categories (family farms, emerging commercial farms, and large-scale commercial farms). The three farm categories were defined not in terms of farm size or legal status, but by the management system and labor supply. In all cases, the emphasis was on commercial agriculture, rather than subsistence-oriented production.

- **Family farms (FAM)** are farms on which family members double as managers. These farms do not employ full-time hired workers on a permanent basis, although they may hire part-time or full-time workers temporarily during peak production periods.

- **Emerging commercial farms (ECF)** also are characterized by the presence of family members who double as managers, but these farms typically employ one to three full-time hired workers. Additional hired labor may also be used during peak production periods.
- **Large commercial farms (LCF)** are managed by specialized managers, who may be either a family member or a hired professional manager. These farms employ three or more full-time hired workers, as well as additional hired labor during peak production periods.

The value chain analysis generated a number of key performance indicators that provide important insights into the international competitiveness of each country with regard to each of the target commodities. These indicators, which are presented in figure 4.1 and tables 4.1–4.6, include the following:

- **Average yield** = average yield (in kilograms/hectare) achieved using recommended production practices and economically efficient levels of inputs. The average yield is a good indicator of physical productivity at the farm level.
- **Farm-level shipment value (SV)** = the value in financial terms of domestic and foreign inputs per unit of output, measured at the farm level. The farm-level SV is a good indicator of the unit value of producing the unprocessed commodity and an important benchmark for use in cross-country comparisons. The unit cost of production is a better indicator than yield for determining competitiveness, because high yields do not necessarily mean low-cost production—sometimes high yields require high levels of expensive inputs. The factors that most influence farm-level SV are precisely those that determine comparative advantage: (a) agroclimatic conditions in the production zone, (b) prior investments in technologies and modifications of the natural resource base through infrastructure, and (c) institutions that shape incentives faced by producers.
- **Import competitiveness ratio** = SV at the main domestic consumption point/import parity price at the main domestic consumption point.
- **Export competitiveness ratio** = SV at the border/export parity price at the border. These competitiveness ratios can be interpreted in much the same way as resource cost ratios used in domestic resource cost

Figure 4.1   Composition of Farm-Level Shipment Values

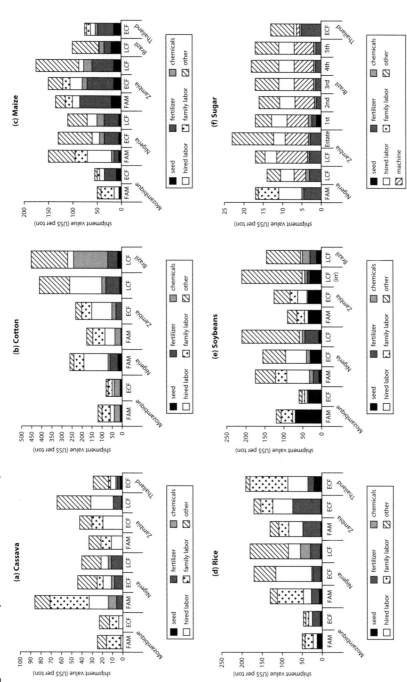

Source: Authors' calculations.
Note: FAM = family farms. ECF = emerging commercial farms. LCF = large commercial farms. Estate = Estate farms (Zambia only). irr = irrigated.

Table 4.1   Competitiveness Indicators from Value Chain Analysis: Cassava (2007)

	Mozambique		Nigeria			Zambia			Thailand
	FAM	ECF	FAM	ECF	LCF	FAM	ECF	LCF	ECF
Domestic consumption location	Nacala		Ibadan			Kasama			Khon Kaen
Port of entry (imports)	Durban		Lagos			Durban			Bangkok
International market source (imports)	via Rotterdam		via Rotterdam			via Rotterdam			U.S. gulf ports
Domestic yields (mt/ha)	1.3	2.5	3.0	3.6	5.0	4.0	4.5	12.0	16.7
SV at farm (US$/mt)	26	22	86	44	40	34	42	63	26
Assembly and processing costs (US$/mt)	103	107	96	138	152	94	87	68	64
SV at consumption point (US$/mt)	129	129	183	183	192	128	128	131	90
Import parity at consumption point (US$/mt)	351		321			501			276
Logistics port to consumption (US$/mt)	50		40			200			15
Logistics international market to port (US$/mt)	140		120			140			100
International reference price (US$/mt)	161		161			161			161
Import competitiveness ratio	**0.37**	**0.37**	**0.57**	**0.57**	**0.60**	**0.26**	**0.26**	**0.26**	**0.33**
Domestic production/processing location	Nacala		Ibadan			Kasama			Khon Kaen
Port of exit (exports)	Durban		Lagos			Durban			Bangkok
International market destination (exports)	Rotterdam		Rotterdam			Rotterdam			Rotterdam
Domestic yields (mt/ha)	1.3	2.5	3.0	3.6	5.0	4.0	4.5	12.0	16.7
SV at farm (US$/mt)	26	22	86	44	40	34	42	63	26
Assembly and processing costs (US$/mt)	103	107	96	138	152	94	87	68	64
Logistics assembly point to port (US$/mt)	50		40			200			15
SV at port of exit (US$/mt)	179	179	223	223	232	328	328	331	105
Export parity at port (US$/mt)	21		41			21			61
Logistics port to international market (US$/mt)	140		120			140			100
International reference price (US$/mt)	161		161			161			161
Export competitiveness ratio	**8.5**	**8.5**	**5.4**	**5.4**	**5.7**	**15.6**	**15.6**	**15.8**	**1.7**

Source: CCAA background studies.

Note: mt = metric ton(s). ha = hectare(s). SV = shipment value. FAM = family farms. ECF = emerging commercial farms. LCF = large commercial farms.

Table 4.2 Competitiveness Indicators from Value Chain Analysis: Cotton (2007)

	Mozambique		Nigeria		Zambia			Brazil
	FAM	ECF	FAM	FAM	FAM	ECF	LCF (irr)	LCF
Domestic consumption location	Nacala		Rotterdam		Katete		Lusaka	Santos
Port of entry (imports)	Durban		Lagos			Durban	Durban	Santos
International market source (imports)	via Rotterdam		via Rotterdam			via Rotterdam	via Rotterdam	via Rotterdam
Domestic yields (mt/ha)	0.6	0.8	0.9	0.9	0.8	1.3	3.0	3.8
SV at farm (US$/mt)	120	84	255	255	182	234	409	447
Assembly and processing costs (US$/mt)	921	957	843	843	865	813	936	919
SV at consumption point (US$/mt)	1,041	1,041	1,098	1,098	1,047	1,047	1,345	1,366
Import parity at consumption point (US$/mt)	1,638		1,530		1,772		1,722	1,465
Logistics port to consumption (US$/mt)	60		—		194		144	—
Logistics international market to port (US$/mt)	168		120		168		168	55
International reference price (US$/mt)	1,410		1,410		1,410		1,410	1,410
Import competitiveness ratio	**0.64**	**0.64**	**0.72**		**0.59**	**0.59**	**0.78**	**0.93**
Domestic production/processing location	Nacala		Rotterdam		Katete		Lusak	Santos
Port of exit (exports)	Durban		Lagos			Durban		Santos
International market destination (exports)	Rotterdam		Rotterdam			Rotterdam		Rotterdam
Domestic yields (mt/ha)	0.6	0.8	0.9	0.9	0.8	1.3	3.0	3.8
SV at farm (US$/mt)	120	84	255	255	182	234	409	447
Assembly and processing costs (US$/mt)	921	957	843	843	865	813	936	919
Logistics assembly point to port (US$/mt)	60		—		194		144	144
SV at port of exit (US$/mt)	1,101	1,101	1,098		1,241	1,241	1,489	1,366
Export parity at port (US$/mt)	1,242		1,008		1,270		1,313	1,355
Logistics port to international market (US$/mt)	168		120		168		168	55
International reference price (US$/mt)	1,410		1,410		1,410		1,410	1,410
Export competitiveness ratio	**0.89**	**0.89**	**1.09**		**0.98**	**0.98**	**1.13**	**1.01**

Source: CCAA background studies.

Note: mt = metric ton(s). ha = hectare(s). SV = shipment value. FAM = family farms. ECF = emerging commercial farms. LCF = large commercial farms. — = not available. irr = irrigated.

Table 4.3 Competitiveness Indicators from Value Chain Analysis: Maize (2007)

	Mozambique		Nigeria			Zambia			Brazil	Thailand
	FAM	ECF	FAM	ECF	LCF	FAM	ECF	LCF	LCF	ECF
Domestic consumption location	Beira		Lagos			Kapiri		Lusaka	Santos	Bangkok
Port of entry (imports)	Maputo		Lagos			Lusaka			Santos	Bangkok
International market source (imports)	Randfontein		via Rotterdam			Randfontein			via Rotterdam	via Rotterdam
Domestic yields (mt/ha)	0.75	2.5	1.3	2.5	5	2.75	3.9	5.8	4.5	3.7
SV at farm (US$/mt)	51	54	151	130	105	136	152	177	101	79
Assembly and processing costs (US$/mt)	63	60	122	143	168	9	67	54	75	18
SV at consumption point (US$/mt)	114	114	273	273	273	145	219	230	175	97
Import parity at consumption point (US$/mt)	314			248		355	369		183	228
Logistics port to consumption (US$/mt)	40		—			25				
Logistics international market to port (US$/mt)	15		120			110	110		55	100
International reference price (US$/mt)	259		128			220	259		128	128
Import competitiveness ratio	**0.36**		**1.10**			**0.41**	**0.62**	**0.65**	**0.96**	**0.43**

	Mozambique		Nigeria			Zambia			Brazil	Thailand
	FAM	ECF	FAM	ECF	LCF	FAM	ECF	LCF	LCF	ECF
Domestic production/processing location	Beira		Lagos			Kapiri		Lusaka	Santos	Bangkok
Port of exit (exports)	Maputo		Lagos			Lusaka			Santos	Bangkok
International market destination (exports)	Randfontein		Rotterdam			Randfontein			Rotterdam	Rotterdam
Domestic yields (mt/ha)	0.75	2.5	1.3	2.5	5	2.75	3.9	5.8	4.5	3.7
SV at farm (US$/mt)	51	54	151	130	105	136	152	177	101	79
Assembly and processing (US$/mt)	63	60	122	143	168	9	67	54	75	18
Logistics assembly to port (US$/mt)	40					25				
SV at port of exit (US$/mt)	154	154	273	273	273	170	219	230	175	97
Export parity at port (US$/mt)	244			8		110	149		73	28
Logistics port to international market (US$/mt)	15		120			110	110		55	100
International reference price (US$/mt)	259		128			220	259		128	128
Export competitiveness ratio	**0.6**	**0.6**	**34.1**	**34.1**	**34.1**	**1.5**	**1.5**	**1.5**	**2.40**	**3.5**

Source: CCAA background studies.

Note: mt = metric ton(s). ha = hectare(s). SV = shipment value. FAM = family farms. ECF = emerging commercial farms. LCF = large commercial farms. — = not available. irr = irrigated.

Table 4.4 Competitiveness Indicators from Value Chain Analysis: Rice (2007)

	Mozambique FAM	Mozambique ECF	Nigeria FAM	Nigeria ECF	Nigeria LCF	Zambia FAM	Zambia ECF	Thailand ECF
Domestic consumption location	Beira		Ibadan			Lusaka		Bangkok
Port of entry (imports)	Durban		Lagos			Durban		Bangkok
International market source (impc	Bangkok		Bangkok			Bangkok		California
Domestic yields (mt/ha)	1.0	3.0	0.9	1.8	2.5	1.5	2.0	2.8
SV at farm (US$/mt)	51	47	130	168	183	129	174	192
Assembly and processing costs (US$/mt)	282	286	548	511	495	362	335	124
SV at consumption point (US$/mt)	332	332	678	678	678	491	509	316
Import parity at consumption point (US$/mt)	433		459			503		645
Logistics port to consumption (US$/mt)	50		40			120		—
Logistics international market to port (US$/mt)	64		100			64		120
International reference price (US$/mt)	319		319			319		525
Import competitiveness ratio	**0.77**	**1.50**	**1.48**			**0.98**	**1.01**	**0.49**
Domestic production/processing location	Beira		Ibadan			Lusaka		Khon Kaen
Port of exit (exports)	Durban		Lagos			Durban		Bangkok
International market destination (exports)	Bangkok		Bangkok			Bangkok		Rotterdam
Domestic yields (mt/ha)	1.0	3.0	0.9	1.8	2.5	1.5	2.0	2.8
SV at farm (US$/mt)	51	47	130	168	183	129	174	192
Assembly and processing costs (US$/mt)	282	286	548	511	495	362	335	124
Logistics assembly point to port (US$/mt)	50		40			120		—
SV at port of exit (US$/mt)	382	382	718	718	718	611	629	316
Export parity at port (US$/mt)	255		219			255		400
Logistics port to international market (US$/mt)	64		100			64		100
International reference price (US$/mt)	319		319			319		500
Export competitiveness ratio	**0.50**	**1.50**	**3.28**	**3.28**	**3.28**	**2.40**	**2.47**	**0.79**

Source: CCAA background studies.

Note: mt = metric ton(s). ha = hectare(s). SV = shipment value. FAM = family farms. ECF = emerging commercial farms. LCF = large commercial farms. — = not available.

Table 4.5 Competitiveness Indicators from Value Chain Analysis: Soybeans (2007)

	Mozambique		Nigeria			Zambia			Brazil
	FAM	ECF	FAM	ECF	LCF	FAM	ECF	LCF	LCF
Domestic consumption location	Namialo		Ibadan			Lusaka			Santos
Port of entry (imports)	Durban		Lagos			Durban			Santos
International market source (imports)	via Rotterdam		via Rotterdam			via Rotterdam			U.S. gulf ports
Domestic yields (mt/ha)	0.5	1.6	1	1.5	2	2	2.5	3.5	2.7
SV at farm (US$/mt)	119	58	176	154	208	91	120	206	145
Assembly and processing costs (US$/mt)	143	204	81	103	49	115	115	61	50
SV at consumption point (US$/mt)	262	262	258	258	258	206	235	268	195
Import parity at consumption point (US$/mt)	451		414			514			254
Logistics port to consumption (US$/mt)	57		40			120			—
Logistics international market to port (US$/mt)	140		120			140			40
International reference price (US$/mt)	254		254			254			214
Import competitiveness ratio	**0.58**		**0.62**			**0.40**	**0.46**	**0.52**	**0.77**
Domestic production/processing location	Namialo		Ibadan			Lusaka			Santos
Port of exit (exports)	Durban		Lagos			Durban			Santos
International market destination (exports)	Rotterdam		Rotterdam			Rotterdam			Rotterdam
Domestic yields (mt/ha)	0.5	1.6	1	1.5	2	2	2.5	3.5	2.7
SV at farm (US$/mt)	119	58	176	154	208	91	120	206	145
Assembly and processing costs (US$/mt)	143	204	81	103	49	115	115	61	50
Logistics assembly point to port (US$/mt)	57		40			120			
SV at port of exit (US$/mt)	319	319	298	298	298	326	355	388	195
Export parity at port (US$/mt)	114		134			114			199
Logistics port to international market (US$/mt)	140		120			140			55
International reference price (US$/mt)	254		254			254			254
Export competitiveness ratio	**2.80**		**2.22**			**2.86**	**3.11**	**3.40**	**0.98**

Source: CCAA background studies.

Note: mt = metric ton(s). ha = hectare(s). SV = shipment value. FAM = family farms. ECF = emerging commercial farms. LCF = large commercial farms. — = not available.

Table 4.6 Competitiveness Indicators from Value Chain Analysis: Sugar (2007)

	Nigeria		Zambia		Brazil					Thailand
	FAM	LCF	LCF	Estate	LCF (first to fifth harvest)					ECF
Domestic consumption location	Numan		Nakambala		Tangará da Serra					Khon Kaen
Port of entry (imports)	Lagos		Durban		Santos					Bangkok
International market source (imports)	New York		Santos		Santos					New York
Domestic yields (mt/ha)	35	50	110	116	114	96	82	75	74	63
SV at farm (US$/mt)	17	14	18	23	18	15	17	18	17	13
Assembly and processing costs (US$/mt)	261	189	221	245	160	143	154	163	159	215
SV at consumption point (US$/mt)	278	203	239	268	178	159	171	181	176	227
Import parity at consumption point (US$/mt)	461		438				246			401
Logistics port to consumption (US$/mt)	60		72				—			15
Logistics international market to port (US$/mt)	155		120				—			140
International reference price (US$/mt)	246		246				246			246
Import competitiveness ratio	**0.60**	**0.44**	**0.55**	**0.61**			**0.70**			**0.57**
Domestic production/processing location	Numan		Nakambala		Tangará da Serra					Khon Kaen
Port of exit (exports)	Lagos		Durban		Santos					Bangkok
International market destination (exports)	New York		Santos		Santos					New York
Domestic yields (mt/ha)	35	50	110	116	114	96	82	75	74	63
SV at farm (US$/mt)	17	14	18	23	18	15	17	18	17	13
Assembly and processing (US$/mt)	261	189	221	245	160	143	154	163	159	215
Logistics assembly to port (US$/mt)	60		72				—			15
SV at port of exit (US$/mt)	338	263	311	340	178	159	171	181	176	242
Export parity at port (US$/mt)	91		126				246			176
Logistics port to international market (US$/mt)	155		120				—			70
International reference price (US$/mt)	246		246				246			246
Export competitiveness ratio	**3.72**	**2.89**	**2.47**	**2.70**			**0.70**			**1.38**

Source: CCAA background studies.

Note: mt = metric ton(s). ha = hectare(s). SV = shipment value. FAM = family farms. ECF = emerging commercial farms. LCF = large commercial farms. — = not available.

(DRC) analysis. A competitiveness ratio of less than 1 indicates that the country is competitive in the production of the commodity. A competitiveness ratio of more than 1 indicates that the country is not competitive in the production of the commodity.

Before presenting the results of the value chain analysis, three limitations should be recognized.

First, each country study was prepared by a different team of analysts, and this affected the comparability of results. Although the overall patterns and main conclusions about costs, returns, and competitiveness are considered reliable, there is a certain margin of error associated with each individual result.

Second, international competitiveness comparisons are of limited value unless the same commodities are compared in the same locations. Because few of the CCAA case study countries currently compete with one another on a head-to-head basis in the same markets, the CCAA value chain analysis necessarily involved some "what if" modeling of counterfactual scenarios that are not currently observable.

Third, in an age of rapidly changing global commodity prices, empirical results can and frequently do become overtaken by events, sometimes in very short order. The results summarized below reflect prices prevailing in mid-2007, when the CCAA empirical work was done. Given that future prices may be more favorable than in 2007 (as discussed above), the estimates of competitiveness are considered to be conservative.

Cassava

In *Mozambique* and *Zambia*, cassava has traditionally been grown as a food crop. It is valued for its resistance to drought and tolerance to poor soils and is often grown on maize-dominated farms as a diversification crop. Almost all of the cassava produced in Mozambique and Zambia is consumed with little or no industrial processing.

In *Nigeria*, the world's largest cassava producer, a very different situation prevails. Cassava is a leading staple in some parts of the country, so per capita consumption levels are higher than in Mozambique and Zambia. Cassava is consumed either fresh or more commonly after processing into flour-like *gari*. In addition to food demand, there is also great demand for industrial products made from cassava, including starches used in textiles, manufactured food and beverages, pharmaceuticals, cosmetics, and pulp industries. It is estimated that more than 40 million tons of cassava are needed to satisfy total domestic demand in Nigeria.

Shipment values for cassava produced in the three African case studies, as well as in the success-story comparator Thailand, are shown in figure 4.1(a). Two results stand out:

First, cassava can be produced in all three of the African case study countries at a cost that is not dramatically higher than the cost in Thailand, which has long exported cassava successfully (in Mozambique, the farm-level SVs are actually lower than in Thailand).

Second, although many analysts have highlighted the vast potential of the small-scale cassava sector in Nigeria, when family labor is assigned a value equivalent to 60 percent of the wage rate for hired labor, small-scale cassava production using traditional labor-intensive production practices and resulting in low yields looks much less attractive compared with medium- and large-scale production.

The results of the competitiveness analysis for cassava in table 4.1 show that in all three of the African countries, domestically produced cassava is extremely competitive in the domestic market, but it is noncompetitive in international markets.[1] This result is not surprising, considering the low value-to-weight ratio of cassava products, the large international transport costs, and the generally weak demand in international markets, where use of cassava as animal feed has declined in the wake of trade policy reforms that have effectively ended the protected European market that Thailand was so effectively able to target during the 1970s and 1980s. Interestingly, at 2007 prices, even Thailand, traditionally the world's dominant cassava exporter, is not competitive in the European market, and in fact Thai cassava exports now go almost exclusively eastward, mainly to China. Although the three African countries are currently not competitive in international cassava markets, the situation could change if cassava were to become an important crop for biofuels production. Studies are under way in Mozambique and Nigeria, among other countries, to explore the economics of cassava-based ethanol production.

Cotton

Cotton is one of the most important smallholder cash crops in Africa and a major export earner for many African countries. Because of high production costs associated with extensive use of fertilizer and pesticides, smallholder production systems are often organized around an outgrower program with ties to the ginning company that provides inputs and technical assistance under contract. The buyer also monitors quality: fiber contamination from polypropylene bags is an important threat to the competitiveness of smallholder cotton in Africa.[2]

Two results stand out for shipment values of cotton, shown in figure 4.1(b).

First, cotton can be produced in the three African counties at significantly lower cost than in Brazil.

Second, cotton produced by smallholders is less costly than cotton produced on large-scale mechanized farms.

The results of the competitiveness analysis for cotton lint summarized in table 4.2 show that in all three of the African countries, domestically produced cotton is competitive in domestic markets, especially in Mozambique and Zambia, where high-grade cottons are produced at extremely competitive prices. This finding is of limited interest, however, given that only a very small percentage of domestic cotton production in the CCAA case study is processed domestically. The real test for cotton is whether it can compete in export markets. The competitiveness indicators for cotton exports are more mixed. Mozambique and Zambia are competitive international exporters, but Nigeria is not (although the export competitiveness ratio of 1.08 suggests that Nigerian farmers are close to being competitive). In Zambia, large-scale commercial cotton producers appear the least competitive, reflecting the low cost of family labor used by family farms (FAM) and emerging commercial farms (ECF), as well as the high cost of irrigation used on large commercial farms (LCF). Interestingly, at 2007 prices, Brazilian cotton is not competitive in international markets, mainly because of the extremely high cost of the pesticides that are used extensively by Brazilian cotton producers.[3]

Maize

In *Mozambique* and *Zambia*, white maize is strategically important as the main subsistence crop and most widely grown agricultural commodity. Maize production systems cover a very wide spectrum of possibilities, ranging from very simple hand-hoe systems using recycled seed and almost no purchased inputs to very intensive commercial systems based on mechanical cultivation and, in some cases, even aerial application of herbicides. Smallholders in Mozambique and Zambia sometimes intercrop maize with other foods, but not to the same extent as in Nigeria.

In *Nigeria*, yellow maize is one of many staples and is typically inter-cropped with other crops such as beans, yam, pumpkin, sweet potato, and vegetables. Intercropping results in lower yields for maize but helps farmers to increase the overall productivity of resources invested in agriculture.

Two results stand out in the shipment values for maize presented in figure 4.1(c):

First, unit production costs for maize vary considerably among the African countries. Farm-level SVs for maize produced in Nigeria and Zambia are generally high compared with farm-level SVs for maize pro-duced in Brazil and Thailand, but they are extremely low for maize pro-duced in Mozambique.

Second, the differences in farm-level SVs for maize among the African countries seem to stem largely from differences in production methods and the associated input costs. Production costs in Nigeria and Zambia are significantly inflated by the cost of fertilizer and other inputs. In Mozambique, the use of purchased inputs is generally very low. This can be related to the generally higher levels of soil fertility in Mozambique, where farmers are able to achieve reasonably good yields—although still lower than in many other African countries—with minimum use of pur-chased inputs.

The results of the competitiveness analysis for maize presented in table 4.3 show that among the African countries, only in Mozambique and Zambia are producers clearly competitive in domestic markets. Domestic production costs in these two countries are lower than the transport-adjusted price of maize produced in neighboring South Africa, the main and most reliable source of imported maize. Maize produced in Nigeria is not competitive in domestic markets, at least not in the major consump-tion centers located in the central and southern parts of the country. In the comparator countries of Brazil and Thailand, domestically produced maize is competitive with imports, although producers in Brazil face stiff competition from U.S. producers. With regard to maize exports, only Mozambique shows a clear competitive advantage, thanks mainly to the limited use of purchased inputs by family farms and emerging commer-cial farms. Maize produced in Nigeria is extremely noncompetitive in international markets. Interestingly, at 2007 prices, even Brazil would have difficulty competing in international markets, which explains why Brazilian maize is now used mainly as an input into the export-oriented poultry and livestock industries. A similar situation prevails in Thailand, where most maize is used to feed animals, mainly poultry.

Rice

In *Mozambique* and *Zambia,* rice is a relatively minor crop grown mainly by smallholders and used for home consumption. By contrast, Nigeria is the largest rice producer in Africa. Even so, with rapid urbanization, domestic production has not been able to keep up with demand growth, and Nigeria is among the largest rice importers in the world.

Farm-level SVs presented in figure 4.1(d) for rice produced in Nigeria and Zambia are quite similar to farm-level SVs for rice produced in Thailand. This suggests that Thailand's ability to export successfully into international markets results from the superior quality of Thai rice and from Thailand's ability to contain logistics costs after rice leaves the farm gate and makes its way to distant destinations. Farm-level SVs for rice produced in Mozambique are extremely low, again reflecting the ability of Mozambican producers to rely on the natural fertility of local soils and avoid use of expensive fertilizers—at least for now.

The results of the competitiveness analysis for rice in table 4.4 show that of the African countries, only in Mozambique are rice producers clearly competitive in the domestic market. Rice producers in Zambia are close to being competitive with imports, with family farmers showing a small advantage compared with emerging commercial farms. Rice producers in Nigeria are clearly uncompetitive and have been able to survive only because import restrictions keep domestic rice prices significantly above the import parity price. With regard to rice exports, none of the African countries is competitive.

Soybeans

In *Mozambique,* soybeans are a new crop that is only recently being promoted by nongovernmental organizations (NGOs) and donor agencies as an alternative to maize and to support an emerging commercial livestock sector. In *Zambia,* soybeans are typically grown by large commercial farmers as a rotation crop with wheat or maize. In *Nigeria,* soybeans are used as both a food and a feed ingredient for livestock, and soybean oil is used locally to manufacture skin lotions, margarine, and other products.

The farm-level SVs presented in figure 4.1(e) for soybeans produced in the three African case study countries are comparable to the farm-level SV for soybeans produced in Brazil, indicating that all three countries have the potential to compete in international markets. However, when soybeans are produced by large-scale commercial producers, machinery costs make up a large share of total production costs (machinery costs appear in figure 4.1(e) as "Other costs"). This suggests that the recent run-up in global energy prices will have the effect of increasing the relative competitiveness of soybeans produced using smaller-scale, more labor-intensive technologies.

In all three of the African countries, soybean producers are competitive in domestic markets (table 4.5). This result stems mainly from the low production costs, with most soybeans in these countries produced by family farmers and emerging commercial farmers who are able to take advantage of low family labor costs. None of the African countries is competitive as an exporter in international markets, where prices are determined by the global export powerhouses, Brazil and the United States.

Sugar

Sugarcane is produced by large-scale commercial farms and parastatals in all three African case study countries. Farm-level SVs for sugar produced in Nigeria and Zambia, presented in figure 4.1(f), are not significantly different from those in Brazil, indicating that the African countries have the ability to be competitive, at least when it comes to primary production (that is, production of sugarcane). The farm-level SV for sugarcane produced in all other countries is slightly lower than the farm-level SVs in all the other countries, mainly because of the very low machinery costs incurred by Thailand's predominantly small-scale sugarcane producers.

The pattern of farm-level competitiveness holds up through subsequent processing stages. In both of the African countries for which data were available (Nigeria and Zambia), refined sugar producers are competitive in domestic markets, as well as in some regional markets. The same is true in the two comparator countries, Brazil and Thailand (table 4.6). The situation is different, however, with regard to export competitiveness: refined sugar produced in Nigeria and Zambia is not competitive in international (European) markets when nonpreferential prices are used. The Thai sugar industry also has experienced an erosion of competitiveness; refined sugar produced in Thailand is no longer competitive in the European market, which is why Thai sugar producers have turned to markets in the east (China and Japan).

Summary of Value Chain Results

The CCAA value chain analysis generated a number of insights concerning the current and likely future competitiveness of the three African case study countries:

The African case study countries are competitive in domestic markets in the production of many of the targeted commodities. High international and domestic logistics costs raise the prices of imported commodities and provide a certain degree of "natural protection" that domestic producers can exploit. Because domestic markets for some of these commodities are large and growing and because significant imports are already taking place, there appears to be considerable room for expansion of domestic production to recapture these markets. Prospects are brightest for rice, soybeans, sugar, and maize.

The African case study countries are generally not competitive in international markets in the production of the targeted commodities. Exceptions are found in cotton, sugar, and maize, which can be exported profitably by some of the case study countries, at least in some years. The same high international and domestic logistics costs that provide a certain natural protection for domestic producers pose a significant barrier when it comes to exporting, because these costs must be absorbed by African producers if their commodities are to be competitive internationally.

Regional markets appear to offer the most promising opportunities for expansion over the short-to-medium term. The CCAA value chain analysis did not formally analyze competitiveness in regional markets, but given the relatively high logistics costs associated with reaching international markets, it is clear that African producers are favorably positioned to serve regional markets relative to the countries that dominate international commodities trade. Demand in regional markets can be expected to grow rapidly as a result of population growth, income gains, and accelerating urbanization. African exporters will be able to expand trade not only by exploiting growth in overall demand but also by displacing imports from outside the region, which currently are considerable.

The African case study countries are able to compete despite generally modest levels of farm-level productivity, in part because labor costs are low. For many of the targeted commodities, unit production costs achieved in the African case study countries compare favorably with unit production costs achieved in the comparator countries. Producers in the African countries are able to achieve comparable unit production costs despite realizing much lower crop yields, thanks mainly to the generally low cost of labor. Although it is good that African countries are low-cost producers, the source of African competitiveness is in a sense lamentable, as the low cost of labor in Africa speaks to the excess supply of labor and the lack of employment opportunities outside of agriculture.

The African case study countries are able to compete despite generally modest levels of farm-level productivity, in part because use of purchased inputs is minimal. Especially in Mozambique and Nigeria, family farmers and emerging commercial farmers still have opportunities to practice extensive agriculture, and they can rely on the natural fertility of recently cleared land, without having to resort to expensive fertilizer. Again, while it is good that African countries are low-cost producers, it must be recognized that the limited use of purchased inputs is made possible by systematic soil nutrient mining, which is unsustainable over the longer term.

The competitiveness of African case study countries is often—but not always—undermined by inefficiencies in domestic and port logistics. Domestic logistics costs in the African case study countries are generally high compared with domestic logistics costs in the comparator countries (Brazil and Thailand). This finding emerging from the value chain analysis speaks to the well-known widespread deficiencies in infrastructure for transport, processing, and storage. Inefficient coordination mechanisms found in the African case study countries impose additional official and unofficial transaction costs.

Smallholders have a critical role to play as a source of competitiveness in the African case study countries. Contrary to expectations, the analysis revealed few obvious scale economies in the African production systems analyzed for the CCAA study. Compared with LCF value chains, FAM and ECF value chains were typically found to have lower shipment values at the farm level and/or final distribution point. This result derives mainly from three factors: (a) the extensive use of low-cost family labor by smallholder farmers, (b) the higher taxes charged on inputs used by large commercial farms, and (c) the higher marginal returns to fertilizer and agrichemicals at the generally low input levels associated with smallholder production. LCF systems can play an important strategic role by contributing to the achievement of the critical mass of product needed to attract local and international buyers, but the value chain analysis shows that investments in smallholder agriculture can be an important source of competitiveness in their own right. An important additional benefit of smallholder-led agricultural growth is the much higher level of second-round demand effects that occur when income gains are realized by smallholder households, as opposed to LCF.

Notes

1. Use of the standardized value chain methodology to make intercountry comparisons is somewhat complicated in the case of cassava because of important differences between countries in the structure of demand. The most important internationally traded cassava products are pellets (used as a feed ingredient) and starch (used as an industrial additive), whereas within the African countries, cassava is traded mainly in the form of processed *gari* (Nigeria) or fresh tubers (Mozambique and Zambia). These differences can be accommodated in the value chain analysis through the use of appropriate conversion factors and relevant price series, but these adjustments introduce another element of uncertainty into the analysis.

2. Polypropylene does not absorb dye, so the presence of even small quantities of this fiber can render large bolts of fabric virtually worthless.

3. An important determinant of the profitability of cotton production is the value of the cotton seed (and how much of that value farmers receive). The relative value of the seed has increased in recent years with the oilseeds boom. In the CCAA analysis, cotton seed was valued based on reported local prices, but the marketing arrangements for cotton seed and potential opportunities to capture additional value from seed were not analyzed in detail.

CHAPTER 5

Factors Affecting the Competitiveness of African Agriculture

Policy Environment

Historically, agriculture in developing countries has been heavily taxed through macroeconomic and sectoral policies (Krueger, Schiff, and Valdés 1988). Up to the 1980s, macroeconomic policies typically provided incentives for the growth of industry through policies of import substitution and protection, which indirectly discriminated against agriculture. In addition, most countries maintained overvalued exchange rates that lowered prices to tradable sectors, including agriculture. At the same time, agricultural sector policies suppressed producer prices of agricultural commodities through controlled procurement prices, export taxation (especially through agricultural marketing boards),.and/or export quotas. Although many governments attempted to reduce the negative impact of these measures on agricultural production incentives by subsidizing input prices and investing in irrigation and other capital inputs, the countermeasures were rarely sufficient to compensate for the huge losses imposed on agriculture through indirect taxation measures, especially overvalued exchange rates. In fact, indirect taxes on agriculture through macroeconomic policies were estimated to be three times the direct taxation of the sector (Krueger, Schiff, and Valdés 1988).

This net taxation of agriculture was highest in the agriculture-based countries of Africa, where it averaged 29 percent and was particularly high for exportables at 46 percent (World Bank 2007c). This high level of net taxation severely depressed growth in the sector; averaging across a large sample of developing countries, it has been estimated that a 10 percent reduction in the level of taxation would have improved agricultural growth by 0.4 percent annually.

Stagnating growth, lack of fiscal sustainability, and macroeconomic instability led eventually to the structural adjustment policies of the 1980s and 1990s. Measures introduced under structural adjustment reform packages typically included the introduction of market-determined exchange rates, privatization of many industries, opening of borders to trade and investment, and improving the business climate. Structural adjustment policies often led to a substantial improvement in incentives to the agricultural sector. Overall taxation of the agricultural sector in agriculture-based countries of Africa decreased from 29 percent in 1980–84 to 10 percent in 2000–04; however, exportables continued to be significantly taxed (World Bank 2007c).

Overview of Net Policy Effects in the CCAA Case Study Countries

The trend observed at the global level of decreasing taxation of agriculture was reflected to a greater or lesser extent in the experiences of the

Figure 5.1   Net Taxation of Agriculture, CCAA Case Study Countries

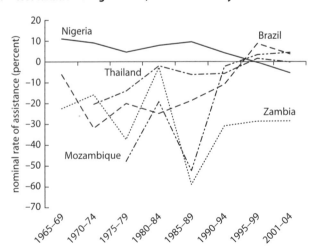

Source: Database on agricultural policy distortions available at www.worldbank.org/agdistortions (accessed January 2, 2009).

five CCAA case study countries (figure 5.1). In both Brazil and Thailand, agriculture was significantly taxed for many years, although not always in the same way. Policies prevailing in Thailand generally were more trade oriented, and agriculture was taxed mainly through the imposition of restrictions on rice exports (designed to maintain low consumer prices for the country's major food staple). In contrast, Brazil maintained a relatively closed economy, characterized by high levels of import protection for both industrial goods and agricultural commodities. Closing the economy did not serve to improve stability, however, because the country experienced a highly volatile macroeconomic environment, characterized by exchange rate instability and overvaluation. At the same time, Brazil also pursued a cheap food policy by controlling prices of food staples. Over time, both Brazil and Thailand adopted policy reforms that leveled the playing field for agriculture, and by the early 2000s, domestic prices of both importables and exportables were close to border prices.

Among the African case study countries, two—Mozambique and Zambia—taxed agriculture extremely heavily through controlled prices, high protection of industry, and overvalued exchange rates. During the 1980s, the level of implicit taxation in these two countries was as high as 60 percent (figure 5.1). Nigeria, on the other hand, imposed high levels of protection on importables (including many food staples), while continuing to tax exportables. The net effect was to protect agriculture, which imposed high prices on consumers and undermined Nigeria's competitiveness in all sectors. In all three countries, macroeconomic and sectoral policy reforms beginning in the 1990s have significantly reduced policy distortions (figure 5.1). However, Zambia stands out as having consistently taxed agriculture, and both Mozambique and Zambia have had quite unstable policy regimes during the transition period. Alone among the five countries, policies in Zambia continue to significantly tax exportables.

Macroeconomic Policies

In all of the CCAA case study countries, domestic macroeconomic policies have played an important role in shaping the fortunes of commercial agriculture. After long periods of turbulence, reforms succeeded eventually in producing greater macroeconomic stability, as reflected in improving macroeconomic scores based on fiscal balance, inflation, and exchange rate stability (figure 5.2). Thailand is something of an exception, because the Thai government has fairly consistently supported a market- and export-oriented policy regime and maintained a sound macroeconomic policy (at least up until the Asian financial crisis of the late 1990s). Brazil

Figure 5.2   Macroeconomic Scores of CCAA Case Study Countries, 1985–2007

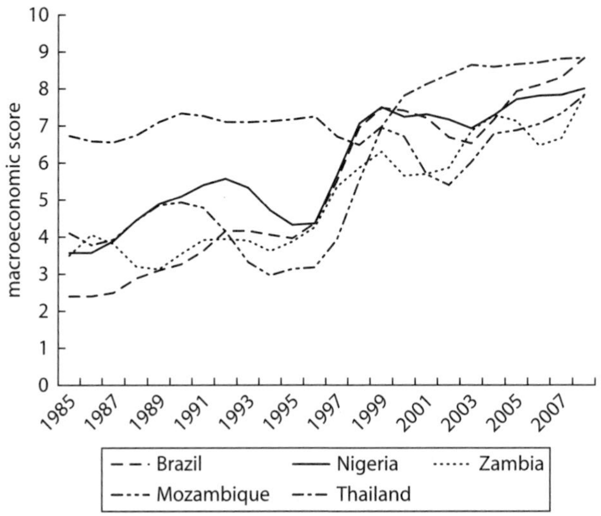

Source: http://www.prsgroup.com/.
Note: The macroeconomic score is the average of the budget balance score, inflation score, and exchange rate stability score provided by the *International Country Risk Guide*.

has had a more unstable macroeconomic environment, but since the mid-1990s, it has experienced a period of relative stability, especially following the devaluation of the currency in 1999. In the three African countries, progress has been remarkably consistent. After pursuing disastrous policies throughout the 1970s and 1980s, all three countries have established relatively sound macroeconomic policy environments. They are not alone in Africa: most Sub-Saharan countries now have fiscal surpluses and inflation rates below 10 percent (Ndulu 2007).

Among macroeconomic policies, exchange rate policies have probably had the biggest impact on incentives in the agricultural sector (Schuh 1976). This has particularly been the case in the African countries, especially Nigeria and Zambia, where the parallel exchange rate sometimes exceeded the official rate by five times or more (Walkenhorst 2009; Robinson, Govereh, and Ndlela 2009). Although all of the case study countries have moved toward market-determined exchange rates, recent exchange rate appreciation in Nigeria and Zambia has resulted from so-called Dutch disease, caused by large inflows of foreign exchange as a result of commodity exports (oil in Nigeria, copper in Zambia). Appreciating exchange rates threaten the competitiveness of exports and make it more difficult for domestic producers to compete against imports.

In a market economy, policy makers generally have limited ability to manipulate exchange rates as a means of encouraging agricultural competiveness, although some countries (for example, Chile) have attempted to temper the effects of Dutch disease by keeping foreign exchange earnings in offshore funds. The broader lesson is that once agricultural competitiveness has been achieved, maintaining that competitiveness can be challenging for reasons that lie beyond the agricultural sector itself.

Agricultural Sector-Specific Policies in Brazil and Thailand

Brazil and Thailand have used a variety of policy interventions to influence incentives in the agricultural sector. These include the following:

Trade policies. Both Brazil and Thailand have imposed taxes on agricultural exports, partly as a fiscal device to generate revenue for government and also as a way of maintaining low domestic food prices. For more than two decades, Brazil taxed all agricultural exports at a standard rate of 13 percent; this tax was removed only in 1996. During the 1970s, Thailand taxed rice exports by as much as 30 percent. Meanwhile, both countries protected import substitutes through tariffs, although at relatively modest levels. Thailand also maintained quantitative restrictions on imports and some exports and continues to do so. For example, it has effectively protected its sugar industry by mandating a "home price" for domestically consumed sugar, while sugar exports are sold at lower prices in foreign markets.

Price policies. The governments of Brazil and Thailand have used price support policies to encourage production of major agricultural products, although the extent to which they have been willing to do so has been limited because the ultimate goal has been to ensure the production of cheap food.

In Brazil, price supports played an important role in shaping the course of agricultural development in the Cerrado by ensuring a minimum level of profitability and reducing risk. During the 1970s and 1980s, support prices were panterritorial, which meant that the government ended up becoming the main purchaser of soybeans, maize, and rice in more remote areas where private sector marketing was discouraged by high transportation costs. In Thailand, policy makers have tended to rely on the discipline of the market to promote international competitiveness. Domestic price supports and price stabilization measures have been used extensively, but they generally have been tied to trends in world prices. That is, price interventions have been more important in stabilizing prices than in setting price levels. For example, many Thai sugar farmers cite price stability as an important factor inducing them to grow sugarcane, rather than other potentially more profitable but also much more variable alternative crops.

In recent years, both Brazil and Thailand have experimented with new approaches to supporting and stabilizing prices of strategically important commodities such as rice and maize. In Thailand, a program has been introduced under which farmers are prepaid a guaranteed floor price for their production, which is then stored in the farmers' own storage facilities until market prices strengthen. In Brazil, use of forward contracting and futures markets is increasingly common among traders, processors, and exporters, all of whom now are able to lock in contracts with producers. Although these approaches have not yet been formally evaluated, they appear to have had some success in stabilizing intraseasonal price swings and in ensuring that farmers are able to gain access to cash without having to rely on forced sales at low postharvest prices.

Production quotas. Production quotas have been used extensively in Thailand, for many crops. As part of its successful effort to reduce the volatility of domestic sugar prices, the Thai government introduced a system of sugarcane production quotas, combined with incentives to move refineries closer to production zones in the northeast. Similarly with cassava and maize, whose prices have remained depressed over many years, rather than maintaining price supports, the Thai government has usually responded by introducing measures to cut back production while promoting diversification into alternative crops.

Input subsidies. From the 1960s through the 1980s, the leading agricultural policy instrument in Brazil was highly subsidized rural credit, with real rates of interest approaching eye-popping negative levels during the period of largest credit supply (up to -36 percent per annum). Araújo, de Janvry, and Sadoulet (2002) estimate that credit subsidies accounted for 12 percent of all agricultural income in some years. Successive Thai governments also used input subsidies and low-cost credit to ensure that farmers were in a position to respond to international prices. It is important to note that in neither case were these subsidies sufficient to offset taxation through macroeconomic and price policies. Subsidized credit may have provided an important stimulus, but it also had significant costs in terms of growth and equity.

In summary, both Brazil and Thailand relied on domestic policies to support the emergence of competitive commercial agriculture. Generally speaking, the policies implemented in Thailand were much more consistent than those implemented in Brazil, showing fewer changes in direction and less extreme swings.

Agricultural Policies in the African Countries

To what extent have African countries been able to use agricultural price, trade, and subsidy policies to stimulate the emergence of competitive commercial agriculture? The literature suggests that only rarely in Africa have targeted agricultural policies been used effectively to overcome market failures or stimulate the emergence of competitive commercial agriculture. This conclusion is borne out by the findings of the country case studies.

Agricultural policies in *Nigeria* have gone through four distinct phases (Walkenhorst 2009).

During the first phase (1960–70), agriculture was still the country's major foreign exchange earner. Agricultural export taxes accounted for a large share of government revenues, so public policy not surprisingly focused on supporting agricultural research and extension and on promoting exports.

The second phase (1970–86) was characterized by heavy government intervention in the agricultural sector, financed initially from oil revenues. In an era of expansive fiscal policies, the government introduced many new agricultural programs involving subsidies, agricultural credit support schemes, and guaranteed minimum prices overseen by a plethora of new national commodity boards. These policies did not yield the anticipated benefits in terms of agricultural development, however, and as a result Nigeria devolved during this period from a net exporter of agricultural commodities to a large importer. During the early 1980s, as oil revenues declined, the high costs of these programs (and similar policies in other sectors) proved increasingly unsustainable.

The third phase (1987–99) was precipitated by a widespread fiscal crisis, which ushered in sweeping structural reforms across the economy. Government expenditures were sharply curtailed, price controls were removed, input subsidies were suspended, and marketing activities were liberalized. National food self-sufficiency became an explicit policy goal, implemented through bans on imports of major food staples, but at a high cost in terms of protection. The nominal rate of protection for rice and maize was more than 200 percent during this period.

The fourth phase (1999 to the present) coincided with the advent of democracy and has been marked by efforts to create a business environment conducive to greater private investment in the agricultural sector. Liberalization measures were further strengthened, with many import duties and restrictions suspended. At the same time, in an attempt to kick-start production, beginning in 2002 the federal government launched a series of Presidential Initiatives for Agriculture targeted at individual commodities. Although the Presidential Initiatives have had some success in stimulating increased production, they have not made Nigerian farmers competitive in world or regional markets.

Nigerian agriculture remains saddled with the legacy of decades of heavy protection. Import bans and tariffs have not only imposed high costs on Nigerian consumers but also severely undermined the competitiveness of Nigerian producers. The government's current strategy of aggressively promoting and partially protecting agriculture during a period of high oil prices is basically sound, provided the interventions focus on improving efficiency. Reducing protection levels and exposing producers to increased international competition could lead to efficiency gains, as it did so effectively in Brazil and Thailand.

Agricultural policies in *Zambia* have also been characterized by extensive state interventionism. Following independence, for many years the agricultural sector operated under strict government control, with pervasive state institutions, input and marketing subsidies, and controls on the prices of foreign currency and credit, all financed with revenues from copper. Agricultural performance was dismal, with bloated parastatals and limited private sector investment. Liberalization began in earnest in 1992. Price controls and subsidies were eliminated, and parastatals were privatized. The macroeconomic policy regime is now largely free of major impediments.

The abrupt retreat of government from the sector has left somewhat of a vacuum in the provision of key agricultural services. Poor service delivery, marketing constraints (especially in outlying areas as a result of poor infrastructure—notably, feeder roads), a void in agricultural finance and credit, and poor accessibility and administration of land today conspire against the emergence of a buoyant smallholder sector. Although some large-scale commercial farmers are able to overcome these constraints, most smallholders cannot, leaving them particularly disadvantaged.

Today, the government continues to intervene directly in the agricultural sector, in part to compensate for these failures. Programs have been implemented in recent years to improve access to fertilizer and to safeguard food security; however, larger farmers have benefited disproportionally from these programs, raising issues of equity. The heavy degree of subsidies also has called into question the fiscal sustainability of these programs (for example, the fertilizer subsidy alone consumes more than one-half of the agricultural budget) and led to criticisms that much-needed investments in public goods are being crowded out. Zambia today has a largely consistent agricultural policy framework favoring the attainment of competitiveness in domestic and international markets, but it has yet to develop efficient programs to build input markets, stabilize maize prices, and invest in core public goods.

Agricultural policies in *Mozambique* have gone through three phases since independence (Alfieri, Arndt, and Cirera 2009).

The first phase (1975–87) was characterized by extensive central planning. Large plantations, processing facilities, and marketing organizations were state owned. The main agricultural policy instrument used during this period by government was controlled prices set well below world prices and aimed at subsidizing consumers.

The second phase (1987–98) was characterized by progressive liberalization and privatization of markets. During this period, a sound macroeconomic policy environment was put in place.

The third period (1999 to the present) has been characterized by a relative lack of direct government intervention in the food crop sector, where domestic prices are now closely aligned with border prices. Government intervention is still strong in selected commercial crops, however, especially in sugar (import tariffs), cashews (export tax), tobacco (geographical concessions), and cotton (minimum prices and geographical concessions).

In sum, Mozambique has to a large extent leveled the playing field in agriculture, with the exception of some key commercial crops. Supply response to the improved policy environment continues to be constrained, however, because of very poor infrastructure and weak capacity in R&D and extension.

Policy Incentives and Growth

The Thailand success story reflects in part a record of relatively sound policies, especially macroeconomic stability and sectoral policies that set incentives broadly in line with prices in international markets. Brazil took longer to achieve macroeconomic stability and agricultural trade liberalization, but these measures, once achieved, led to a boom in agricultural exports. As Lopes et al. (2008, 96–7) conclude, "The outstanding performance of Brazil's agriculture from the mid-1990s to 2004 was a result of the major reforms in macroeconomic and sectoral policies." At the same time, the experiences of both countries highlight the difficult challenge faced by policy makers in attempting to manage a successful commercialization process while at the same time safeguarding national food security and ensuring low domestic food prices. This was most recently demonstrated by the response of Thailand's government to the global food crisis of 2008, when it reinstated quotas on rice exports.

The stimulatory effects of favorable policies were especially pronounced in Brazil and Thailand, but they have been observable as well in the African countries. Recent increases in agricultural growth rates in many African countries have been correlated with improved macroeconomic scores (World Bank 2007c) and a reduction in the relatively higher taxation of importables relative to exportables (figure 5.3). Improved performance of specific subsectors within agriculture also has been associated with policy liberalization (for example, as in the cotton subsector in Zambia, where annual exports increased from 4,000 tons in 1990 to 54,000 tons in 2005). Important opportunities still remain, however, for improvement in the incentives facing African agriculture, especially in the many countries where exportables are still significantly taxed.

The fact that the same policy reforms that led to a takeoff in commercial agriculture in Brazil and Thailand have had less impact in the African countries suggests that other factors may be constraining commercial agricultural growth. As will be discussed below, in Africa many of the ingredients needed to support a sustained supply response are lacking, especially technology, infrastructure, and market institutions.

Because many of these ingredients require sustained investment over decades to have impacts, the critical question is, What can governments do in the short-to-medium term to stimulate an agricultural supply response? Reminiscent of the approaches used in Brazil and Thailand in an earlier era, many African countries continue to provide targeted interventions in key commodities, such as fertilizer subsidies and price supports. How these programs can be better designed and whether they can be made fiscally sustainable are open questions.

Technology

Since the regions selected for this study are relatively land-abundant it is not surprising that area expansion has been the major driver of growth in all five of the case study countries. This was the case even in Brazil and Thailand, especially during the early phases of their emergence as agricultural export powerhouses. Between 1971 and 2006, soybean area in Brazil increased by 4.6 percent annually, and sugarcane area in Thailand increased by 4.7 percent annually (figure 5.4). Close examination of the historical production data reveals, however, that the sources of production

Figure 5.3 Nominal Rates of Assistance, CCAA Case Study Countries

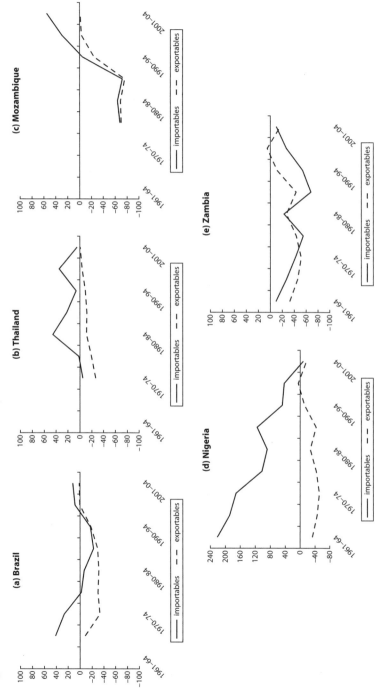

Source: Database on agricultural policy distortions available at www.worldbank.org/agdistortions (accessed January 2, 2009).

Figure 5.4   Decomposition of Production Growth, CCAA Selected Commodities

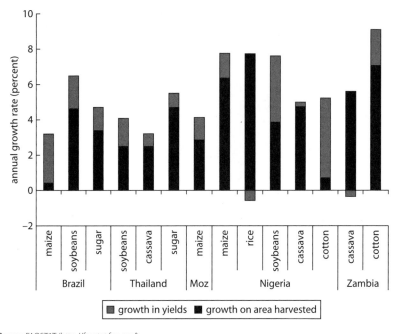

Source: FAOSTAT (http://faostat.fao.org/).
Note: Includes only commodities with growth rates above 3 percent from 1971 to 2006. Moz = Mozambique.

growth in these two countries have changed over time, with yield growth accounting for an ever-larger component of overall growth.

In the African case study countries, production of many of the target commodities has increased since 1971 at rates exceeding 3 percent annually. In most cases, the main source of production growth has been area expansion, even during the most recent period. Examples include the rapid increase in maize and cassava production in Nigeria and, to a lesser extent, the increase in rice production in Mozambique and cassava production in Zambia. Cotton and soybeans in Nigeria represent the only instances in which yield increases have made major contributions to production growth.

In almost all of the six target commodities, the difference in yields achieved in Brazil and Thailand compared with the yields achieved in the three African countries is wide and growing (figure 5.5).[1] The difference in yields illustrates the critical importance for African countries of investing in the adoption of improved technologies, which will be needed to establish competitiveness not only in world markets but even in

Figure 5.5   Yield Indices for the Selected Commodities

(Brazil 1971–75 = 100)

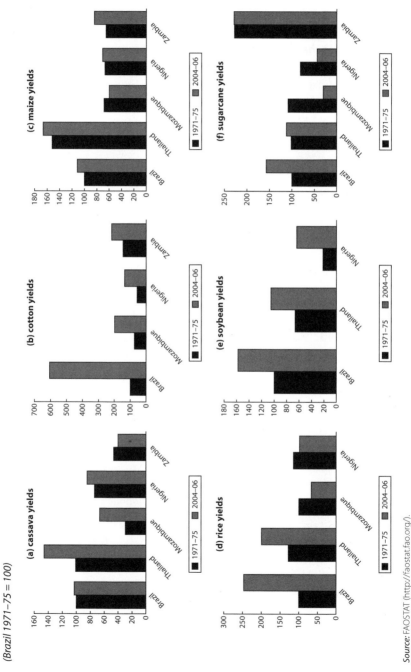

Source: FAOSTAT (http://faostat.fao.org/).

domestic and regional markets. The Brazilian and Thai experiences with agricultural commercialization point to the vital importance of getting the basic production technology right.

Getting the Technology Right in Brazil and Thailand

The competitiveness of Brazilian agriculture can be attributed in large part to the widespread adoption of modern varieties and improved crop and soil management technologies, whose development was made possible by sustained public investment in agricultural research. In Brazil, an important early breakthrough was the selection of modern forage grass varieties that today cover the 21 percent of the Cerrado region that is planted to improved pasture. The introduction of these forage grass varieties was followed by the development of some 40 soybean varieties suited to the low latitude tropics and that catalyzed the soybean revolution in the Cerrado. Modern varieties adapted to the Cerrado, including some genetically modified organisms, have also been developed for cotton, cassava, maize, and wheat (box 5.1).

Box 5.1

The Cerrado Soybean Revolution: A Many-Faceted Technology

Although the Cerrado region is famous for its soybean production, the bulk of Brazil's soybean crop is still produced in the south of the country, where it was first introduced. The spread of soybeans to the Cerrado involved a number of innovations: the initial focus was on adapting cultivars to the day length of the low-latitude tropics. Brazilian soybeans also benefited from the nitrogen-fixing bacteria inoculation practices that were imported from North America and fine-tuned by local researchers. Beginning in the 1980s, disease resistance was increasingly included in the research agenda. The development of integrated crop management practices led to a sizable reduction in pesticide use. Soil fertility management research led to the identification of more efficient fertilizer and lime application techniques. Soil management and crop rotation permitted no-till planting substitution for conventional seeding, with positive effects upon system sustainability. EMBRAPA's partnership models with farmers' associations provided financial support to genetic improvement programs. In 1997, the Cultivar Protection Law led to new research by the private sector: the Mato Grosso Foundation and companies such as Monsoy, Syngenta, Pioneer, and Milenia.

The development of improved cultivars was important, but it was not enough. Modern varieties would not have been successful had they not been introduced along with improved crop and soil management practices that made the nutrient-deficient soils of the Cerrado highly productive. The Oxisols found in roughly one-half of the Cerrado are highly acid and low in phosphorus, calcium, magnesium, and potassium. Scientists at EMBRAPA, working closely with colleagues in other national and international institutions, developed cost-effective techniques to detect acidity and fertility problems, as well as measures to overcome them (especially the use of gypsum and phosphorus). In addition, an innovation network comprising public research organizations, private firms, and farmer organizations collaborated successfully in adapting conservation farming methods developed in the south of Brazil to the conditions of the Cerrado. Conservation farming integrates a range of practices to allow fragile soils to be managed sustainably. Conservation tillage also significantly reduces production costs, especially after the price of Roundup herbicide fell in the 1990s (Ekboir 2003). These soil management innovations set the stage for the huge expansion in the area planted to soybeans that has helped make Brazil the world's leading soybean exporter.[2]

In similar fashion, research played an important role in propelling the cassava industry in northeast Thailand. Scientists from the Rayong Field Crops Research Institute (Rayong-FCRC), with important input from the Colombia-based International Center for Tropical Agriculture (CIAT), generated the technologies needed by farmers to respond to changes in growing conditions and in market demand. Six improved cassava varieties introduced beginning in 1975 (of almost 350 varieties developed by Rayong-FCRC and CIAT) currently account for 64 percent of the area planted to cassava in Thailand. These varieties can be harvested early (thereby permitting double-cropping), are resistant to common pests and diseases, and feature highly improved root quality. The latter is particularly important because gross root yield is difficult to increase because of the poor soil conditions prevailing in the areas in which cassava is grown; therefore, improvements in starch and/or dry-matter content help to increase the output of processed product at a given root yield level (Hershey et al. 2001). More recently, cropping systems research has generated improved management practices for soil nutrient conservation and erosion control to combat declining soil fertility.

Localized Successes in Africa

Improved technologies for production of the CCAA-selected commodities have also been introduced in Africa, although the results have been somewhat mixed:

- Improved disease-resistant and early-maturing maize varieties were a major driver of maize production growth in Nigeria during the 1980s. Extensive adoption of hybrid maize similarly led to robust maize production growth in Zambia. However, maize intensification programs in these countries were public-sector-managed and underwritten by large subsidies on fertilizer and credit that proved both inefficient and unsustainable. Nevertheless, these experiences, as well those registered in Kenya, Malawi, and other countries, demonstrated that significant productivity gains can be achieved in smallholder agriculture if farmers can be provided with the right technology and inputs, as well as assured markets at remunerative prices (Byerlee and Eicher 1997).

- Rapid adoption of cassava varieties with improved resistance to cassava mosaic virus led to dramatic increases in cassava production in Nigeria during the 1990s. The development of a regional program for biological control of mealybug averted a mealybug disaster in Nigeria and more broadly across Africa (Zeddies et al. 2001). Expansion of cassava was also fueled by the shift in demand for cassava foods such as *gari* and *fufu*, which have become major consumption items in urban areas. In Nigeria, mechanical graters for *gari* preparation released women's labor (previously tied up with the fermentation of cassava) to plant more cassava and greatly increased the returns to labor from cassava production (Nweke 2004). But in contrast to Thailand, Nigeria is not yet a significant producer of processed cassava products, such as livestock feed and starch.

- Promotion of soybean recipes in Nigeria led to increased local trading of soybean food products, with attendant improvement in the nutritional status of many Nigerians, particularly infants and school children. Increased demand for soybean-derived products in turn led to increased production of soybeans. Nigeria, with more than a half million hectares of soybeans, is the only significant producer of soybeans for human consumption in Africa.

- Rice research yielded a promising breakthrough during the 1990s in the form of New Rice for Africa (NERICA) rice varieties, which are based on interspecific hybridization of Asian and African rice species. NERICA varieties feature improved drought and weed tolerance, and they yield well under low-input conditions. By 2007, NERICA varieties were being grown on about 200,000 hectares, mostly in Côte d'Ivoire and Guinea.

It is worth noting to note that the research that led to these technological breakthroughs was not conducted by publicly funded African national agricultural research institutes. Although national research systems were important partners in this research, all of the technologies, except for hybrid maize, were initially developed in international agricultural research centers, especially CIAT and the Africa Rice Center (WARDA).

These success stories from Africa featuring the introduction and uptake of improved crop varieties unfortunately have not been matched by corresponding success stories featuring the introduction and uptake of improved crop and soil management practices. Despite the very serious problems of soil degradation and soil-fertility mining in Africa, there are no examples of breakthroughs in soil management technologies comparable to the breakthroughs that proved so critical in the Brazilian Cerrado. Many African governments have attempted to increase soil nutrient management practices by promoting packages of improved practices with the help of massive subsidies for fertilizer and credit, but the cost-effectiveness of these programs has yet to be demonstrated. Perhaps the most promising achievement to date has been the adoption by about 80,000 farmers in Zambia of nitrogen-fixing tree legumes in maize-fallow systems. Many more such successes in crop and soil management will be needed in Africa to ensure sustainable productivity growth.

Given low population density and labor scarcity, mechanization will also be important to commercialization of agriculture in the African Guinea Savannah, just as it was in Brazil and Thailand. No special incentives are needed to facilitate mechanization, although access to finance will be important for initial purchase of machinery. The experience of many countries shows that where machinery use is profitable, rental markets develop quickly, allowing small farmers to mechanize many operations efficiently. Usually rental markets develop first for tractors used for land preparation and planting (Pingali, Bigot, and Binswanger 1992). Offering special incentives, as was done in Brazil through subsidized credit, not only is unnecessary but also risks leading to premature and larger-scale mechanization, with negative implications for employment.

Although the development of mechanical technology can be left to the private sector and farmers, public research systems have an important role in developing appropriate tillage practices to sustainably manage fragile tropical soils. The development of locally adapted zero tillage methods in different parts of Brazil is an example of an outstanding success in this regard. The promotion of mechanized farming without research support, as has occurred in some parts of Africa, ultimately leads to soil degradation and declining yields (for example, the semimechanized rainfed systems of the Sudan).

Investing More and Better in Agricultural Research

The vast literature on the returns to investment in agricultural research leaves little doubt that such investment generates consistently high returns (Alston et al. 2000). Although it is well known that agricultural research often generates large spillover benefits, this does not mean that individual countries can refrain from investing in agricultural research without suffering severe consequences. Agricultural technology must be adapted to local conditions; thus, even if a country chooses to rely mainly on imported technology, it is likely to experience problems unless it is willing to make a minimum investment to ensure that the imported technology is properly adapted. Adaptive research is especially needed in Africa, where agroclimatic conditions are particularly complex and varied and where the incidence of pests and diseases is higher than in other regions. Recent work by Pardey et al. (2007) has shown that the "technological distance" between growing conditions prevailing in Africa and those prevailing in developed countries is unusually large, so technologies travel even less well to Africa than they do to other developing regions.

Brazil has arguably the strongest national research system in the world for tropical agriculture. The Brazilian national research system received a systematic and long-lasting impetus in 1973 with the creation of EMBRAPA as a national agricultural research public corporation. By the 1990s, EMBRAPA had an annual budget of more than US$300 million and was employing more than 2,000 scientists, most with advanced degrees. EMBRAPA is a highly professional organization, with considerable autonomy and flexibility to provide incentives to attract and keep the best scientists. Individual states in Brazil also have their own public research organizations, and there is also a thriving private R&D sector. In the 1990s, EMBRAPA introduced national competitive funding to tap complementary expertise from other research providers, especially in universities, as well as to provide incentives for more effective interinstitutional collaboration.

Spending on agricultural research has been very low in Africa compared with that in other regions. In 2000, total spending on agricultural

R&D for all of Sub-Saharan Africa was lower than total spending in India and less than one-half of total spending in China (Pardey et al. 2007). To further complicate matters, agricultural research in Africa is highly fragmented, in part because researchers are spread across a large number of small and medium-size countries. Even though Africa, India, and the United States have roughly the same cropped area, in Africa there are 390 public research institutes, compared with 120 in India and only 51 in the United States. Although the total number of agricultural scientists employed in Africa is similar to the number employed in the United States, the average number of scientists working in a given institute is only 30 in Africa, compared to 180 in the United States. The dispersion of agricultural scientists in Africa across so many small institutes makes it difficult to assemble the critical mass of researchers needed to address the generally more complex problems of African agriculture.

Comparison of Brazilian and Nigerian agricultural research systems further demonstrates the huge gap in R&D capacity. Although there are many more farmers and workers employed in agriculture in Nigeria than in Brazil, Brazil spends 40 times as much on agricultural research and has 4 times the number of scientists and 4 times the spending per scientist. The R&D capacity gap, already vast, is likely to increase in future, as spending per scientist in Nigeria has been trending downward (Beintema and Ayoola 2004) (figure 5.6).

The situation in the two other African case study countries is even more bleak. During the 1990s, Zambia's public agricultural research system lost one-half of its crop scientists, while the public agricultural research system in Mozambique started from an extremely weak human resource base after independence. With the possible exception of South Africa, it is hard to think of a single country in Africa in which strong political leadership has resulted in sustained support to national research systems, as has been the case in Brazil.

Public research institutes need more than increased funding to be effective. They also need appropriate governance structures, as well as incentive systems capable of eliciting superior performance from researchers and management. Where appropriate governance structures and incentive systems are lacking, even generous levels of overall funding will have little impact. In Nigeria, for example, the national agricultural research system has experienced a decline in capacity despite repeated pronouncements of government support and despite considerable donor funding. In Zambia, public research institutes are still managed as line departments within the Ministry of Agriculture, rather than enjoying autonomous status.

Figure 5.6   Agricultural R&D Spending, Brazil and Nigeria
(US$ 000 PPP)

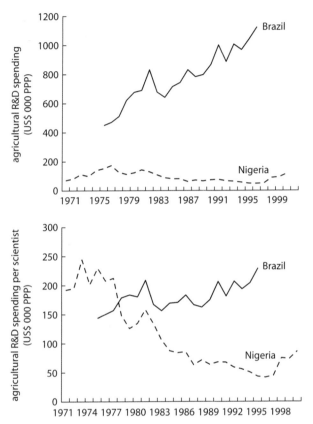

Source: www.asti.cgiar.org.

The efficiency of agricultural research in Africa could be increased by consolidating many of the existing small programs into fewer, larger programs that can support the critical masses of researchers and resources needed to capture economies of scale. Regional and international organizations can play a central role in helping to overcome the small-country problem. International organizations in fact already play a major role, with many of the successes achieved to date having been associated with international agricultural research centers such as the International Institute of Tropical Agriculture (IITA), the Africa Rice Center (WARDA), and Centro Internacional de Mejoramiento de Maís y Trigo (International Maize and Wheat Improvement Center; CIMMYT). The challenge will be to coordinate international, regional, and national research efforts to improve efficiency and eliminate wasteful duplication of effort.

Building More Pluralistic Systems

An important lesson emerging from Brazil and Thailand is that many agricultural research functions that are initially supported with public funds can gradually be transferred to private firms. In the same vein, the performance of many public research institutes in Africa can no doubt be improved through the establishment of closer links with private sector players. Managing the transition from public to private management poses challenges, but these challenges are not insurmountable. Where research is organized along commodity lines, one option is for stakeholders to take over the management of the relevant research institute in return for paying the running costs through levies. This has happened, for example, in the tea sector in Tanzania, where the Tea Research Institute is now widely regarded as the best-performing research institute in the country (Kangasniemi 2002). Likewise, the government of Zambia has established research trusts as a way of fostering public-private partnerships that can respond to the needs of commercial farmers.

One area in which the private sector can almost certainly play a more active role is in the area of crop varietal development and seed production. In both Brazil and Thailand, public-private partnerships have become increasingly important in supporting plant-breeding research, and many private seed companies now routinely form research alliances with public breeding institutes. Creating an environment conducive to the private sector is important to capture advances in biotechnology for crops such as maize, soybeans, and cotton, as has been the case in Brazil. These technologies also have important environmental impacts (facilitating, for example, the adoption of conservation tillage or reduction in pesticide use), but an effective regulatory system for transgenic technologies is still lacking in nearly all Sub-Saharan Africa countries.

Extension and Supporting Services

A final important lesson emerging from Brazil and Thailand is that research by itself cannot lead to sustained productivity changes. Technology generation must be complemented by sustained efforts in agricultural extension, seed supply, and the development of input and output markets.

Thailand, with its traditional focus on smallholder agriculture, has long placed strong emphasis on agricultural extension. The Department of Agricultural Extension (DoAE), established in 1967, maintains an extensive network of regional, provincial, and district offices throughout the Northeast Region. In 1999, DoAE implemented a new system in which farmers set the development priorities and extension officers serve as facilitators and coordinators, as well as learning partners of farmers. Service centers and technology-transfer centers in each subdistrict have been established to work with farmers. The success of the new system has yet to be established, however.

In Nigeria and Zambia, extension efforts during the 1980s and 1990s were organized around the training-and-visit (T&V) system promoted by the World Bank. Although the T&V system had enjoyed considerable success in some Asian settings, it proved less effective in the heterogeneous conditions of African agriculture, and it was also not financially sustainable. In Nigeria, the World Bank alone invested more than US$1 billion in support to agricultural extension delivered through state-level Agricultural Development Programs, with generally disappointing results. More recent efforts to revive extension have emphasized empowering farmer organizations to contract extension services from NGOs (Nigeria) or from private advisory services providers (Zambia, Uganda).

In Mozambique, reform of the public agricultural extension system is fairly recent, but still some success has been achieved in developing a pluralistic system involving extension workers from the private sector, NGOs, and government. The Mozambican approach emphasizes working with farmers' associations, deemed to be both faster and more cost-effective. Although this approach shows promise, clearly much remains to be done: a recent survey revealed that only 9.4 percent of rural villages have an extension office or post, and even in those villages, only 20 percent of households reported contact with extension staff. Large distances and poor road infrastructure have been identified as the main factors preventing better outreach (Gemo, Eicher, and Teclemariam 2005).

Involvement of the private sector can help solve one of the most intractable problems of agricultural intensification—ensuring efficient production and dissemination of improved seed. In Brazil and Thailand, these activities are now largely in private hands, even for self-pollinated crops. Private seed companies are now very active in producing hybrid maize seed in Nigeria, and they are emerging in Zambia. However, inefficient parastatal seed companies and the lack of incentives or a suitable investment climate for the private sector mean that access to improved seed is a perennial problem for commercial producers. Cassava, a vegetatively propagated crop, presents its own unique dissemination challenges, although there have been some successful programs for widely distributing improved planting materials, for example in Nigeria.

Conclusions

Six major conclusions emerge from this brief review of technology generation and dissemination experiences in the CCAA case study countries:

1. Adoption of improved technology is critical not only for developing a competitive commercial agricultural sector but also for ensuring that the fragile natural resource base associated with Guinea Savannah systems is protected.
2. Crop yields in the African countries are generally much lower than crop yields in Brazil and Thailand, and the gap has been widening. However, there are pockets of success in each of the three African countries that demonstrate that those countries' soils and climates can be managed to produce yields similar to those realized in equivalent areas in Brazil and Thailand.
3. Adoption of improved crop varieties has been important everywhere as a catalyst for agricultural productivity change, but adoption of improved varieties alone has rarely been sufficient to achieve a sustained breakthrough in productivity. Improvements in crop and soil management practices are also needed. Identifying sustainable management systems adapted to the heterogeneous production conditions of Africa remains a huge challenge, but as demonstrated by the experience of Brazil, the potential payoffs are enormous.
4. Although agricultural research is critical for developing a competitive commercial agricultural sector, research alone cannot ensure success. Increasingly, innovation involves close interaction among a range of actors—the private sector, NGOs, extension, and farmer organizations. As these actors emerge and develop into vibrant innovation networks, the public sector must adjust priorities and approaches to provide complementary support.
5. Mozambique, Nigeria, and Zambia, like most African countries, are massively underinvesting in agricultural research. Investment in agricultural R&D must increase at all levels—international, regional, national, and subnational levels. International and regional research is especially important in Africa to achieve scale economies.
6. Increased investment must be accompanied by serious efforts to reform research and extension systems to be more pluralistic, dynamic, and demand driven. No country in Africa has moved far in this reform process.

Mobilizing political support for renewed public investment in African agricultural research and extension and sensitizing political leaders to take an active interest in the performance of their national research systems should be a key objective of organizations such as NEPAD and those who fund research, such as ministries of finance, international financial institutions, and bilateral donors.

Infrastructure

Infrastructure investments played a big role as an early driver of the development of the Cerrado region of Brazil and the Northeast Region of Thailand. Governments in both countries invested heavily in roads, railroads, electricity, water supply, and communications, which today are all very well developed, even in many rural areas.

Up until the 1960s, the Cerrado region was connected to the rest of Brazil only via railroads and a few roads, with small urban centers located along many rail lines. After the founding of Brasilia in 1961, spending on infrastructure increased. The Second National Development Plan included a series of special investment programs that benefited the Cerrado. These multisector programs resulted in the rapid development of transportation and storage facilities, energy generation and transmission capacity, agricultural research and extension facilities, and communications infrastructure. Public investment in infrastructure slowed during the years of economic crises. Today, the government faces a challenge in maintaining the large stock of infrastructure in a region that still has extremely low population density, and it is turning increasingly to public-private partnerships and private concessions as a way of supplementing public funds.

Infrastructure investments in the Northeast Region of Thailand accelerated sharply beginning in the 1950s, when thousands of kilometers of roads were constructed to link large towns. The Friendship Highway, financed by the United States during the early 1960s, spanned the entire region and served as the backbone of an eventual network of secondary and tertiary roads that linked most of the provincial and district centers and connected isolated villages with major highways. In addition to serving national security purposes (an explicit objective of the road network was to combat the spread of Communism from Laos and Cambodia by promoting development of rural communities), the road network provided a convenient means for rural people to migrate to Bangkok and other urban areas to the south in search of employment. By 1991, rural roads in the Northeast Region constituted 44 per cent of all rural roads in the country. Development of the road system was accompanied by investments in railways and airports, which served to dramatically reduce the cost of moving people and goods. Investments in transportation infrastructure were accompanied as well by investments in rural electrification, made possible by the abundant availability of local hydropower. By the 1980s, very few villages in the Northeast Region lacked access to electricity.

The experiences of Brazil and Thailand stand in marked contrast to the experiences of most African countries, where the low stock and extremely poor quality of transport infrastructure poses a major barrier to the movement of people and goods. Compared with those for rural inhabitants in the two Asian countries, rural inhabitants in the three African countries face extended travel times in attempting to reach a town of 5,000 or more people (table 5.1).

Africa's notoriously high transport and logistics costs derive primarily from an absence of well-maintained roads, but additional contributing factors include inefficient operating procedures and high transaction costs. Before the 1980s, most transport businesses in Africa, including railways, trucking companies, bus services, and civil aviation companies, were publicly owned and operated. As heavily regulated public enterprises, they were generally slow to respond to changes in demand for transportation services, and because they charged low tariffs, they were usually unprofitable. Beginning in the 1990s, the transport industry in many parts of Africa has been largely deregulated and privatized. Concessions for operating trucking companies, bus services, railways, ports, and airports have become common. The relatively few public enterprises that remain have been given more autonomy, and arbitrary regulation has been replaced by regulation through consensual performance contracts. In the highway sector, establishment of sustainable institutions designed to ensure maintenance of existing infrastructure—autonomous road agencies

Table 5.1   Travel Time to Towns of 5,000 or More Inhabitants, CCAA Case Study Countries

	High access (0–1 hour)	Medium access (2–4 hours)	Low access (>=5 hours)	Total
	(percent of the rural population)			
Brazil	36.8	55.7	7.5	100.0
Thailand	69.2	26.9	3.9	100.0
Mozambique	18.4	39.5	42.1	100.0
Nigeria	24.5	63.7	11.8	100.0
Zambia	4.3	24.0	71.7	100.0

Source: J. Nelson, 2006, Market Accessibility Surfaces for Africa, Latin America and the Caribbean, and Asia. Unpublished data, made available through personal communication.

and dedicated road funds—has become the norm, with positive results beginning to emerge.

If the cost of building and maintaining "hard" infrastructure in the transport sector has come down, the same cannot be said about many "soft" costs that lead to African countries having much higher overall logistics costs. Unofficial tariffs and bribes imposed by the police and others at road checkpoints and border posts remain a serious problem in many parts of Africa. A study funded by the Economic Commission for Africa reported: "Along the West African road corridors linking the ports of Abidjan, Accra, Cotonou, Dakar, and Lome to Burkina Faso, Mali, and Niger, truckers paid US$322 million in undue costs at police customs and gendarmerie checkpoints in 1997, partly because the Inter-State Road Transport Convention had not been implemented" (Economic Commission for Africa 2004). Because the size of these charges is often commensurate with the value of the commodities being transported, there is a real danger that if profit margins begin to improve, the gains will be nullified by increased extractions. Actions are needed to ensure that governments crack down on these illicit practices.

The situation for Africa as a whole is borne out in the three CCAA case study countries. In *Mozambique*, roads and railways constructed under the Portuguese colonial government were oriented not only to facilitate the transport of agricultural commodities from inland production zones but also to facilitate transshipment of commodities from the neighboring countries of Malawi, Zambia, and Zimbabwe. North-south trade within the country was minimal. The current stock of transport infrastructure reflects the colonial legacy; even today, no north-south rail system exists in Mozambique. The deficiencies of the rail network are hardly made up by exceptionally good roads; the density of the road network (3.9 kilometers of road per 100 square kilometers of land area) is the lowest in all of southern Africa. It costs nearly US$7,000 to truck a standard container from Maputo to Pemba, nearly 2.5 times the amount it would take to ship the same container from Dubai (US$2,550) or Guangzhou, China (US$2,550). Maritime transport services are equally deficient. No shipping line provides a direct link between Maputo and Durban. As a result of the road, rail, and maritime impediments and costs between the northern and southern sections of the country, agricultural produce mainly circulates within the northern and southern regions and not between them.

The situation could soon change, however, because major investments in infrastructure undertaken since the end of the war could greatly reduce domestic transport costs. These investments, which include construction of a major bridge on the Zambezi River and the rehabilitation of the main road linking the northern part of the country to Maputo, have the potential to better link crop production surplus areas in the north (including Zambezia Province) to the important domestic markets located in the south. During the decade before 2003, the proportion of roads in good-to-fair condition increased from 10 percent to 70 percent; the proportion of impassable roads decreased from 50 percent to only 8 percent; and the proportion of unpaved roads in good-to-fair condition rose from 20 percent to 51 percent (World Bank 2004). Radio and telecommunications also have improved greatly. By 2005, there were 800,000 mobile phone subscribers, many of them outside of Maputo, and the quality of service had improved substantially compared with that of earlier years. All provincial capitals and many district capitals now have Internet access.

In *Nigeria*, infrastructure plays a critical role in ensuring efficient operations in the value chains of all the selected commodities, because transport costs account for a significant proportion of the final shipment values. High transport costs can be attributed partly to the high cost of fuel and partly to the poor condition of most roads. More than one-third (37 percent) of the federal highway network is classified as being in poor condition, and nearly two-thirds (60 percent) of rural roads are classified as poor. The coverage of the national road network remains extremely deficient. To put things into perspective, Nigeria's road density would have to rise sevenfold from its current level of 97 kilometers of road per 1,000 square kilometers to match the road density of India in 1950. The situation with regard to maritime transport services is hardly more encouraging. Nigeria's ports infrastructure and customs facilities are undersized and overtaxed, with capacity constraints and procedural roadblocks making transit times much longer than in most other international ports. On average, 17 days are needed in Nigeria to clear imports, and 15 days are needed to process exports.

Belying the country's status as a major oil producer, energy costs in Nigeria are very high by international standards. Firms in Nigeria typically pay twice as much for energy as firms in India. The high energy prices prevailing in Nigeria reflect inefficiencies in generation and transmission, with much of the country's energy infrastructure now being antiquated and overwhelmed.

In *Zambia*, a landlocked country, high internal transportation costs have a major bearing on the opportunities for trade and investment. It is no accident that a relatively large share of Zambia's agriculture exports is made up of relatively high-value commodities such as sugar, tobacco, horticulture products (fruits, vegetables, cut flowers), coffee, paprika, and cotton lint. These higher-value commodities provide exporters with greater scope for making a profit even after high transport costs have been absorbed. The limited coverage and generally poor condition of Zambia's rural road network restrict opportunities for profitable investment in outlying areas. Small-scale farmers located far from the main road network are particularly affected, because the high cost of bringing inputs to the farm and taking products to market often leave them with little choice but to produce mainly for home consumption. Transport costs are also a constraint for commercial farmers, many of whom must maintain their own feeder road network at considerable expense and effort.

Transportation by road is the most common way of moving agricultural commodities in and out of Zambia. In this respect, it should be noted that large differences exist between front- and back-load rates along most major trucking routes. Between Lusaka and Johannesburg, for example, typical prices quoted for northbound freight are around US$90 per ton, compared with US$45 per ton for southbound freight. These lower prices for back-load freight provide good opportunities for exporters. Rail freight is also available, but the cost of shipping by rail is about the same as the cost of shipping by road, and rail service is much less predictable.

In Africa generally, even where roads are relatively well developed, transport costs far exceed those in other regions (box 5.2). High transport costs can be attributed to a number of factors: higher vehicle costs, higher fuel prices, higher accident rates, and a variety of informal taxes and tariffs. High transport costs do provide a certain level of de facto protection to African producers selling into inland domestic markets, but they also increase the cost of imported inputs (especially fertilizer and fuel).

In summary, the infrastructural development experiences in Brazil and Thailand contrast sharply with those of most African countries. Whereas the governments of Brazil and Thailand invested heavily in linking rural areas through transport networks and energy grids, governments in most African countries have been able to establish transport and energy infrastructure mainly in and around urban centers or along selected rail corridors. Vast areas in the African Guinea Savannah remain poorly served, with limited access to transport and energy services. This has hampered the ability of many African producers to access even domestic urban markets, much less export into subregional and international markets. High domestic transport and logistics thus represent enormous obstacles that currently threaten the ability of African producers to compete effectively in export markets, especially those for low-value agricultural commodities.

Box 5.2

Road Freight Transport Costs Are Higher in Africa Than in Asia

Not only are roads (on average) of lower quality in Africa than in Asia and the road density much lower, but road-freight transport costs are much higher per ton/kilometer even on roads of comparable quality (Platteau and Hayami 1996). Hine and Rizet (1991) reported that long-distance road freight transport costs in Francophone Africa (Côte d'Ivoire, Cameroon, and Mali) were four to five times higher than comparable costs in Pakistan. Southern African road freight transport costs were also high, while data from India and Vietnam showed costs similar to those in Pakistan.

Four factors contributed to these differences.

First, new vehicle prices tend to be much higher in Africa than in Asia—for example, prices in Tanzania are two to three times higher than the prices of vehicles of similar capacity in Indonesia. This partly reflects the common practice in Africa of allowing dealers to hold exclusive rights on the importation of vehicles and spare parts, and it partly reflects the fact that Asian dealers typically import low-specification vehicles, since they can rely on well-developed artisanal industries for local modification.

Second, fuel prices are often lower in Asia than in Africa.

Third, trucks are driven many more hours on average per year in Asia compared to Africa. In part, this undoubtedly reflects the lower general level of business in African economies. However, Hine and Rizet (1991) also highlight the role played by trucking associations in Africa in informally dividing up work among local trucks. By contrast, Asian trucks make extensive use of highly competitive freight-forwarding agents to secure business for them.

Fourth, Asian drivers are given a much greater degree of responsibility for business performance than their counterparts in Africa. This not only encourages them to use the freight-forwarding agents but also means that they drive at much lower speeds, thereby incurring lower fuel costs and reducing the costs associated with accidents.

Irrigation

Because good water control significantly increases the returns to investments in farm-level production inputs such as improved seed and fertilizer, irrigation was a major driver of the early successes of the green revolution in Asia and Latin America. Conversely, the relative scarcity of irrigation in Africa has been a major hindrance to the spread of improved seed-fertilizer technology in that region.

Irrigation is undoubtedly a key driver of agricultural productivity growth, but it is not equally important everywhere. In areas where rainfall is adequate for crop production and where it is reasonably reliable, the importance of irrigation is not as great. Mainly for that reason, irrigation was not a critical factor underlying the agricultural transformation of the Brazilian Cerrado, and in the Northeast Region of Thailand it was important only for rice, a crop with high water requirements.

In Brazil, only about 2.95 million hectares are irrigated, representing roughly 7 percent of all cultivated land. Of the total area under irrigation, about 40 percent is located in the Cerrado region. Very little of the irrigation infrastructure found in the Cerrado consists of large, publicly funded schemes; most of the irrigation in the region is privately financed and involves small-scale pumping operations.

Farming systems in the Northeast Region of Thailand are mostly rainfed, but irrigation has been expanding and now accounts for about 17 percent of the cultivated area. The Thai government began investing in irrigation during the 1960s, focusing initially on the construction of six large dams on tributaries of the Mun River, the region's major water course. In 1977, the Royal Irrigation Department (RID) launched a small-scale water resource development project in the Northeast Region, under which weirs and small reservoirs were constructed and turned over to subdistrict councils for operation and maintenance. The main beneficiary of irrigation in the Northeast Region has been rice, production of which nearly doubled from 5.3 million tons in 1975 to 10.4 million tons in 2005, even though the area planted increased only by 25 percent, from 4 million hectares to 5.2 million hectares. Irrigation is much less important to producers of cassava and sugarcane, which explains why irrigation development was not a major driver of the Northeast Region's export success. On the other hand, irrigation undoubtedly has played an important role in improving the welfare of rural households by helping farmers diversify their productive activities and protect against weather-induced risk.

Irrigation statistics for the African case study countries are summarized in table 5.2. In *Mozambique*, existing irrigation schemes can potentially serve about 118,000 hectares, but only about one-third of these schemes are currently operational. Rehabilitation of nonoperational schemes and expansion of rural drinking water supplies have been targeted by the government as urgent priorities. Provision of water, especially for small-scale,

Table 5.2   Current and Potentially Irrigated Area, Mozambique, Nigeria, and Zambia

	Potentially cultivatable area	Actual cultivated area	Potentially irrigable area	Actual irrigated area	Irrigated share of cultivatable area	Irrigated share of cultivated area	Irrigated share of irrigable area
	(000 ha)	(000 ha)	(000 ha)	(000 ha)	(percent)	(percent)	(percent)
Mozambique	36,000	4,435	3,072	118	0.33	2.66	3.85
Nigeria	61,000	33,000	2,330	293	0.48	0.89	12.58
Zambia	16,350	5,289	523	156	0.95	2.95	29.81

Source: World Bank 2007b.
Note: ha = hectares.

low-cost irrigation, as well as the operation and maintenance of existing systems, would be very helpful in reducing the country's vulnerability to droughts.

In *Nigeria*, even though lack of water is a major constraint to production, the country's vast irrigation potential remains largely unexploited. Between 2 million and 2.5 million hectares are considered potentially irrigable, but currently only about 290,000 hectares are under irrigation, representing less than 1 percent of the cropped area. Irrigation is used quite extensively in the production of wheat and sugarcane, but it is used much less extensively in the production of rice and vegetables. Recently the World Bank–supported Fadama Development Projects have successfully developed low-lying *fadama* lands using small-scale private or community-based irrigation.

In *Zambia*, estimates of the technically irrigable area range as high as 500,000 hectares. Thus far, only about 150,000 hectares have been developed for irrigation, predominantly on large commercial farms. Government-developed and -managed irrigation schemes have in general performed poorly, although some donor-supported projects have enjoyed some success in helping smallholders build dams, construct gravity-fed water furrows, and acquire treadle pumps to improve year-round water access for both crops and livestock.

Irrigation may not be as critical in the Guinea Savannah as in other more arid production environments, but the potential contribution of irrigation to African agriculture should not be underestimated. Commercial farmers in southern Africa have long known that even a single preplanting irrigation can make an enormous difference in enabling timely planting and ensuring that crops get off to a vigorous start, which can significantly affect eventual yields and reduce risks.

Irrigation thus can significantly improve productivity and (eventually) competitiveness in the African countries.

Institutions

Successful commercialization of agriculture depends on well-functioning markets. Arguably, the toughest challenge facing those who seek to promote commercial agriculture is to put in place the institutions to make markets more efficient and less risky.

Product and Factor Markets

Experience from around the world makes clear that competitive commercial agriculture is unlikely to develop unless markets for inputs and outputs are working effectively. Markets must be able to perform a number of key functions:

- Drive down transaction costs so that input and output prices offered actors throughout the value chain are as attractive as possible, given costs of production and transport
- Ensure that market prices of inputs and outputs approximate long-run economic prices, so that patterns of growth in commercial agriculture are efficient
- Assure that the markets convey, through price and other signals (for example, terms of contracts), the information needed to ensure that the various stages of the value chain are well coordinated in terms of volumes and qualities of products
- Provide incentives for the adoption of technically efficient and economically profitable new technologies
- Avoid transmitting excessive risk in the system (for example, through transmission to farmers of every short-term fluctuation in global markets), which may discourage efficient long-term investment in the value chain, particularly among more risk-averse actors.

The importance of well-functioning markets was clearly demonstrated during the agricultural transformation processes that took place in Brazil and Thailand. Neither country achieved success in commercial agriculture simply by exposing farmers to the unfiltered prices prevailing in world markets. As discussed earlier, policy makers in both countries attempted to provide incentives and reduce price risks by setting minimum support prices and facilitating forward contracting. Policy reforms implemented in Brazil beginning in the 1990s phased out price supports, which were largely replaced by premiums paid to traders to make up for any difference between the support price and the market price. Processors also offered forward contracting tied to provision of loans and in turn reduced their risks through operations on futures markets. Successive Thai governments also implemented targeted domestic price supports and price stabilization measures, although with a somewhat lighter touch and with more reliance on private traders than in Brazil.

In both countries, vertical integration and contract farming have emerged as important for reducing farmers' price risks and providing inputs and credit. This is most developed in industries with a relatively small number of processing firms, such as sugar and cassava in Thailand and soybeans in Brazil.

In Africa, marketing costs are often high because production is distributed across large areas, because the quantity marketed per farm is small, and because infrastructure is poor. For the many food staples that are consumed mainly on-farm, a small proportion of total production enters markets, making markets thin and hence volatile. The thinness of these markets makes market stabilization very difficult and costly, especially in countries where high transportation costs result in a large wedge between import and export parity prices, thereby limiting the ability to use trade policy to stabilize prices (as was done in Thailand).

All three of the African case study countries have at times used panterritorial pricing for some commodities. Panterritorial pricing seriously affected the spatial distribution of production and forced state agencies to intervene in markets to perform an arbitrage role. This was seen most clearly in Zambia, where relatively high panterritorial prices for maize led to widespread maize production even in areas located far from major consumption centers. Until the early 1990s, a parastatal, NAMBOARD, was largely responsible for maize marketing and storage; predictably, it incurred very high fiscal costs.

After a series of reforms introduced during the 1990s, a Food Reserve Agency was established in Zambia and charged with stabilizing prices through local purchases and sales and imports. But government efforts to lend stability to output markets have sometimes had the opposite effect, by introducing uncertainty about whether policies will be maintained. Operations of the Food Reserve Agency have often sent confused signals to markets and undermined private sector incentives. In some years, this has actually increased price volatility because private agents were discouraged and government agencies did not deliver (Nijhoff et al. 2003). In

Mozambique, where government intervention has been minimal and borders are relatively open, price instability has been lower than in Zambia (figure 5.7).

Because agriculture in the African Guinea Savannah is so dependent on unpredictable rainfall, and because poor infrastructure prevents markets from dealing efficiently with weather-related production shortfalls, price volatility poses a major risk for producers and discourages intensification (Byerlee, Jayne, and Myers 2006). Pilot schemes implemented in Malawi to test innovative weather-indexed insurance instruments and forward contracting techniques (using the South African Futures Exchange) show promise of cheaper and more market-friendly ways to manage risks.

Although all three of the African CCAA case study countries have used price supports, they have been less successful than Thailand in using price policy to align domestic prices with the long-term trend in world prices and smoothing short-term price fluctuations. Managing prices in this way requires considerable analytic skill to track evolving trends in world prices, as well as bureaucratic and political flexibility to adjust support prices as a consequence of the forecasted trends.

Figure 5.7   Wholesale Maize Prices, Southern Africa, 1994–2003
(US$/kg)

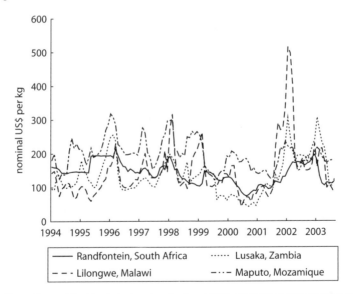

Sources: Mozambique and Zambia: wholesale maize prices from Ministry of Agriculture; Malawi: retail maize prices from Ministry of Agriculture; South Africa: wholesale white maize price data from SAFEX, Randfontein.
Note: kg = kilogram.

In Africa, all three of the CCAA case study countries have used input subsidies to stimulate the development of commercial agriculture. Nigeria and Zambia, having larger nonagricultural sectors than Mozambique, have been able to finance such subsidies more easily than Mozambique (Nigeria particularly during its oil boom of the 1980s). Nigeria and Zambia also have had greater need for subsidies to offset the Dutch disease that resulted from strong oil and copper prices. These subsidies have had significant opportunity costs to the economy, however. For example, in Zambia, fertilizer subsidies absorbed 37 percent of the Ministry of Agriculture and Cooperatives budget in 2005/06, crowding out expenditures on research and extension that could have led to more sustainable increases in agricultural productivity. The bulk of these subsidies appear to have been captured by medium-scale farmers, which may have had the unintended effect of fostering land consolidation, as was the case with credit subsidies in Brazil (Jayne et al. 2006). There is also little evidence that the use of subsidies in the African countries had a "learning effect," inducing farmers to try new technologies of which they were previously unaware. Rather, the subsidies made it profitable for farmers to adopt technologies, such as fertilizer, which they previously knew about but had chosen not to use because of unfavorable output/input price ratios.

Reforms introduced during the 1990s in all three countries significantly reduced the level of input and output subsidies, with the exception of the fertilizer subsidies in Zambia. Reintroduction of fertilizer subsidies is currently under discussion in Nigeria and Mozambique as part of the response to the current high food prices.

A key feature of agricultural markets that can affect performance, and that policy makers often try to influence, is market structure. In the presence of scale economies, information asymmetries, and missing public goods, farmers in Africa are often faced with missing or incomplete markets (for example, for inputs, outputs, and credit). Missing or incomplete markets can potentially be overcome by linking input and output markets, as occurs in the case of many contract farming systems, where large-scale oligopsony or monopsony trading organizations act as system coordinators. Historically, these organizations (for example, the cotton companies in Francophone Africa) have not only purchased crops from farmers, but they have also supplied production inputs, financed agricultural research, provided extension services, built feeder roads, and even supported functional literacy programs. Oligopsony and monopsony trading organizations are often criticized as exploiting farmers, leading to calls that they be subjected to increased competition. But too much competition can prove counterproductive, because it may allow farmers to default on their debts by selling their crops to an organization other than the one from which they received inputs and other services on credit. A critical balance has to be struck. The dilemma is how to strike a balance between the vertical coordination advantages of these larger actors and their potential capacity to exploit farmers by extracting monopsony rents. The formation of effective farmer organizations to negotiate prices and other contract conditions is also necessary, as the cases of Brazil and Thailand sugar clearly show.

Some commodity subsectors are organized as local monopolies, either because high postharvest perishability encourages combining production and processing activities (for example, tea) or because policy makers have chosen to promote this form of organization (for example, privatized cotton sectors in Mozambique, Burkina Faso, and Côte d'Ivoire). Under these circumstances, processors normally have strong incentives to invest in service provision to smallholder suppliers, so the role of the state can be limited to (a) ensuring that there is an ongoing program of research to support the development of the sector; (b) setting the rules of the game for local monopoly concession (re)tendering, to ensure that this process provides investors with both the confidence and the incentives to invest in service provision; and (c) implementing a "competition policy" to ensure that smallholder producers receive a fair price for their output, if this is not adequately guaranteed by the rules of the game established for the monopoly concession. These tasks are not easy, but they can be performed by a committed central government agency.

Other commodity subsectors function as oligopolies. Here again, processors normally will have incentives to invest in service provision to smallholder suppliers. Assuming that there is a basic level of trust among the oligopolists, informal coordination can facilitate input credit recovery and ensure that sufficient incentives exist for extension provision and maintenance of quality control. Under these circumstances, it should be possible to limit the role of the state to (a) and (c) above.

Still other commodity subsectors function as competitive markets, with large numbers of buyers. In these subsectors, private coordination among buyers may well be unachievable. As a result, there are likely to be few, if any, incentives for interlocked preharvest provision service and output purchase. Thus, unless the state plays an active role in providing key services, such as extension, these may simply not be provided, limiting commercialization. The arrested green revolution in maize in eastern and southern Africa and the highly competitive Tanzanian and Ugandan cotton sectors provide powerful examples of these difficulties.

Dorward, Kydd, and Poulton (2005) ask, in the context of cotton systems in Africa, whether small producers and companies respectively are better off within a more competitive or a more concentrated (but better coordinated) industry, such as provided by contract farming, if the latter can deliver input credit to producers and services to producers, but the former cannot. These authors conclude that households that are able to access credit from the concentrated firms fare better under a concentrated system that is able to deliver credit, even though under the monopolistic or oligopolistic systems, the seed cotton prices they receive are up to 40 percent lower than under competitive systems. Their improved benefits arise because they receive better services, count on more reliable input supplies, and achieve higher yields. Yet the recent decline of these "tighter systems," resulting in part from lack of discipline on internal management and political pressures that led to slow adjustment of farmer prices to falling world prices, raises questions about their sustainability. Considerable experimentation and learning are often required to develop locally appropriate systems, as seen in cotton in Zambia and Malawi (box 5.3).

Financial Markets

As commercial agriculture expands, farmers need greater access to financing. Demand for purchased inputs, on-farm investments, and postharvest services typically grows faster than production itself. To some extent, the investments that accompany agricultural commercialization can be financed using savings, profits from other enterprises, or loans, but because of the large scale of needed investments, self-financing usually cannot cover all of the increased investment needs.

Facilitating access to credit for commercializing agriculture poses a major challenge, particularly among smallholders. Given the risks and information asymmetries that characterize agricultural markets, formal financial institutions are often reluctant to lend to smallholders, who frequently lack collateral or other means of securing loans. Attempts to reduce the cost of credit to farmers by subsidizing credit often leads to poor capacity to mobilize local savings and excess demand for loans. The excess demand results in the loans being rationed on the basis of influence or on the ability to absorb high transaction costs, which frequently leads to the bulk of the lending being captured by larger or more influential farmers. Government mandates to target loans to particular sectors or groups are frequently evaded by banks. Government-supported lending agencies created to overcome these problems frequently experience high

Box 5.3

Reducing Risk in Smallholder Cotton Production Systems

Smallholder cotton production has expanded rapidly in Zambia, especially as the two major ginning companies have solved many of the problems around the risk of side selling by farmers to avoid repaying input loans, while at the same time reducing transaction costs per unit of output. The main player in the Zambian cotton industry, Dunavant Cotton Ltd., changed its outgrower schemes to the so-called distributor model that uses a network of locally based distributors who are contracted by the company and work on the basis of a commission. The distributor, typically a larger farmer (not a Dunavant employee), is required to put up collateral as part of the agreement and is fully responsible for the selection of the outgrowers, the provision of inputs and extension support, recovery of credits, and collection of the crop from the outgrowers. At the end of the season, the distributor receives a commission from the company based on credit recovery rates, volumes of the crop, and proper grading. Under the distributor system, the company's per unit transaction costs have been lowered by reducing the number of directly employed extension staff, reducing side selling and farmers' defaults, increasing the numbers of farmers mobilized, and promoting informal village-based interest groups. These organize deliveries and collections and negotiate with the distributor and the company, with no associated costs or levies to the companies. The same system has now been transferred to the company's operations in Mozambique and has made the company an important new player in an industry characterized by antiquated ginning equipment and organizational structures. The entry of such new operators, combined with better monitoring of the concessions (reintroduced at the end of the war) by the state and emerging producer organizations, may finally lead to improvements in the condition of farmers who, historically, receive the lowest seed-cotton prices in the region.

Source: Keyser 2007.

costs and low loan recovery rates, resulting in poor sustainability of the programs.

Brazil and Thailand used very different approaches to provide financing to commercial farmers. These approaches were a function of, and reinforced, the markedly different structures of agriculture in the two countries. Especially during the import substitution period, Brazil provided massive amounts of state credit as the main compensatory policy instrument to offset the taxation of agriculture that was taking place via overvalued exchange rates and other import substitution policies. The net effect of all these policies was to provide only a modest level of support to agriculture, but large-scale mechanized farming was particularly favored by state-supported commodity purchasing programs, cheap credit programs, and free-for-all land policies.

In Thailand, the state also provided credit to farmers, but in this case the financial system was targeted mainly at small farmers. The Bank for Agriculture and Agricultural Cooperatives (BAAC) has been the most important source of institutional lending into the agricultural sector, with 55–70 percent of all farmers borrowing from BAAC in different years. Collateral is not needed for small annual loans, as long as borrowers guarantee each other via group lending. Repayment rates for smaller loans have been good. For larger loans and longer-term loans, collateral is needed. When BAAC operates its own credit programs, the interest rates charged on agricultural loans are normally in line with prevailing market rates, typically in the range of 8–15 percent, depending on the borrower's credit rating. When BAAC serves as the implementing agency for special government credit programs, interest rates may be subsidized. Roughly 10 percent of all BAAC lending has consisted of subsidized lending. A striking feature of Thailand's agricultural credit system is that it has been both large and fiscally sustainable.

In the CCAA African case study countries, the experience with agricultural credit programs has been generally disappointing. In *Mozambique*, the agricultural credit system is still poorly developed. Access to formal sources of finance is very limited for most farmers, except through interlinked markets with firms that have large concessions for cash crops, such as cotton. Only 3.5 percent of rural households have access to credit, much of which is provided not by financial institutions, but rather by companies managing large cash-crop schemes. Limited amounts of credit are also available to some institutional clients through local banks, although this tends to be expensive. In December 2006, local banks were charging a base interest rate of 20.8 percent per year for long-term credit, even though inflation was only 8.1 percent per year. Collateral requirements are demanding; most banks in Mozambique accept a mortgage only on a building, not movable property. Lending into the agricultural sector is uncommon; only about 10 percent of the total portfolio of commercial banks goes to agriculture, including agroindustries, and loans are rarely made to smallholders.

In *Zambia*, extremely low population densities, poor infrastructure, and the high inherent risks of rainfed agriculture make for one of the most inhospitable environments for rural finance in the world. Mainly for those reasons, credit in Zambia is still inordinately expensive and often unavailable, not only for farmers but even for rural nonfarm enterprises.

In *Nigeria*, things should be different. In principle, the country's higher population density and considerable oil wealth provide a good opportunity for building a largely self-sustaining financial system with significant outreach. But the current system is still far from such a state. The federal government and many state governments have made many attempts over the past 30 years to make financial services more accessible to farmers. Among other things, they have created specialized rural financial institutions, introduced compulsory agricultural lending targets, directly supported agricultural lending through government development projects and institutions, approved on-lending schemes for agricultural cooperatives implemented via commercial banks and state cooperative apex bodies, made opening of new urban bank branches contingent on the parallel opening of rural branches, supported agricultural loan guarantee schemes, and introduced debt payment moratoria. Despite good intentions, however, most government involvement with credit was unproductive. The initiatives succeeded in increasing levels of loan disbursement, but most failed to achieve adequate levels of loan repayment, and as a result, they proved unsustainable.

In summary, agricultural credit systems in Africa are in general poorly developed, and they have rarely been able to provide the liquidity needed to meet the demands of commercial agriculture. Where agricultural credit programs have been launched in Africa, they have sometimes succeeded in channeling subsidized credit to producers, but the impacts in terms of commercial agriculture have been minimal. Many rural financial institutions supported using public funds have proved unsustainable and have had to be shut down or drastically reformed.

Business Climate, Investment Climate, and Transaction Costs

Brazil. Brazilian policy to develop the Cerrado was based on creating incentives for private farmers. The large public investment in road infrastructure, for example, encouraged complementary private investment in land development. Initially, panterritorial pricing suppressed private incentives to invest in storage and marketing, with the result that the public sector played a large role, although the private sector incentives to invest in marketing increased with the reforms of the 1990s. Similarly, public-private partnerships expanded in the 1990s in the area of agricultural research.

Labor and tax regulations were among the main constraints to private sector expansion. In 2007/08, Brazil ranked 72nd out of 131 countries on the Global Competitiveness Index (GCI), with the four top constraints to doing business cited as tax regulations, tax rates, restrictive labor regulations, and inefficient government bureaucracy.

Thailand. Thai efforts to develop agriculture in the Northeast Region were characterized by strong public-private partnerships. Through the National Development Plans that guided development efforts throughout the country, the Thai government advocated a relatively free and well-functioning market with good support to the private sector. Efforts were made to allocate responsibilities among the public and private sectors, based on their perceived comparative advantages. Government efforts focused on infrastructure development, research, education, extension, information dissemination, and policies affecting access to credit and land. Government has also supported the creation of farmer groups, occasionally mediating among these groups and the private sector (for example, the sugar companies). At the same time, the roles and functions of private entrepreneurs and merchants were crucially important because they provided good access to marketing facilities, together with needed private investment, to achieve production and marketing potentials for the region.

Although Thailand has made large strides in improving its business climate (currently ranking 28th out of 131 countries on the GCI), problems remain in policy instability and implementation. The four largest constraints on the GCI list are policy instability, inefficient government bureaucracy, government instability, and corruption. In contrast, physical infrastructure, labor force quality, and tax rates rank very low or not at all.

Mozambique. The business climate in Mozambique shows signs of improving, but it is still ranked very low compared with the business climate in many other developing countries. The IFC's *Doing Business 2009* (IFC 2008) ranked Mozambique 141st out of 181 countries for ease of doing business, and the *Global Competitiveness Report 2007–2008* (World Economic Forum 2007) ranked Mozambique 121st out of 127 countries in terms of business competitiveness. Somewhat surprisingly, considering the country's large size and underdeveloped road system, infrastructure ranks only fifth in importance as a business constraint; access to financing, inefficient government bureaucracy, corruption, and restrictive labor regulations all ranked higher.

Nigeria. Nigeria compares poorly with many other developing countries with regard to key variables that affect competitiveness in the agricultural sector (Yee and Paludetto 2005). These variables include availability and cost of credit, availability and cost of public utility services (especially electricity and water), quality and cost of labor, rigidity of the labor market, poor infrastructure, cumbersome port procedures, and a high burden of regulatory compliance. The IFC's *Doing Business 2009* (IFC 2008) ranked Nigeria 118th out of 181 countries for ease of doing business, and the *Global Competitiveness Report 2007–2008* (World Economic Forum 2007) ranked Nigeria 84th out of 127 countries in terms of business competitiveness. Despite recent government efforts to address the problem, corruption continues to add considerably to the cost of doing business in Nigeria. Firms in Nigeria frequently express lower confidence in the consistency of government officials' enforcement of regulations than firms elsewhere in Sub-Saharan Africa. Crime and security concerns further exacerbate the unfavorable business climate, particularly at the downstream stages of the value chain (processing, transportation, storage). The percentage of Nigerian firms rating crime and theft as a severe obstacle to business operation and growth (36 percent) is fourth highest among all countries in Sub-Saharan Africa. Taken together, these factors pose severe obstacles to businesses and undermine the competitiveness of Nigerian agriculture.

These problems affecting the business climate more generally are consistently borne out by case studies of individual value chains. For example, the recent study by Mamman (2004) of livestock supply chains in Sokoto state concluded that efficient functioning of the chain is constrained by the following factors: inadequate capital and lack of access to formal credit; lack of basic facilities, such as water, electricity, and secured environment in the cattle market; inadequate space for the display of cattle in the market; numerous police checkpoints where bribes have to be paid by the drivers while transporting animals from the north to the south; and high rates of taxes and levies imposed by state and local governments. The landmark study by Nweke, Spencer, and Lynam (2002) found that inefficient and costly logistics services weaken supply chains for perishable commodities such as cassava, the processing of which is highly time sensitive.

Zambia. The business climate in Zambia is still ranked very low compared with that of many other developing countries, but there are signs that it may be improving. The IFC's *Doing Business 2009* (IFC 2008) ranked Zambia 100th out of 181 countries for ease of doing business, and the *Global Competitiveness Report 2007–2008* (World Economic Forum 2007) ranked Zambia 106th out of 127 countries on the Business Competitiveness Index. The most problematic business factors include access to financing, inadequate infrastructure, corruption, and high tax rates. One noteworthy feature of the business climate in Zambia is the uncertainty introduced by frequent and unpredictable public interventions in markets for politically important commodities such as maize and rice, which have been subject to arbitrarily imposed export bans and price controls. Large grain-trading companies in South Africa have demonstrated a reluctance to do business in Zambia, citing the difficulty of ensuring that the commodities they buy actually exist and are available for export.

Human Capital

Successful commercialization of agriculture is unlikely to happen in the absence of human capital. Producers will not be able to make the transition from subsistence-oriented farming to commercial farming unless they have the skills, knowledge, and experience to access and exploit new technology, establish and manage a business enterprise, and identify and exploit market opportunities.

Agricultural Education and Training

The experiences of Brazil and Thailand show that agricultural education and training (AET) plays a crucial role in developing and sustaining commercial agriculture. AET involves both university-level programs and vocational training in agriculture, the latter being particularly important because actors throughout the value chain need to learn how to use new technologies and more sophisticated management techniques involved in commercial agriculture. AET directly raises agricultural productivity by developing the capacities of farmers and the other actors throughout the value chain and indirectly by generating human capital for support services and by training the next generation of agricultural researchers.

With the help of strong donor support (particularly from the United States Agency for International Development [USAID] and the World Bank), Brazil and Thailand invested heavily in building and strengthening their agricultural universities during the 1960s and 1970s. During the 1960s, the Brazilian government strengthened undergraduate programs in agriculture by training more than 1,000 academic staff. In 1970–71, more than 900 Brazilian graduate students were studying agricultural sciences in the United States. The results of the heavy public investment in capacity building were reflected in the changing staff profile at the agricultural University of Fortaleza, in the state of Ceará, to the east of the Cerrado.

In 1963, only 2 percent of the faculty held advanced degrees; 10 years later, that number had risen to 82 percent. EMBRAPA similarly began upgrading its staff soon after its creation in 1973, drawing on both over-seas training and the increased domestic capacity to offer advanced degrees (Eicher 2006; World Bank 2007a). Thailand, with substantial assistance from the Rockefeller Foundation and USAID, similarly engaged in a major upgrading of academic staff, beginning in the 1950s. Between 1950 and 1986, an estimated 15,000 Thais pursued short-term training and longer-term graduate education in the United States (Eicher 2006). During this period, both Brazil and Thailand put in place salary structures and other incentives to reduce brain drain from the newly strengthened universities and provided the laboratory and library facilities to make them productive.

Similar efforts at capacity building were mounted in Africa, but they have not been sustained. During the 1960s, a few African countries, including Ethiopia, Ghana, Kenya, Nigeria, and Sierra Leone, took advan-tage of donor support to create agricultural universities, inspired by the U.S. land grant model. For example, following Nigeria's independence in 1960, USAID granted contracts to four U.S. universities (Michigan State, Wisconsin, Kansas State, and Colorado State) to help build four agricul-tural universities in Nigeria based on the land-grant model. The essence of the land-grant model—the linking of teaching, research, and extension within a single organization—proved elusive, however, mainly because of the institutional reporting structure in Nigeria, under which universities reported to the Ministry of Education, with few links to the Ministry of Agriculture. Consequently, even though these efforts did help to strengthen undergraduate education, the contributions to research and extension were much weaker. In northern Nigeria, Kansas State's collab-orative program with Amadou Bello University in Zaria initially proved more successful, thanks to the decision of Nigerian political leaders to transfer the research functions formerly located within the Ministry of Agriculture to the university, along with five senior researchers charged with promoting a two-way flow of information from farmers to researchers and a flow of technology from researchers to extension agents and farmers. After some initial successes, the initiative lost support because policy makers became distracted by the Nigerian civil war, the oil boom, and political strife.

Overall, the expansion of higher-education facilities in Africa has been impressive; the number of public universities grew from 20 in 1960 to roughly 300 today. Of these, at least 96 teach agriculture and natural resources management. The distribution of these universities throughout the region is very uneven, however; 26 universities offering agricultural and resource management courses are located in Nigeria. In contrast, Zambia benefited from much lower levels of assistance during the 1960s and 1970s for development of its agricultural higher-education program, and Mozambique, which became independent much later, hardly at all. A major achievement of the expansion of university-level training in Africa, combined with overseas advanced-degree training, was the Africanization of most agricultural education and research organizations on the continent, as expatriates were largely replaced by nationals (Beintema and Stads 2006). Secondary (vocational) training programs in agriculture have expanded much more modestly, representing only about 3–5 percent of total enrollment in vocational programs in Africa.

For a while, the number of programs offered in agriculture expanded steadily, but more recently the resources to offer quality programs have largely evaporated. The initial institution-building achievements of the 1970s and 1980s in Africa in the area of AET have given way to neglect since the 1990s. With the retreat of donor support for African agriculture in the 1990s, support for formal AET programs in Africa dried up, accounting for just 0.7 percent of agricultural sector aid between 2000 and 2004. Government funding tended to follow donor priorities, with the result that salaries and research resources for faculty have plummeted, forcing many academics to give nominal attention to their teaching duties while pursuing consulting or other jobs to supplement their incomes. At the same time, as the African countries went through structural adjustment and employment opportunities in public agricultural research and extension staffs fell, curricula in the agricultural faculties and in agricultural technical training programs often failed to evolve, leading to an imbalance between curricula and job-market demands. The ultimate cost of the government and donor pullback from AET has been to distance African professionals from global knowledge networks and the cutting edge of technology transfer. It has also left a severely depleted and aging human resource pool in African agriculture, particularly for the next generation that will need to replace many African agricultural scientists who were trained in the 1970s and 1980s and who are now nearing retirement. A major political and financial commitment to rebuilding capacity and human capital in these systems is needed, particularly in view of the fact that such investments had to be sustained over several decades in Brazil, Thailand, and most other countries that have been able to transform their agricultural sectors. The optimal configuration of AET institutions will differ by country, however. Nigeria is sufficiently large to host several world-class programs, but smaller countries such as Zambia and Mozambique will need to look more to regional programs.

Producer Organizations

The development of a modern commercial agricultural sector is typically associated with a rise in producer organizations, created as farmers seek better forms of horizontal and vertical coordination. By joining together into organizations, farmers can take advantage of economies of scale, more easily access technical and financial services, and gain a stronger political voice. Farmers who are members of producer organizations often find it easier to borrow from financial institutions; buy inputs in bulk and negotiate lower prices from sellers; augment the quantity of produce being offered for sale and extract higher prices from buyers; and capture scale economies in transport and storage to reduce unit costs. In addition to empowering individual farmers (for example, by representing their collective interests in decision-making forums), producer organizations can help establish and enforce quality standards.

Strong producer organizations are still relatively rare in Africa. As civil-society organizations that can eventually compete with the authority of the state, producer organizations were often suppressed, at least up until the spread of democracy during the past two decades. During the immediate postcolonial period, many attempts were made to introduce farmer cooperatives, but these were often top-down creations of the state and frequently failed. Only recently, as democratization has afforded greater space for civil-society organizations, a new wave of producer organizations has started to emerge, frequently with the help of donor support.

Even under favorable circumstances, the development of formal organizations capable of delivering real benefits for farmers, especially smallholders, tends to be a long and complicated process. Informal farmer groups often form as commercialization takes hold, sometimes almost spontaneously, but the development of strong and sustainable self-managed producer organizations requires a substantial investment of money, time, and expertise. External partners can sometimes play an important role in supporting the process. Increased access to financial and other services are important initial outcomes, but long-term benefits, such as improved access to credit, market integration, and skills enhancement, are unlikely to follow unless the association develops the capacity to become financially sustainable and maintain strong and transparent management.

Generally speaking, effective producer organizations thrive in democratic environments that provide a favorable climate for civil-society organizations in general. In Brazil and Thailand, producer organizations now are active in defending smallholder rights (including rights to land), but in many parts of Africa, producer organizations are still poorly developed. Few producer organizations in Africa have developed sufficiently and gained the commercial acumen needed to take on a major role in service delivery. And while farmer organizations in some African countries are becoming increasingly influential stakeholders in agricultural policy discussions, they have rarely demonstrated the ability to generate the strong political will in favor of agriculture that propelled development of the Brazilian Cerrado and the Northeast Region of Thailand. Still, producer organizations in some African counties—including Nigeria and Zambia—are probably more advanced today than were the producer organizations found in Brazil and Thailand at the beginning of the 1960s.

Notes

1. A significant exception is sugarcane produced in Zambia, where very high yields reflect ideal growing conditions and private estate management.

2. The progress in varietal improvement and crop and soil management has been symbiotic. Improved varieties were important in achieving the payoff to intensification of crop management, especially the response to improved soil fertility. Later breeders have been selecting varieties that are better adapted to planting under zero tillage.

CHAPTER 6

Potential Social and Environmental Impacts of Commercial Agriculture

Commercial agriculture will not be able to realize its potential as a powerful driver of sustainable pro-poor growth if the rise of commercial agriculture turns out to be socially divisive, environmentally unsustainable, or both. For this reason, African policy makers will need to pay close attention to potential social and environmental impacts associated with the agricultural commercialization process and ensure that the transformation of subsistence-oriented farming systems into market-oriented farming systems takes place in ways that contribute effectively to welfare objectives and environmental goals.

Potential Social Impacts

Commercial agriculture in Africa is unlikely to contribute effectively to national policy objectives of broad-based growth and poverty reduction unless care is taken to ensure that the wealth created by commercial agriculture is shared widely. This implies that policy makers will have to pay close attention to the factors that affect the size and distribution of benefits generated as a result of the commercialization process.

Employment Generation, Income Gains, and Access to Social Services

Expansion of commercial agriculture, whether practiced by small-scale family-run farms or by large-scale agribusiness enterprises, affects social welfare through three main pathways: (a) by affecting employment opportunities and incomes of those directly involved in the transformation of farming and associated value chains; (b) by affecting prices of food and fibers, which tend to make up a large part of the consumption baskets of the poor; and (c) by generating income gains that can be tapped through taxation or voluntary investment to finance delivery of improved social services (for example, health and education). Although the first two pathways are only loosely dependent on government intervention, the third pathway—harnessing income gains to finance the delivery of improved social services—depends critically on the existence of well-functioning markets, as well as on the presence of effective public finance systems and/or civil-society organizations that can appropriate some of the expanded agricultural income and invest it effectively in needed social infrastructure.

To what extent did the wealth created by agricultural commercialization in Brazil and Thailand translate into greater employment opportunities, income gains, and improved social infrastructure for the poor? As discussed earlier in this report, the rise of commercial agriculture in the two countries was based on completely different models: the rise of commercial agriculture in Brazil was driven by large-scale agribusiness enterprises, while in Thailand it was driven by the rapid proliferation of commercially oriented small-scale family farms. Did the fact that the two countries used different models affect the efficiency and distribution of the benefits? And what are the implications for the African case study countries?

Brazil. The rise of commercial agriculture in the Cerrado region had generally positive effects on poverty and social well-being. The development of the Cerrado region created significant new employment opportunities, especially in fast-growing urban centers. Large welfare gains accrued to a significant group of the Brazilian poor inside the Cerrado region and in other regions, who benefited from large reductions in the prices of basic staples that resulted from the huge expansion of agricultural production in the Cerrado. The real value of the food consumer price index declined by a total of 80 percent in the 30-year period before 2005. This translated into a substantial increase in the real incomes of the poor. In addition, the agricultural sector generated a huge trade surplus for Brazil—ranging from US$10 billion per year during the 1990s to US$40 billion per year during the early 2000s. This surplus was critical in ensuring Brazil's solvency and helped the country avoid the long and deep recessions (with large impacts on the poor) that many other emerging economies faced during this period.

Since the 1960s, the population of the Cerrado region has grown at twice the rate seen elsewhere in the country. Rapid population growth, combined with increasing mechanization of agriculture, resulted in substantial urbanization and related growth of nonagricultural activities. The high rates of agricultural and nonagricultural growth fueled substantial investments in health and education infrastructure. For example, the region's share of health facilities reached 7 percent in 2000, commensurate with its share in the nation's population. There was also concerted public investment in schools. From the 1970s through the 1990s, the number of inhabitants per school was close to the national average, but the gains were eventually eroded, and by 2000 the number of inhabitants per school in the Cerrado region (892) was once again considerably higher than the national average (579). Nevertheless, the literacy rate in the Cerrado region rose from 56 percent in 1970 to 87 percent by 2000, the latter well above the national average.

In 2000, health and education outcomes in the Cerrado region, as measured by infant mortality rates, life expectancy, and literacy rates, were comparable to Brazilian national averages. Housing indicators in the Cerrado region were better than the national average, despite important migration and heavy population flows into the region over the previous 30 years. The proportion of *favela* (slum) homes in the Cerrado region fell from 0.58 percent in 1980 to 0.44 percent 2000. In contrast, for Brazil as a whole, the proportion rose from 1.62 percent to 3.04 percent over the same period.

But these social benefits came at a cost. Some of the region's indigenous peoples and many early settlers—smallholder farmers as well as landless farm laborers—lost their lands, livelihoods, and in some cases their lives as the result of the expansion of large-scale mechanized agriculture. Furthermore, large-scale commercial producers substituted capital for labor, fueled by heavy credit subsidies that made capital artificially cheap and reduced the employment impacts of the expansion in rural areas. Finally, although agricultural commercialization in the Cerrado led to strong overall income growth throughout the region, the distribution of income followed the general pattern of increasing concentration seen elsewhere in Brazil. For example, in Goiás state mean agricultural income per capita grew by 138 percent over the period 1970–80, but the Gini coefficient increased from 0.439 to 0.582. During the same period, absolute poverty (as measured by the percentage of the agricultural population earning less than the minimum wage) fell from 82 percent to 52 percent before rebounding to nearly 60 percent by the end of the 1980s. The increasing concentration of income in the face of strong income growth was caused by the steady concentration of landholdings, along with the policy-induced agricultural mechanization that prematurely reduced employment of unskilled labor in agriculture.

Thailand. Because expansion of commercial agriculture in Thailand was based on smallholder farming, including settlement of previously uninhabited land, and involved land reform that secured the settlers' rights, Thailand experienced fewer negative social impacts than did Brazil. Even though income distribution became more concentrated in the Northeast Region as a whole over the period 1980–2002 (the Gini ratio increasing from 0.474 to 0.527), concentration of incomes *decreased* in the agricultural sector, with the Gini ratio falling from 0.416 to 0.396, which is lower than in other regions of Thailand. Absolute incomes rose for both farmers and farm laborers: between 1977 and 2001, real farm incomes increased by 119 percent, and real farm wages by 103 percent. As a consequence of the broad-based income growth, the headcount poverty rate, which stood at 56 percent in the Northeast Region in 1988, had plunged to 17.2 percent by 2004. Because poverty rates fell even faster in other regions of Thailand, however, poverty has become more concentrated in the Northeast Region, which in 2004 was home to 51 percent of Thailand's 7 million poor.

Importantly, agricultural commercialization in Thailand stimulated rapid expansion of downstream (off-farm) segments of many agricultural value chains. Unlike in Brazil, off-farm enterprises in Thailand did not have access to highly subsidized credit, so they avoided labor-displacing technology and consequently generated large numbers of jobs. The number of "factories" in the Northeast Region, 78 percent of which were rice mills, expanded from 1,908 in 1975 to 43,747 in 2000, at which time they accounted for more than 324,000 jobs. The rapid expansion of both agricultural and nonagricultural employment also induced labor migration into the area from neighboring Laos, mainly of poor, young, single women. Although outmigration from the Northeast Region to the Bangkok metropolitan area increased in response to continued population growth in the Northeast Region, outmigration was lower in villages where agriculture was more commercialized.

During the 1960s and 1970s, Thailand's economy was more open than Brazil's, so the expansion in domestic agricultural production did not have as dramatic an impact in driving down domestic food prices as it did in Brazil. Nonetheless, Thailand used export quotas and taxes to hold down domestic prices of staples, especially rice, thereby benefiting poor consumers.

Although health and education had been important national priorities in Thailand since the 1960s, poverty alleviation per se became an important goal during the Fifth National Plan (1982–86). Beginning in 1982, poor villages were identified, and development projects were introduced by five major government ministries (Agriculture and Agricultural Cooperatives, Education, Health, Interior, and Commerce). Education in remote areas in Thailand began to be promoted as early as 1961. Although educational indicators for the Northeast Region still lag behind those of other regions, there is no doubt that education in the Northeast Region has improved over the past 40 years. This improvement is the product of national policy and was financed largely through the national budget, but the growth of commercial agriculture in the Northeast Region likely contributed. Increased household income, derived in part from commercial crop production, enabled parents to send their children to school and buy school uniforms, books, and other necessary materials for use in the school.

Other social indicators of the Northeast Region, such as the number of patients per doctor, the number of telephone lines per 1,000 people, the percentage of households having access to electricity and piped water, have improved. Compared with those of Bangkok, however, a large gap still remains (NESDB 2006; World Bank and NESB 2005).

Last but not least, the growth of commercial agriculture also contributed to, and was facilitated by, greater integration of the Northeast Region into Thailand's political system. Although this integration was initially pursued in response to the communist insurgency, the formation of farmer organizations dedicated to marketing commercial crops improved the political and economic bargaining power of farmers. The Northeast Region emerged as a potent political constituency representing an important voting base for many political parties. As a major political force, the Northeast Region has benefited from continuous political patronage and frequent promises of development support. Farmers from the Northeast Region have mounted many protests in recent years and made numerous demands on the central government, and some of their leaders have become prominent players in the national political arena.

The experiences of Brazil and Thailand show that expansion of commercial agriculture can bring significant employment opportunities, income gains, food price declines, and reductions in poverty. Of critical importance for African policy makers, the social impacts of expanded commercial agriculture in both countries were critically influenced by a small number of key factors:

- The macroeconomic environment, especially interest and exchange rates (this influenced the incentives to mechanize and thereby shaped employment opportunities, not only in farming but also throughout the value chain)
- The land-tenure system and distribution of land holdings (this determined who benefited directly from increased primary production)
- The extent to which provision of agricultural services (for example, extension, finance, input supply) reached small-scale and women farmers
- The divergence between import-parity and export-parity prices (this established the degree to which expanded domestic production reduced domestic food prices—thus increasing the real incomes of the poor)
- The flexibility of the marketing systems (this determined how much domestic prices declined in response to expanded production)
- The capacity and the willingness of the national and local governments and farmer organizations to tap some of the growth from commercial agriculture to finance collective investments in health and education
- The effect of the growth on the political and social integration of the previously isolated regions with the rest of the country.

Although some of the lessons emerging from the Brazilian and Thai experiences are fairly straightforward, others are more ambiguous, and there is room for debate about what is the best strategy for fostering rapid and inclusive growth. Four issues warrant deeper discussion, especially in light of recent controversies over the commercialization of agriculture in Africa: (a) the optimal scale of the farm operation, (b) land tenure and land administration, (c) gender impacts of agricultural commercialization, and (d) food security impacts of agricultural commercialization.

Farm Size and Commercial Agriculture: Is Bigger Necessarily Better?

Recently there have been many media reports about the scramble for agricultural land in Africa. This scramble—sometimes referred to as a "land grab"—was first triggered by the biofuels boom and later stimulated even further by the global food price explosion. The first wave of investor interest, driven mainly by biofuels speculators, has been examined by Cotula, Dyer, and Vermeulen (2008), while the second wave, motivated by the desire to invest in land for food production, is analyzed in Grain Briefing (2008). Both of these documents list numerous initiated, pending, or completed land acquisitions by mainly foreign investors in the developing world, including Africa. Although biofuels speculators come from all corners of the globe, in cases where the investments have been motivated by food security concerns, the potential investors have tended to be China, the Republic of Korea, India, various Persian Gulf States, and a handful of other countries that have limited land and/or water resources. These countries have expressed interest in securing access to land that can be used to produce food that would be used to augment their own national food supplies. It is not clear how many of the intended or completed land acquisitions have resulted in actual farming projects. The collapse of global commodity prices that occurred during the second half of 2008 may have taken the wind out of many of these initiatives.

The debate over the relative advantages and disadvantages in Africa of large-scale versus small-scale farming models has been further stimulated by the leading development economist Paul Collier, who has published several provocative articles in which he has characterized advocates of small-scale farming in Africa as romantics who are ignoring the degree to which the international food system and agricultural production technology have changed in favor of larger-scale ventures (for example, see Collier 2008a, 2008b).

Information and analysis presented in this report make clear that there is enormous potential for competitive commercial agriculture in Africa and that the more favorable prices expected to prevail over the longer term are likely to make investments in African agriculture even more attractive in future. Therefore, the recent upsurge in investor interest is to be welcomed. What is not clear, however, is whether the large-scale farm models contemplated for such investments have been fully thought through.

Past experience is not very encouraging. For decades, empirical data from all over the world have consistently shown that large farms dependent on hired managers and workers are less productive and less profitable (per hectare) than small farms managed by families and operated primarily with family labor. The results of the CCAA value chain analysis are fully consistent with these broader data. What this means is that farm-level agricultural production (primary production) is normally subject to diseconomies of scale. This finding is admittedly counterintuitive: one would assume that there are scale economies associated with use of large machines, better access to capital and credit, increased power to negotiate favorable prices for inputs and outputs, stronger incentives to stay abreast of rapid technical change, and the ability to self-provide infrastructure and services.

Probably because the finding is so counterintuitive, an enormous amount of work has focused on examining the decreasing scale economies in agriculture and exposing the reasons for the relative efficiency of the family farm (for a summary of the literature, see Binswanger, Deininger, and Feder [1995]). The theoretical literature shows that the main source of the superior productive efficiency of small farms derives from the greater incentives felt by family labor to work hard. In addition, the heterogeneity of land quality, even within small farms, and the fact that production occurs under highly variable weather conditions, put a premium on close management and supervision of farm operations by family members who have a strong incentive to maximize returns. The productivity advantage is therefore not so much associated with smaller farm size per se, but with the incentives felt by management and labor. The recurring empirical finding that primary agricultural production is usually characterized by decreasing economies of scale shows that the advantage conferred by these greater incentives are in practice rarely offset by the lower information, financing, and marketing costs and other advantages typically enjoyed by larger-scale operations.

Exceptions to the lack of economies of scale arise in the so-called plantation crops, such as sugar, oil palm, tea, bananas, and horticultural crops grown for export. After the harvest, these crops need to be processed very quickly and/or transferred to a cold storage facility; otherwise, they experience rapid declines in quality—and hence value. Assuming that the farm operations of planting and harvesting can be successfully coordinated with the off-farm operations of processing and shipping, the economies of scale associated with the processing and/or shipping of these crops are transmitted to the farm level (Binswanger and Rosenzweig 1986).

The coordination problem associated with plantation crops is typically solved using one of three organizational models: (a) production takes place on a large-scale farm or plantation, over which the processing firm has direct control; (b) production is assured by small-scale family farmers working under contract with the processor; or (c) production is assured

by a mix of the two farm types, usually constituted as a nucleus estate sur-
rounded by family farmers. In Thailand, the contract farming model is
universally practiced for plantation crops. The economies of scale that can
be realized through the use of agricultural machinery are realized in
Thailand and in many other parts of the developing world through the
use of contract-hire services for machinery. In Thailand and elsewhere,
access to information and credit is provided by specialized institutions
that cater to smallholders, and infrastructure is provided by the public
sector. Brazil features a mix of the plantation, contract farming, and
mixed production models, often within the same commodity subsector.
All three modes of organization also can be found in African sugar, oil
palm, and tea production.

Some proponents of the large-scale farming model have argued that
even if large-scale farming is not more productive, it is easier to introduce
and easier to scale up rapidly, making it more suitable for jump-starting
agricultural growth. This argument is not supported by empirical evidence, however. Over the past 15 years and more, rapid growth in agriculture has not been positively correlated with large-scale farming
models. Over this period, Brazil's agricultural growth rate of about 4 percent has been exceeded by those of China, Vietnam, and no less than
eight Sub-Saharan African countries (Angola, Benin, Burkina Faso, Côte
d'Ivoire, Ghana, Liberia, Mozambique, and Nigeria), all of which feature
agricultural sectors dominated by small-scale farming (Hazell et al. 2007).

Yet, if large-scale agriculture is less efficient, how does it continue to
survive? If there are few economies of scale outside of the plantation
crops, why are there such apparently successful large-scale farming sectors in eastern and southern Africa (and also in other parts of the developing world, most notably Latin America)? Should small-scale family
operations not have driven the large operations out of business, thanks to
their greater productive efficiency? Binswanger, Deininger, and Feder
(1995) showed that the early spread of commercial agriculture in Latin
America and in the settler economies of Kenya, South Africa, and
Zimbabwe involved the systematic appropriation of high-quality land by
settlers, combined with displacement of the indigenous population to
areas with typically lower soil fertility and locational disadvantages. To
further undermine the competition from indigenous farmers, smallholders were often prohibited from producing cash crops or excluded from
marketing cash crops via monopolistic marketing boards. In addition,
public infrastructure, research and extension services, and subsidized
credit were focused on the large-scale farms. Finally, to help the large-scale

farms attract labor, taxes were imposed on the indigenous population that, in the absence of a commercial crop, they could pay only by selling their labor to the large-scale farms as workers or tenants. It was only thanks to discriminatory rules of the game—that conferred settler farms with extreme privileges—that the large-scale commercial farms of Africa and Latin America were able to prosper. Far from involving low fiscal costs, the subsidies directed to these farms were usually very high (typically, they were financed from mineral exports).

The experience of large-scale farming in Africa was reviewed in several of the papers commissioned as background pieces for the CCAA study. The paper on the experience of the Commonwealth Development Corporation (CDC) shows a 50-year history of support to the introduction of large-scale farming all over Africa. Of all the ventures studied, about one-half failed outright—for technical reasons, economic reasons, or both. Not surprisingly, most of the successes involved plantation crops (including timber and wood products). Some of the successful ventures used the contract farming or nucleus estate models. The CDC considered food crop production to be better undertaken by the smallholder sector and only rarely ventured into food crops, recording a few rare successes and many failures. No large-scale venture supported by the CDC ever managed to achieve export competitiveness in food crops. High costs of machinery and high overhead costs associated with expatriate management were usually the main obstacles. The only large-scale farming ventures that have ever managed to produce food crops for export have been the large-scale commercial farms that were created with extremely high levels of state support under colonialism or apartheid.

The legacy of past failures with large-scale agriculture in Africa does not mean, however, that large-scale agriculture must necessarily fail in the future. Agricultural production and marketing conditions are changing rapidly, often in ways that apparently provide advantages to larger-scale operations. Technical change is ever more rapid, economies of scale associated with mechanization keep rising, quality standards continue to tighten, traceability of output back to the farm of origin is becoming more important, and finance remains out of reach to many smallholders in Africa. These and other developments have the potential to impart advantages to large-scale ventures.

Examples of where these changing conditions are encouraging the emergence of large-scale farming are beginning to appear in Africa. Maertens and Swinnen (2006) and Maertens (2008) describe how, in Senegal, tightening phytosanitary requirements have caused production for export of fruits and vegetables to shift toward larger farms. Larger-scale plantation operations that contract with farmers for primary production and rely on hired labor to carry out assembly, grading, and packing operations generate much higher incomes for participating farmers and hired workers compared with incomes earned by nonparticipants. The higher incomes have significantly reduced poverty in surrounding communities. Tyler (2008b) described a similar experience—consolidation of production among large-scale commercial conglomerates working with contract farmers—in the Kenya horticulture sector. Although these emerging success stories do point to the potential viability of large-scale commercial farming ventures in Africa, it is important to remember that they represent special cases of highly perishable products produced for export into markets characterized by very demanding quality standards.

Another example of successful large-scale commercial farming in Africa involves irrigated production of sugar. Tyler (2008a) shows that technical efficiencies achievable with the help of large-scale irrigation infrastructure impart cost advantages to large-scale irrigated sugar production compared with rainfed production. Mainly for this reason, irrigated sugar production is almost always undertaken by large-scale enterprises. In contrast, rainfed sugar production continues to be dominated by smallholders, who often work under contract to a centralized processing facility. Contract farming is widely and successfully practiced for rainfed sugar production in many countries, including all five of the CCAA case study countries.

Advocates of large-scale farming sometimes point out that under the large-scale farming model, the costs of many services normally provided by the state are internalized by private farms. But historical experience does not bear out this argument. On the contrary, large-scale and corporate farms have been extremely successful in convincing the government to construct infrastructure, provide input and credit subsidies, extend tax privileges, and allow concessional access to land, often on a massive scale.[1] Many of the firms that have recently begun to express interest in launching large-scale agribusiness ventures in Africa similarly are looking for government support in the form of free or low-cost land, tax privileges, concessional financing, and supporting infrastructure such as access roads and port facilities. Where such support has not been forthcoming, as in the case of the Zimbabwe farmers who moved to Mozambique, the ventures have often failed, and the farmers have withdrawn.

If past experience with large-scale commercial agriculture in Africa has been mixed, the same can be said for small-scale commercial agriculture.

Clearly there have been some unequivocal success stories, cases in which growth in smallholder agriculture has generated important economic and social benefits and has served as a powerful source of poverty reduction. Some of the best-known examples have been the cotton production systems of Francophone West Africa. Grimm and Günther (2004) highlight the importance of smallholder cotton production to the reduction of poverty in Burkina Faso. Tefft, Staatz, and Dioné (1997) described how the rapid expansion of smallholder commercial cotton and rice production in Mali during the export- and import-substitution booms that followed the 1994 CFA franc devaluation resulted in substantial increases in school and health clinic construction, fueled in part by higher local revenues. In both countries, smallholder cotton producers are also the major producers of rainfed food crops, and the expansion of cotton production has had major spillover effects in increasing cereals production. Given the large wedge between import- and export-parity prices in many African countries, the potential for expanded staple food production to drive down real prices for consumers, most of whom are poor, is substantial.[2]

Experience from throughout the world suggests that the development of smallholder-led commercial agriculture is much more likely to succeed when smallholder farmers have ready access to technology and inputs, including credit, market information, and marketing services. Under contract farming, some of these services are provided by the contractor, and their costs are privately financed. In the absence of contract farming, they have to be financed partly or entirely by the state, either at the national level or at the local level. Many different models exist for the provision of these services: farmers' organizations, NGOs, private sector providers contracted by government, or government services of local or national governments.

What, then, is the bottom line regarding farm size and commercial agriculture? Based on the available evidence, there is little to suggest that the large-scale farming model is either necessary or even particularly promising for Africa. Although some have pointed to the apparently successful settler farms of eastern and southern Africa, closer examination reveals that in many cases these were created by expropriating land from indigenous populations and nurtured with streams of preferential policies, subsidies, and supporting investments. The more recent experience of the CDC and other attempts at fostering large-scale farming in Africa were hardly more encouraging, except in typical plantation crops. The CCAA background papers on commercial farming in Africa and the CDC show not a single case where large-scale farms, outside of the settler economies, have ever achieved competitiveness in the export of food crops.

The argument in favor of large-scale agriculture is further undermined by the finding of this study that the most promising markets for Africa's farmers are domestic and regional markets for basic food crops and livestock products. The main opportunities for large-scale farming thus appear to be plantation crops, including sugarcane and oil palm, which currently are the most efficient sources of biofuels. With these two crops, the large-scale plantation farming model will have to compete with contract farming (except perhaps in irrigated sugar) or the mix of nucleus estates with contract farming.

Value chain analysis suggests that the case in favor of large-scale farming in Africa is strongest in the presence of three particular sets of circumstances:

- When economies of scale are present, as in the so-called plantation crops (for example, sugar, oil palm, tea, bananas, and many horticultural crops grown for export). After being harvested, these crops need to be processed very quickly and/or transferred to a cold storage facility; otherwise they experience rapid declines in quality and hence value. If the farm operations of planting and harvesting can be successfully coordinated with the off-farm operations of processing and shipping, the economies of scale associated with the processing and/or shipping of these crops are transmitted to the farm level.
- When Africa's producers must compete in overseas export markets that have very stringent quality requirements and demand backward traceability of output all the way to the farm level, and in which contract farming is not feasible (for example, because of poor enforcement of contracts).
- When relatively fertile land must be developed in very low population-density areas (which include vast tracts of Guinea Savannah land). Without a large agricultural population representing a potential labor force, expansion into these areas will necessarily require mechanization. Although mechanization of smallholder agriculture is possible through the use of draft animals or hired machinery services, even if these technologies can be made available, development of relatively unpopulated areas still may require significant in-migration from other areas of higher population density, to which there may be political obstacles. Under such conditions, large-scale mechanized farming may be the best model, even for the production of staple foods.

In all three of these cases, allocation of extensive tracts of land to large-scale farming enterprises is likely to engender land-tenure problems. Because there are virtually no areas that are entirely unused and unclaimed, the land-tenure problems will often pose enormous challenges—challenges that may be as difficult to resolve as the political issues surrounding in-migration of farmers and agricultural workers from elsewhere.

That large-scale farming is in most cases unlikely to be the most appropriate avenue for the commercialization of African agriculture does not mean that there are not important investment opportunities awaiting in the sector. However, for the foreseeable future, the main opportunities for private investors, domestic or foreign, will remain in seed development, input supply, marketing, and processing. At the same time, many opportunities exist for engaging family farmers in agribusiness ventures through contract-farming arrangements or via organizations of small farmers. For this reason, the future of smallholder production remains bright.

Land Rights, Land Ownership, and Land Use

The land consolidation that accompanied the growth of commercial agriculture in the Brazilian Cerrado offers a cautionary tale for African policy makers. Ineffectual land policies and failed settlement programs, combined with subsidized credit and marketing interventions up until the mid-1980s, resulted in a skewed distributional outcome in terms of land ownership and farm income that has not been corrected by the series of land reforms introduced since the 1990s. This contrasts sharply with the systematic land reform and land-titling policies pursued by Thailand over the past 30 years that maintained or increased equity in land ownership and contributed to rapid and inclusive rural growth. For the African case study countries, the challenge is whether they can construct sets of institutions and equitable enforcement structures that will enable smallholders to access land and engage successfully in profitable commercial agriculture. Failure to do so can have huge costs, as evidenced by the land-tenure–induced crises witnessed recently in Côte d'Ivoire and Zimbabwe, among other countries. This challenge is likely to increase in importance in future years, given the growing demand for land to be used for commercial farming. The government in Mozambique is already struggling to respond to requests for land concessions for biofuel plantations that exceed the cultivated area of the country (Boughton, pers. comm.). Although all three of the African case study countries have laws on the books that in theory should prevent exploitation of traditional land users and facilitate efficient and equitable use of land, whether these laws will be implemented effectively will depend on (currently weak) administrative and judicial institutions. Critical also will be ensuring that the voice of smallholder farmers is not drowned out by the voices of other actors in the economy.

Two land-related issues typically arise whenever there is a boom in commercial agriculture:

- How can land rights be secured for the local population, so that local farmers can participate effectively in the commercialization process and share in the resulting income gains, rather than being evicted or marginalized?
- How can domestic and foreign investors be provided with access to land that typically is already claimed and used by some indigenous group?

In considering these issues, it is useful to consider the history and arrangements for access to land in the five CCAA case study countries.

Brazil. Well before the agricultural transformation of the past three decades, the settlement of the Cerrado region was fraught with conflict. During the 1950s, land sales in Mato Grosso do Sul exploded, and weak regulation of the process allowed the same piece of land to be sold multiple times to different people. Poor farmers in general were left no other option but to take over a small tract of land as *posseiros* (informal landholders or tenants). As the development process ran its course, indigenous peoples were often displaced or even exterminated.

In subsequent decades, as the settlement of the Cerrado region progressed, the agrarian structure changed. The number and size of farms increased, and land-tenure arrangements evolved. In all areas, formal farm ownership increased rapidly as *posseiros* were forced off the land and leasing and sharecropping fell. The rapid expansion in farmed area coincided with a rise in land ownership and a parallel displacement of other types of land tenure. Even though land prices were relatively low, the rights of existing landholders were not well protected, and the presence in the region of *grileiros* (land grabbers) made things worse. Many smallholder *posseiros* lost their land in disputes with *grileiros* and large landholders.

Many commentators have argued that from a social development point of view, the development of the Cerrado region represents a missed opportunity. The government's policy objective of developing a new type of agriculture based on small family farms geared to production for the domestic market degenerated into a largely unregulated and increasingly corrupt scramble for land, with speculative claims being exerted over large areas by wealthy and powerful interest groups and backed up by massive litigation. The land policy failures were aggravated by the enormous subsidized credits to the large farms and the state-dominated marketing system. The intended beneficiaries, not only local populations but also poor immigrants from other parts of Brazil, never achieved the planned level of participation.

Thailand. The land settlement experience in the Northeast Region of Thailand was generally much less contentious than the land settlement experience in the Brazilian Cerrado. The difference can be explained in part by the fact that during the 1960s, when commercialization in the Northeast Region began to accelerate, there were relatively few disputes over land. The impressive expansion in cultivated area recorded in the Northeast Region was achieved largely through clearing of previously uninhabited forest areas. Some 3 million hectares of forest were cleared in the Northeast Region, initially through logging and burning, with the land subsequently being used for rice and upland crop farming. Later, as the population grew and the land frontier became exhausted, many farmers who lacked formal title to the land they were cultivating came under risk of being evicted. Political protests became increasingly common as farmers started to demand legal rights to the land (Pinthong 1992).

Mainly in response to the increasing conflicts over land, in 1975 the Thai government launched an agricultural land reform program under the aegis of the Agricultural Land Reform Office (ALRO). Farmers were initially given rights to cultivate a piece of land; if the land was used continuously for a prescribed period, the occupant was allowed to transfer those rights legally by sale. Between 1975 and 1988, farmland ownership increased from 7.1 million hectares in 1975 to 8.7 million hectares in 1988 (OAE 1973–2005, 1981, 1985, 2001, 2006). Besides the security inherent in owning land, a further advantage to having legal title was to provide many rural households with access to formal credit.

Land-tenure reform in Thailand gained additional momentum in 1984 with the launching of the Land Titling Program (LTP) by the Department of Land, with support from the World Bank and the Australian government. The LTP granted secure land tenure to eligible landholders, with the expectation that security of tenure would enhance access to institutional credit and provide farmers an incentive to make long-term investments to improve productivity. By 2001, the LTP had issued 8.5 million titles over about 4.87 million hectares. Evaluation studies found positive impacts on land prices (127 percent increase), access to institutional credit with cheaper interest rates (132 percent increase), and amount of credit received (75–123 percent increase). Use of purchased inputs, yield per unit area, and value of production have increased on titled land (Burns 2004; Leonard and Ayutthaya 2003). Quite clearly, land-tenure security, land reform, and associated measures to improve land productivity have been important drivers of competitive commercial agriculture in Thailand.

Land-tenure arrangements in Brazil and Thailand thus were somewhat similar at the outset of the agricultural commercialization experiences, but they evolved in very different fashions. In both countries, an initial lack of clarity concerning rights to land encouraged unauthorized occupation of land followed by subsequent appeals for granting of ownership rights, but in Brazil control of the process was effectively captured by powerful interests that were able to secure rights to large blocks of land at the expense of smallholders. By contrast, in Thailand small-scale producers were more effective in protecting their interests, with the result that ownership rights ended up being more widely—many would say also more equitably—distributed.

In light of the very different experiences of Brazil and Thailand in terms of land policies, it is instructive to examine the current situation in the African CCAA case study countries and to speculate what is likely to happen in these countries with respect to land ownership and use.

Mozambique. The impacts of agricultural commercialization on land tenure in Mozambique are difficult to predict with certainty. The population density in Mozambique is still very low, and large regions of the country are not being used for continuous cultivation. Smallholders predominate: in 2005, more than 99 percent of the total estimated 3.28 million holdings consisted of small-scale family farms. Although there is considerable potential in Mozambique for a smallholder-led agricultural revolution, future growth of large-scale commercial agriculture brings very high risks of land conflict and dispossession of smallholders similar to what happened in the Brazilian Cerrado when commercial crops became competitive in external markets.

These risks have been recognized by Mozambican policy makers and have led to the passage of very progressive and largely appropriate legislation designed to protect land ownership rights of smallholders. Land-tenure arrangements are subject to the 1995 National Land Policy, a key feature of which is to give customary tenure the force of formal legal rights. Many African countries, including (for example) Malawi, Tanzania,

Uganda, and Zambia, have similar provisions in their land policies or land laws. In Mozambique, local communities are empowered to decide procedures for land titling and use, so long as these procedures do not conflict with principles enshrined in the national constitution (including gender equity). In most communities, use rights can be acquired through formal request or through occupation by individuals and groups according to customary norms. Individual testimony is accepted as proof of occupation, and there is no hierarchy in either entitlement method or proof type. The law is also sympathetic toward private investors wishing to access land, both nationals and foreigners, and in fact the two categories are treated similarly, apart from the fact that foreigners may not claim land-use rights through occupation. Potential investors must prepare a development plan for farmland they wish to acquire, consult with the communities who would be impacted by their land acquisition, and reach agreement with them on how they will participate in the benefits of the development (or at least how they will be compensated). Once these agreements are reached, a provisional lease is granted that is valid for two years. Upon satisfaction of the development plan, definite land leases can be granted for up to 50 years, and they are renewable, inheritable, and transferable subject to administrative authorization. One condition for the award and the continuation of land leases is the presentation and the completion of a development plan.

Although the National Land Policy provides a solid legal basis for using land for commercial purposes, in practice the process by which leases are granted is not transparent, making it prone to corruption. The consultation process is often perfunctory, and the benefits agreed upon may not be realized in practice. Temporary leases may not be converted to definitive leases, and despite its expiry, the provisional land lease may in practice be used as a quasi-ownership right. In practice, the allocations of land are also often much larger than can reasonably be expected to be put under productive use. It would be better to put a ceiling on such allocations of land to avoid a future need for redistribution. On the other hand, many commercial farmers (defined as farmers who cultivate more than 50 hectares) complain that the procedure for securing land leases is cumbersome and costly because of the administrative process to confirm the viability of the development plan. The National Land Policy also has not always been able to deal effectively with conflicts between smallholders who practice extensive shifting cultivation and commercial farmers. These conflicts have erupted with some regularity in highly productive areas, such as the fertile flood plains along the Limpopo and Zambezi Rivers. Few effective partnerships have been formed between smallholders and large commercial farmers, and smallholders have on occasion been displaced without proper consultation or payment of compensation.

In summary, while Mozambique has enacted laws and regulations designed to avoid socially disruptive commercialization along the lines of what happened in Brazil, it is not clear that the government has the capacity and the willingness to enforce these laws and regulations effectively.

Zambia. With its low population density and high proportion of small-scale family farms, Zambia is in a similar situation to Mozambique's. The main difference between the two countries is that Zambia's agricultural sector also features a significant commercial farm sector, which is concentrated mainly in a narrow corridor running from north to south along the main rail line.

Since independence, Zambia has struggled to reform its land legislation. Currently, the government is in the process of elaborating a new land policy and land law. In the meantime, two land-tenure systems remain in effect: customary and leasehold. Customary land tenure applies to land held under common ownership by communities. Land subject to customary tenure arrangements is inheritable and transferable between individuals and families, but it cannot be sold. Most smallholder production takes place on land held under customary tenure arrangements; this land accounts for 62 percent of the national territory. Leasehold land tenure applies to land that has been registered with the state according to the terms of the Land Act of 1995. All land theoretically is eligible for state registration, so land held under customary tenure arrangements can potentially be converted to leasehold land. As in Mozambique, the process involves preparation of a development plan and consultation and collaboration with affected communities. In leasehold land-tenure systems, title to land can be assigned to anyone, as long as land registration and titling procedures are followed. The title is given for a period not exceeding 99 years, after which the lessee is required to apply for renewal of the title. Most large-scale commercial production takes place on land held under the leasehold system of tenure.

Over time, land held under customary land-tenure arrangements is gradually being converted to leasehold land. Whether or not the conversion process benefits smallholders remains to be seen. Theoretically, those using land under customary land-tenure arrangements are eligible to file for state registration, but the process will have to be easily negotiable by smallholders if they are to avoid being marginalized by the commercialization process.

Nigeria. With an average population density exceeding that of the Northeast Region of Thailand and an agricultural sector dominated by small-scale family farms, Nigeria's path to land-tenure security can usefully borrow from the Thai experience. Yet the country's legacy of very uneven application of legislation governing access to land suggests that an outcome closer to the experience of Brazil is likely.

In Nigeria, access to land can be acquired through two different legal frameworks: customary law or statutory law. Customary law varies considerably between, and even within, the main ethnic groups. Although most systems of customary law effectively regulate access to land for productive uses, the recurrence of certain common problems suggests that customary systems have difficulty dealing with challenges such as the increasing fragmentation of landholdings as they are passed between generations through inheritance, the granting of land-use rights to "strangers" born outside of local communities, and the distinction between rights to land and rights to trees found on the land. Under the stimulus of population growth and commercial pressures, many customary land-tenure systems are spontaneously changing to provide greater security of individual tenure.

Under statutory law, individuals may apply to local government authorities to be issued certificates of occupancy to land. The 1978 Land Use Act (LUA) invests proprietary rights to land in the state, allows the granting of user rights to individuals, and empowers administrators to allocate land rights in lieu of market forces. In theory, every person or corporate body has a statutory right to receive an allocation of land. Because acquisition of land under the LUA does not depend on being a member of a kinship group or on social status, the LUA theoretically provides a mechanism through which commercial investors can access land, but this does not happen much in practice because land application procedures are tedious and confusing.[3] Land allocation under the LUA is seen to a large extent as based on having the right contacts. This becomes an issue for the poor, who frequently lack the right contacts and who therefore rarely get an allocation for agricultural purposes. Women's access to agricultural land in most rural areas is through a husband, brother, or father. Women's land-use rights are secondary rights, and because access to land by women is dependent on the continuing goodwill of male decision makers, it is usually very uncertain.

Because implementation of the statutory laws enshrined in the LUA is inconsistent, various parallel land-tenure systems continue to operate around the country. Arua and Okorji (1997) report that individual, communal, and public ownership of land are often implemented side by side. Rather than seek formal allocations from the local government, people access land by a variety of other means, including allocations by the family head from the communally owned plot; inheritance; rental; purchase or freehold; gift or pledge; and sharecropping. The LUA does not recognize informal contracts, so most of these are legally insecure.

In summary, the lack of a clear and fully functioning land-use policy in Nigeria poses an obstacle to sustainable management of land resources and opens the door to the sorts of abuses that accompanied land consolidation in the Brazilian Cerrado.

Comparing among the three African CCAA case study countries, while policy makers in Mozambique and Zambia have put in place land policies and land laws that are designed to strike a balance between protection of rights of traditional users (specifically including women) and provision of access to new users, policy makers in Nigeria still have not implemented effective land policy reforms and associated legal reforms. However, even in Mozambique and Zambia, where customary land rights and women's rights are protected under the law, implementation is lagging in terms of administrative capacity, community involvement in the granting of land concessions, conflict resolution mechanisms, and access to the courts. As a consequence, the allocation of land to commercial farmers remains problematic, either because the process is still cumbersome and uncertain or because it continues to be dominated by speculative grabbing of excessively large tracts. Speculative land allocation can be controlled by strong community involvement in land allocation, imposition of a ceiling on individual ownership, and/or well-designed land taxes, but none of the CCAA case study countries has these elements in place. Land administration capacity also remains excessively centralized and highly inadequate to the task at hand in all three of the case study countries. Strong political will is needed, not only to ensure adherence to the law but also to decentralize and radically strengthen land administration capacity and governance.

Food Security

For many households in Africa, agriculture plays a critical role in ensuring food security. Food markets tend to function poorly, especially in remote areas with weak infrastructure, so households in these areas must rely on their own production to meet their consumption requirements. The policy challenge is to achieve a balance between addressing food security directly (for example, by trying to improve subsistence farming and/or providing safety nets) and addressing food security indirectly (for example, by focusing on the more entrepreneurial producers in favorable production environments who can deliver food security by producing more and cheaper food and by creating better income opportunities for the landless poor).

To what extent, if any, does shifting to commercial agriculture conflict with the pursuit of food security objectives in subsistence-oriented rural households? Simple comparisons of returns and incomes from crops grown for market and food crops produced for own consumption at home generally show that in "normal" years, returns are higher from crops grown for market. Yet if returns from crops grown for market are generally higher than those from food crops produced for own consumption, why don't smallholder households specialize in production of such crops? Although there are some cases in which households devote their entire available land to a single cash crop (for example, in sugar and tea production in Kenya), households more commonly use most of their land to cultivate food crops for own consumption, even when returns to production for market are apparently higher (von Braun and Kennedy 1994; Peters and Herrera 1994).

Three reasons can potentially explain the preference of many rural households to produce for own consumption.

First, local culture may place a premium on own food production (for example, when it is considered the mark of a good head of household to provide family members with home-produced food). There may also be a gender division of labor within the household, such that women have prime responsibility for food production and provision while men engage in off-farm activities and control production of crops for cash. Culture and social institutions eventually evolve in response to changing market conditions (for example, the development of local food markets), but they may do so only with a considerable lag (Binswanger and McIntire 1987; North 1990).

Second, the extent to which households can participate successfully in cash crop production may be limited by small land endowments, lack of access to capital for inputs, or lack of human capital. Alternatively, households may have only limited ability to bear risk, which may constrain their use of purchased inputs. Especially during early stages of supply chain development, output markets may be unreliable (characterized not only by price volatility but also by questions about whether traders will come at all). This is a particular problem where producers are being encouraged to make investments in tree crops that may yield their first harvest only after several years, as illustrated by the struggles of the liberalized cashew industry in Mozambique (McMillan, Horn, and Rodrik 2002). Too, cash crops and food crops may respond differently to rainfall shocks, justifying a diversified production approach (Ellis 2000). In some cases—especially in hilly areas—cash crops and food crops may be grown on separate plots with different agroecological characteristics (Poulton 1998; Pandey et al. 2006).

Third—and perhaps most important—many poor households are reluctant to give up food crop production entirely because they worry that if they commit themselves entirely to cash crop production, they may later discover that food prices in local markets are higher than expected, compromising their ability to purchase enough food to satisfy household consumption needs.

For a number of reasons—higher transport costs, weaker market integration, greater rainfall shocks, less irrigation capacity, and an absence of effective public policies for grain price stabilization—grain prices tend to be much more volatile in African markets than in Asian ones (Dawe 2001; Hazell, Shields, and Shields 2005). Where food markets are unreliable, inefficient, or highly volatile, farm households will seek to feed themselves first and sell only what they can produce beyond this (Fafchamps 1992; Jayne 1994). According to von Braun and Kennedy (1994, 3–4): "Subsistence production for home consumption is chosen by farmers because it is subjectively the best option, given all constraints. In a global sense, however, it is one of the largest enduring misallocations of human and natural resources, and, due to population pressure and natural resource constraints, it is becoming less and less viable."

Mainly for this reason, improvements in the functioning of markets for staple foods (the major wage good in most low-income countries) may be particularly important in creating incentives for smallholders to allocate a greater proportion of their resources to nonfood cash crops. In the absence of reliable food markets, these households focus first on meeting their food needs, driving the households closer toward autarky. This, in turn, reduces the per-household production of cash crops, thereby increasing assembly costs and lowering competition in assembly resulting from low volumes, which undermines the competitiveness of smallholder commercial agriculture. In such instances, if commercial agriculture is to grow, it will likely be by increasing the scale of farm operations. Failure to reduce transaction costs frequently induces greater vertical integration, which again favors larger-scale operations.

A number of empirical studies have attempted to shed light on this question of whether investing in cash crops necessarily entails a reduction in food security. For example, Govereh and Jayne (2003) show that cotton-growing households in Gokwe North (Zimbabwe) produce maize more intensively than non-cotton-growing households. Although cotton-growing households devote less land to maize than non-cotton-growing households (so that more can be devoted to cotton), food production is similar across both types of households. Govereh and Jayne (2003) also concluded that there can be positive spillover effects from widespread cash crop production that benefit food production (for example, an increase in the number of input stockists). In Senegal, Goetz (1993) found that groundnut production could have important benefits for food production through a complex set of interlocked arrangements covering land, hired labor, and groundnut seed. Although these findings appear to fly in the face of conventional wisdom, they are actually quite consistent with the idea that food crop production needs to be assured before a commitment can be made to cash crop production. If adoption of a cash crop occurs only when concerns related to food security have been allayed, then negative outcomes of cash crop production on food security are unlikely to be observed.

Generally speaking, the empirical literature does not offer definitive proof one way or the other as to whether concerns about food security act as a constraint on smallholder commercialization. However, it is interesting to note that some companies involved in cash crop promotion have sought also to assist smallholder producers to access more food, because they realize that concerns about food security act as a constraint on cash crop production. For example, Compagnie Malienne de Développement des Textiles (the parastatal cotton company in Mali, CMDT) has achieved some success in stimulating maize production not only by undertaking initial varietal selection work but also by making maize seed and maize fertilizer available to cotton producers. In addition, some CDC-supported ventures that have operated outgrower schemes have devoted a portion of their land to producing staples that are then made available to outgrowers as well as to workers, so as to encourage them to expand the share of their land that is planted to the particular cash crop being promoted.

The policy implications of these observations will be addressed later. For now, it is important to note that widespread production of crops (other than staple foods) for market may be enhanced either by interventions that improve the efficiency of food markets and/or by interventions that raise the productivity of food production by net deficit households.

Gender Impacts

Does agricultural commercialization affect men and women in different ways, or is it gender-neutral? The impact of agricultural commercialization on intrahousehold relations is discussed extensively in the literature on the social impacts of expanding smallholder production of cash/export crops. A recurring theme is that expanding the production of crops for export can undermine women's access to resources, especially land; place additional demands on women's time and labor; reduce the traditional autonomy of women in the household, making them more dependent upon the goodwill of male heads of household; undermine household food security; and increase child labor.

Studies in Africa and elsewhere have shown that the shift from production of subsistence food crops to production of cash crops has sometimes been linked with an increase in preschool malnutrition rates (von Braun and Kennedy 1994). It is unclear, however, to what extent these findings can be generalized. The relationship between the commercialization of agriculture and household nutrition is complex, and studies that include baseline data from before the introduction of cash crops are few and far between. One study that does include such baseline data is reported by Kennedy and Oniang'o (1990) in their examination of the health and nutrition effects of sugarcane production in southwestern Kenya. The data suggest that the significantly higher incomes enjoyed by smallholders as a result of their participation in sugar outgrower schemes increased households' aggregate calorie consumption, but higher incomes did not translate into better results in terms of child nutritional status and rates of preschool morbidity and growth. Studies in Mali (summarized by Tefft and Kelly [2004]) point to family structure, land-tenure rights of women, community organization, and the effectiveness of local government as factors that affect the degree to which increased incomes from smallholder commercial agriculture translate into better or worse child nutritional status.

Other studies that have examined the gender impacts of agricultural commercialization have similarly produced mixed results. In Kenya, a study of smallholder production of French beans for export shows how gender conflict led to deterioration in bean quality and ultimately to smallholders losing their contracts to supply beans (Dolan 2001). Another study carried out in Kenya estimated that up to 30 percent of all tea plots are neglected because of disputes over female labor (Sorensen and von Bulow 1990). Gender conflicts have similarly been identified in other studies of smallholder farming in Kenya (for example, Davison

1988; Mackenzie 1993; Francis 1998), including studies relating to the production of tea (Sorensen and von Bulow 1990; Ongile 1999), sugar (Oniang'o 1999; Kennedy and Oniang'o 1990; Rubin 1990), horticulture (Dolan 2001, 2002), and tobacco (Francis 1998; Heald 1991). In The Gambia, conflicts over land and labor have led women to withdraw their labor from irrigated rice production schemes that the government and donors were trying to develop in the country's wetlands (Carney 1993).

These impacts may not be inevitable, however. Intrahousehold cooperation is important if the smallholder household is to act as an efficient agricultural production unit. Under conditions where labor is scarce or production prices are high, women may have some bargaining power with respect to their labor. In relation to tobacco production in Kenya, Heald (1991) notes that higher prices encourage greater cooperation between men and women. In relation to Kenyan tea production, Sorensen and von Bulow (1990) found that because women's labor is crucial to production and because of the difficulties of hiring labor, women do have a certain amount of bargaining power when it comes to negotiating their labor input and influencing the way that tea revenues are spent. Under a restrictive set of conditions, therefore, the gender concern may be somewhat attenuated.

In the three African case study countries, the predominant gender issues related to the commercialization of agriculture stem from women's limited access to land, intrahousehold distribution of income, and the importance of informal agricultural employment to women and their livelihood strategies. In Nigeria and Zambia, the basis of customary land-usage rights—biased against women—still hold sway in the regulatory systems. Even in Mozambique, where the Land Act cannot violate constitutional principles such as gender equality, empirical evidence shows that in many areas, women still do not enjoy equal rights to men. At times of divorce or inheritance, they very often lose all rights to land they have been farming and using to support their families. Moreover, "the current focus on facilitating market mechanisms in the field of land rights does not adequately take into account concerns and questions related to ways women actually access land, for example, through inheritance" (Ikdahl et al. 2005, xi–xii). In Zambia and Mozambique, informal employment in the agricultural sector is dominated by women, so attention needs to be paid to the role of women as both productive and primary processing activities are commercialized. Finally, experience with commercial agriculture in Africa has shown that improved incomes do not always result in improved family welfare, given the tendency for men to control cash crop income. Indeed, far from improving welfare, the rise of commercial agriculture has been seen to increase the vulnerability of women and children as their former productive assets (that is, land and labor) and activities become diverted to commercial agricultural activities over which they exert only limited control.

Potential Environmental Impacts

The conversion of land to agricultural uses and the resulting impacts on the environment have attracted a lot of attention and commentary, some of it more evidence-based than the rest. Much of the commentary has been overtly critical of agriculture, which is blamed for many negative environmental impacts. It is certainly true that agriculture—especially intensive commercial agriculture—can have negative impacts on the environment. For example, the rise of commercial agriculture is often associated with an expansion in cultivated area, made possible in many cases through conversion of natural forest, savannah, or grassland, with attendant losses of native flora and fauna. Similarly, the rise of commercial agriculture is frequently associated with intensification of agricultural production methods, which can place pressure on water resources, cause pollution from misuse of chemicals, and lead to degradation in resource quantity or quality and damage human health.

But the environmental impacts attributable to the rise of commercial agriculture are not necessarily negative. On the contrary, the commercialization of agriculture also has potential to bring benefits for the environment. Most notably, increasing the productivity of intensive commercial production systems can relieve pressure for agriculture to expand into marginal zones, protecting them from eventual damage caused by unsustainable extractive production methods.

How do these issues play out in the context of agricultural commercialization in the Guinea Savannah? What environmental impacts have been associated with the agricultural commercialization processes that have taken place in Brazil and Thailand, and what are the implications going forward for the three African case study countries?

Brazil. Up until the 1960s, agriculture in the Cerrado region featured mainly two types of production systems. A relatively large proportion of the land was devoted to extensive ranching operations, which were oriented toward the production of feeder cattle that were then driven to other regions of the country for finishing. Crop production was concentrated in a relatively small number of pockets and characterized by small-scale semisubsistence farming oriented to the production of food staples. Sustained public investment in regional development led to a major expansion of agriculture, which impacted the region's flora and fauna and also affected soil and water resources.

Conversion of natural Cerrado land to agriculture is commonly linked to the expansion of soybean production, but in fact relatively little land has been cleared expressly for the purpose of growing soybeans. The typical method of extending the agricultural frontier in the Cerrado starts with logging, followed by burning of logged areas to clear the land for seeding as pasture. Over time as soils degrade, the profitability of raising cattle declines, until eventually farmers decide to switch to production of soybeans and other row crops.

Throughout most of the Cerrado, the predominant agroecology was originally savannah and woodland savannah with low trees and shrubs of limited timber value, although there were also large areas covered by transitional Amazonian forest. Agricultural expansion led to a large amount of land conversion from these woodlands and forests to agriculture. In Mato Grosso alone, the area of cleared forest increased from around 100,000 hectares in 1975 to more than 6 million hectares in 1983, during the period of heaviest effort to develop the state. Between 1994 and 2000, land conversion continued at a high rate. Today more than one-third of the land surface has been converted to agricultural uses. In addition to restricting the range of many native plant species, the expansion of commercial agriculture also affected indigenous animal populations. The Cerrado region is home to roughly one-third of Brazil's animal species, representing about 5 percent of the world's fauna. Intense human activity, closely related to the agricultural transformation of the region, reduced the habitats for many species.

In addition to causing biodiversity losses, the intensification of agriculture in the Cerrado may have adversely affected soil resources. The popular soybeans-maize rotation greatly intensifies land use, leading to increased risk of soil compaction and surface erosion. Soil losses associated with agricultural intensification in the Cerrado have varied, depending mainly on the type of cultivation practice used. Production of soybeans using conventional tillage methods results in average soil losses of 25 tons/hectare/year, while use of conservation tillage methods (including zero-till) reduces average soil losses to as little as 3 tons/hectare/year (Conservation International 1995). The cumulative effects of these losses can be very large. It is estimated that farming in the Cerrado has caused average soil losses of 20 tons/hectare/year, or 1 billion tons/year in total

(Ribemboim 1997). More recently, the rate of soil degradation in the Cerrado has slowed dramatically following the widespread adoption of conservation tillage (Ekboir 2003).

Agricultural intensification in the Cerrado also impacted water resources. This is not easily documented, however, because data on hydrologic impacts are scarce. The paucity of hydrologic data is particularly striking because parts of three important river basins have their sources in the Cerrado—Amazon, São Francisco, and Paraná. Concerns about the impacts of agriculture on water resources relate mainly to the likely silting of rivers and to the possible introduction of agrochemicals in river water.

Thailand. No comprehensive assessment has been undertaken of the environmental impacts of commercial agriculture in the Northeast Region of Thailand. The few studies that have been carried out have consisted mainly of plot-level experiments and village-level analyses. Despite the limited scope of these studies, the picture that emerges is one of accelerating environmental problems associated with the expansion of commercial agriculture. The main negative environmental impact has been the loss of forest land, with the attendant losses of biodiversity. Other negative environmental impacts have been documented at individual sites, including enhanced soil erosion, declining soil fertility, and degradation of wetlands.

Most of the Northeast Region was originally covered by open deciduous woodlands and savannah, with some evergreen forests confined mainly to mountain slopes. As recently as 1961, the forested area in the Northeast Region was estimated at around 70,000 square kilometers, representing about 42 percent of the Northeast Region's total land area. Beginning in the early 1960s, an aggressive logging policy led to a dramatic decrease in forested area. By 1980, more than one-half of the forests in the Northeast Region had disappeared. Deforestation continued even after the implementation in 1989 of a nationwide logging ban. By 1998, the forest cover had declined to about 12.4 percent of the total land area.

Active promotion by the government of Thailand of upland cash crop production was a major contributor to the rapid deforestation process that occurred in the Northeast Region. Forest clearing in frontier areas was also encouraged as a strategy for combating communist insurgents who had taken refuge in forested areas at the time, but the expansion of commercial agriculture was the primary cause. Between 1950 and 1984, agricultural land use in the Northeast Region increased by 53 percent

(Hafner [1990], cited in Neef and Schwarzmeier [2001]). Upland farming was extended more than sixfold, rising from around 0.28 million hectares in 1961 to 1.75 million hectares by 1989 (Bello et al. 1998). Massive increases in cassava production were achieved mainly through area expansion; the area planted to cassava rose from 460,000 hectares in 1974/75 to 1 million hectares in 1988/89. Because the population of the Northeast Region grew only modestly during this period, it is clear that much of the deforestation occurred not in response to population growth, but rather in response to the government-supported shift from subsistence farming to cash crop production.

The rapid expansion of cultivated area is likely to have resulted in the loss of native forest species, including plants used in traditional Thai herbal medicine. The exact extent of biodiversity losses remains unknown, however, because the Region's dominant ecosystems had never been properly surveyed (FAO 2001).

The expansion of commercial agriculture was also a major cause of soil erosion, particularly in upland areas. Annual soil losses from upland cassava and sugarcane plots are estimated to average around 20 tons/hectare, double the U.S. Soil Conservation Service's soil loss tolerance threshold of 10 to 12 tons/hectare. The extensive soil losses observed in upland cropping systems stem from the limited amounts of ground cover that characterize these systems, combined with frequent cultivation practices. In contrast, soil erosion is much less of a problem in lowland paddy fields, most of which receive continuous inflows of nutrients eroded from higher parts of the landscape (Vityakon et al. 2004).

Erosion, in turn, has affected soil fertility. Continuous tillage of cultivated soils has led to chemical degradation in some areas, resulting in reduced levels of organic carbon and a decline in cation exchange capacity. Soil organic matter is particularly difficult to restore in these tropical and subtropical environments, where regular disturbance of the soil texture occurs during the preparation of seedbeds and weed control. Studies carried out in the Northeast Region have consistently shown that soil organic-matter levels are generally much lower in upland fields than in lowland paddy fields. In the upland fields, the degradation of soil organic-matter pools tends to be more severe under cassava than sugarcane, because with sugarcane production more organic residues are recycled (Vityakon 2007). Many farmers compensate for soil-fertility declines in upland fields by applying chemical fertilizers that, if they do not form part of an integrated soil nutrient management strategy, can lead to chemical imbalances. Agrochemicals, in the form of inorganic fertilizers, herbicides, and insecticides, today are used in the production of most commercial crops in the Northeast Region. Although this has increased yields, farmers complain that continuous use of chemical fertilizer raises production costs and increases dependency on external resources.

Agricultural commercialization also has affected the quality and quantity of water resources in the Northeast Region. Increasing reliance on irrigation has led to reduced water flows in several major river systems, leading to increased siltation and undesirable changes in water temperatures. Leaching of agrochemicals into surface watercourses, as well as into the water table, has led to deterioration in the quality of water resources. Crops grown in upland areas, especially sugarcane, are grown with high doses of agrochemicals, so leaching of chemical residues into waterways is common. Increased use of agrochemicals has negatively impacted rice-fish systems that contribute significantly to the farmer's diet, and direct pesticide poisoning has also become a serious health problem for many northeastern farmers (Panyakul 2001). In spite of these problems resulting from agrochemical use, however, water quality in the most important rivers in the Northeast Region remains good (OEPP 2002).

Changes in water quality and quantity have had unintended effects. One consequence of the changing water balance has been a marked increase in soil salinity, which affects some 12 percent of the region (Williamson et al. [1989], cited in Bell and Seng [2004]). Accelerated deforestation has contributed to the dilution of below-ground salt deposits and facilitated the diffusion of salt through natural and artificial waterways (Bello et al. 1998).

Over the years, the government of Thailand has introduced risk mitigation measures that have served to attenuate some of these negative environmental impacts. For example, tree-planting programs have slowed soil erosion and stopped or even reversed salinization processes in some upland areas. Restoration of soil fertility can be achieved through various methods. Introduction of certain favorable crop rotations can help to reduce soil nutrient mining and maintain crop-yield levels. The problem of soil-fertility declines is well recognized by farmers, many of whom have developed local practices to reverse chemical degradation based on the use of termite mound materials and, more recently, the application of materials dredged from lakes (Nobel and Suzuki 2005). Organic farming is also being promoted as an environmentally friendly alternative to conventional, high-input agriculture.

CCAA African case study countries. In many parts of Africa, as elsewhere in the world, agricultural intensification—including intensification associated with the rise of commercial agriculture—has impacted the environment. The impacts tend to be portrayed in negative terms: one hears much talk about deforestation and associated biodiversity losses, degradation of soil and water resources, and adverse health effects associated with the use of crop chemicals. But even if there is a widespread perception that the environmental impacts of commercial agriculture are inevitably negative, that perception is not always supported by evidence. Thus there is a need to better understand the environmental impacts potentially associated with commercialization of agriculture, as well as the lessons learned from past experiences that might allow negative environmental impacts to be attenuated in the future through improved policies and better technical interventions.

In the three African case study countries, clearing of land for agriculture has impacted biodiversity, although it is difficult to say to what extent, because the process has not been well documented. In *Mozambique*, the natural resource base is still largely untouched, so the potential for both development and for damage are correspondingly high. Forests, grasslands, mangroves, freshwater lakes and rivers, coasts, the intertidal zone, and littoral waters, as well as the wildlife these habitats support, provide many goods and services and constitute the livelihood base for many. Most of these natural assets are in a healthy condition, partly as a result of low population densities and low levels of economic development (Hatton, Telford, and Krugmann 2003). Natural forests cover approximately 60 million hectares, or 75 percent of the total land surface. Significant areas of savannah and scrubland also occur. Biodiversity is high in Mozambique; the country boasts 5,500 plant species, 205 mammals, 170 reptiles, 40 amphibians, and fully two-thirds of all the bird species found in southern Africa (Chemonics International 2008). Fortunately, the government maintains a reasonable number of protected areas, including forest reserves and wildlife sanctuaries, but sustainable resource management remains a problem. Uncontrolled harvesting of wood and plant species occurs in many areas, however, and hunting of animals is widespread. Compared with those of other African countries, the rate at which land is being converted to agricultural uses is relatively low. About 4 percent of the country's forest cover was lost between 1990 and 2005. Deforestation rates have not increased significantly in recent years, averaging 0.3 percent per year between 2000 and 2005 (FAO 2005).

Nigeria, too, is rich in biodiversity. The country claims 7,895 species of plants and more than 22,000 species of vertebrates and invertebrates.

Nigeria's plants include many species with traditional value as food items or medicine and for various domestic uses. Nigeria is also an epicenter for wild varieties of important crop plants, including cowpeas, rice, yams, and groundnuts (ARD 2002). Loss of biodiversity is principally related to human activities, including agriculture (especially shifting cultivation, based on slash-and-burn methods), fuelwood collection, logging, and grazing. In contrast to Mozambique, deforestation is a major environmental concern. Between 1990 and 2000, the annual deforestation rate averaged 2.8 percent, which is very high compared with the average rates for African countries (0.8 percent) and all low-income countries (0.7 percent). During 2000–05, Nigeria ranked among the top 10 countries with respect to annual net losses in forest cover. The so-called "forest reserves" extend over 9.6 million hectares, but have to a large degree been so degraded as to remain reserves in name only, extensively deprived of tree cover, and (in some areas) well advanced toward desertification. Much of the remaining forest is secondary forest, either regrowth on abandoned farm land or planted tree crops such as cocoa or rubber.

In *Zambia*, 14 ecosystems can be distinguished, falling into 4 main categories: forest, thicket, woodland, and grassland. These ecosystems support a rich set of flora and fauna. The Zambian national biodiversity action plan lists 8,017 species of organisms (MENR 1999). Of these, at least 170 are considered rare, and a further 31 are considered vulnerable or endangered (Douthwaite, Chitalu, and Lungu 2005). Zambia has a number of wild plant species that are related to cultivated crops, including wild relatives of rice, cowpeas, sorghum, sesame, and various cucurbit species. As in the other case study countries, in Zambia the data on deforestation are poor. Woodland and forest cover about 68 percent of the country, with wetlands covering a further 27 percent. Man-made ecosystems account for only 3 percent of the total area. Natural ecosystems have been widely degraded by human influence, and especially by fire, shifting cultivation, and harvesting of fuelwood (Douthwaite, Chitalu, and Lungu 2005).

In all three CCAA case study countries, practices linked to agriculture—both subsistence and commercial—have contributed to the degradation of soil and water resources, although there is considerable variability among countries.

With regard to impacts on soil resources, the situation in *Mozambique* is not as alarming as in other neighboring countries, in part because only 4.5 million hectares out of 36 million hectares of arable land are used annually for agriculture. Many areas used for small-scale farming have experienced moderate-to-high nutrient mining, caused by low levels of inputs used for crop production. Areas of greatest erosion potential tend to be those situated at higher altitude (between 200 and 1,500 meters) and with sloping land surfaces.

In *Nigeria*, land degradation poses a major environmental threat. Clearing of land for agricultural use has exposed soils to the elements and resulted in accelerating rates of erosion. In 1997, the government estimated that more than 90 percent of the nation's agricultural land was suffering from some form of erosion. Erosion in turn has had a predictably negative effect on soil fertility. Most soil-fertility problems in Nigeria can be attributed to continuous intensive cultivation using traditional low-input production technologies, combined with burning of crop residues and/or persistent overgrazing (FAO 2002). A major obstacle to addressing environmental degradation problems in Nigeria is the lack of detailed knowledge about land degradation, soil productivity losses, depletion of grazing reserves, and deforestation rates. As a result, only limited progress has been achieved in developing and disseminating sustainable agricultural production technologies. Resource-conserving technologies such as use of crop rotations, agroforestry practices, and integrated crop-livestock systems have had low rates of adoption, either because the technologies have been lacking, because farmer awareness has been low, or because incentives to adopt have been weak.

In *Zambia*, no hard data exist on the extent and distribution of erosion. In some provinces, farmers testify consistently that soil erosion is increasing, and they acknowledge that the fertility of their fields has declined over the years. Many scientists agree with these observations and attribute declining productivity to continuous application of inorganic fertilizers without liming and to cultivation of maize without crop rotation.

Impacts of agricultural intensification on water resources in the three African case study countries are not well documented. In *Mozambique*, more than 100 major river systems have been identified. Surface water resources are abundant, and groundwater potential is considerable, although water withdrawals are less than 1 percent of renewable water resources. Agriculture is the main consumer of water, accounting for 87 percent of all withdrawals. Irrigation potential is estimated to be 3 million hectares (FAO 2000), compared with only about 40,000 hectares currently being irrigated. Water pollution is generally not a significant problem, because agricultural production systems are still dominated mainly by smallholders, who tend to use very modest quantities of fertilizer and crop chemicals.

Nigeria also possesses significant water resources. Estimates of the potential for irrigation range from 1.6 million hectares (FAO) to 2.5 million hectares (government of Nigeria). In the past, the lack of environmental concerns in the planning and implementation of water resource projects resulted in the destruction of extensive areas of low-lying fadama lands, with predictable consequences for fisheries and wildlife habitats. Future development projects could divert still more water from the wetlands for irrigated agriculture in upstream areas, negatively affecting irrigated agricultural production in the floodplain. Expansion of irrigated crop production in low-lying fadama lands has led to a lowering of the water table in some areas. Data on the severity of agriculture-related water pollution are scarce, but fertilizer consumption levels are sufficiently low that pollution from agriculture is likely to be low as well.

In *Zambia*, total renewable water resources amount to about 105 cubic kilometers/year, of which about 80 cubic kilometers/year are produced internally. Currently, about 160,000 hectares are irrigated, representing roughly 30 percent of economical irrigation potential. Most irrigation infrastructure in Zambia is used to support commercial agriculture, especially sugar, wheat, and coffee. Water pollution is common in proximity to industrial sites, as well as in densely settled urban areas. The only significant agricultural source of water pollution is the sedimentation arising from cultivation near rivers and streams.

Implications of the Environmental Analysis

The Guinea Savannah zone, which is characterized by medium-to-high agricultural potential, extends across about 700 million hectares in Africa, nearly three times the area of the Brazilian Cerrado. Of these, only 48 million hectares are currently being cropped. Although not all of the African Guinea Savannah zone is suitable for agriculture, clearly it represents one of the world's largest underused agricultural land reserves. There is no question that to feed the world, meet the growing demand for agricultural raw materials, and generate the feedstuffs needed for production of biofuels, a significant share of this zone will eventually have to be converted to agriculture, probably under more intensive land-use systems than are currently prevalent.

The fact that land conversion and agricultural intensification associated with the rise of commercial agriculture should impact the environment comes as no surprise. Environmental change is an inevitable outcome of economic growth and development. Economic activity, including commercial agriculture, qualitatively transforms the physical environment within which it takes place—that is inevitable. The amount of harm done to the environment depends on the technology used and on the value that is attached to different aspects of the environment.

When assessing the likely environmental impacts of commercial agriculture in Africa, it is important not to lose sight of the counterfactual—the environmental effects of agriculture that would occur in the absence of commercialization. Localized environmental damage caused by commercial agriculture may be warranted if it precludes the incurrence of much greater damage elsewhere, by allowing the same agricultural output to be produced on less land or less valuable land. The likely environmental impacts of commercial agriculture therefore need to be assessed in the context of the wider environmental problems relating to agriculture, especially those stemming from unsustainable practices associated with low-productivity subsistence farming practiced by smallholders forced by population pressure to clear forests, shorten fallows, or move into fragile areas.

The commercialization experiences of Brazil and Thailand (and indeed of many other countries) show clearly that the rise of commercial agriculture is associated with significant conversion of forests and bushland to agricultural uses, which brings some risk of environmental problems. For example, inappropriate use of chemical fertilizer (not only underuse but also overuse) can cause soil problems. Environmental problems also may be associated with the irrigation that often accompanies intensive farming, as when the dams used to control and store water cause damage to natural habitats and biodiversity by preventing valuable nutrients from flowing downstream, or when irrigation systems lead to the salinization of cropland. Finally, inappropriate use of pesticides can reduce biodiversity and pollute streams, rivers, and groundwater through toxic runoff. In addition to the damage they cause to ecological systems, pesticides can also harm the health of farmers and agricultural workers.

Although some of these problems do not yet apply to much of African agriculture, where the main environmental problems have more to do with inadequate levels of intensifications and insufficient use of modern inputs, there clearly are lessons to be learned from the experiences of Brazil, Thailand, and many other countries about some of the environmental problems associated with agricultural intensification and how to avoid or minimize them. At the same time, it is important to remember that by increasing the yields of staple food crops, the green revolutions of the 20th century reduced the pressure to convert natural habitats into agricultural land. This inevitably came at some environmental cost, but arguably a lower one than might have been incurred if the green revolution had not taken place.

Notes

1. The amount of land requested for large-scale farming ventures is often far larger than what can reasonably be expected to be farmed by a single entrepreneur. Where land allocations are too large, they lead to underutilization of land in large-scale farms and subsequent pressures for land reform.

2. On the other hand, the large wedge between import- and export-parity prices makes price stabilization difficult because prices can vary over a very wide range before being tempered by imports or exports.

3. The recent granting of land-use rights to Zimbabwean commercial farmers in Kwara state indicates that the process can be expedited.

CHAPTER 7

Conclusions and Recommendations: Opportunities and Challenges

If Africa's farmers and agribusiness firms cannot become competitive in rapidly growing domestic and export markets, African agriculture will not be able to realize its potential as a powerful engine of pro-poor growth. The CCAA study was undertaken to explore the feasibility of restoring international competitiveness to African agriculture.

The CCAA study results, summarized in this report, highlight the enormous potential found in Africa's Guinea Savannah zone for expanding commercial agriculture and creating new wealth. Potential exists as well in other zones, but the other zones are not nearly as large. This final section briefly reviews that potential, recaps the challenges that will need to be overcome if it is to be realized, and outlines in general terms the steps needed to make it a reality.

Bright Prospects for Commercial Agriculture in the Guinea Savannah Zone

Africa's Guinea Savannah zone contains probably the largest area of underutilized agricultural land in the world. This land could be tapped to produce food, agricultural raw materials, and biofuels feedstocks, not only for Africa but also for other regions. Land in the Guinea Savannah zone has generally good agricultural potential, and population densities are low in many areas, so there is scope for expanding the intensive production systems needed to support a dynamic commercial agriculture. Producers in the Guinea Savannah zone are focusing on the production of relatively undifferentiated bulk commodities, similar to producers in the Cerrado region of Brazil and the Northeast Region of Thailand when those two regions launched their agricultural revolutions. Bulk commodities are well suited to this physical environment, and their production imposes relatively modest quality demands on farmers and other actors in the value chain as they seek to break into regional and international markets.

The detailed CCAA case studies carried out in Mozambique, Nigeria, and Zambia suggest that the prospects for commercial agriculture in these countries today are as good as or better than they were in Brazil and Thailand during the period when those two countries were going through their agricultural revolutions. The positive outlook for the successful development of commercial agriculture in the African countries is grounded in five main factors.

Rapid Economic Growth and Strong Demand Prospects

For the first time in more than 40 years, economic growth rates in Africa are now above 6 percent (on average), translating into per capita income growth rates above 3 percent. Accelerating rates of income growth in Africa, combined with still high population growth rates and rapid urbanization, provide very diverse and ample market opportunities in domestic and regional markets. The substantial and growing reliance of many African countries on food imports provides considerable scope for import substitution, and capturing these nearby markets is less demanding logistically and in terms of product standards than breaking into international markets. World market prospects also look stronger because of growing demand in Asia and Africa and expansion of biofuels production. Indeed, demand for oilseeds and for biofuels feedstocks is already spurring private investment in Africa in the production of these commodities. Just as Brazil emerged as the world's largest soybean exporter and Thailand as the world's largest exporter of rice and cassava, Africa could be a global leader in many bulk commodities in the 21st century.

Favorable Domestic Economic Policy Environments

In Mozambique, Nigeria, and Zambia—and indeed in many other African countries—the macroeconomic environment is now generally favorable to agriculture. Because of the spread of macroeconomic stability, introduction of market-determined exchange rates, and opening of trade regimes, economic growth rates have sharply accelerated. These same factors and the elimination of many export taxes have sharply reduced the net taxation of agriculture across Africa, although a number of countries, including Zambia, still tax their export sectors. The better macroeconomic environment and lower inflation also are leading to reductions in nominal and real interest rates that should be helpful to economywide investment, and especially to agricultural investment, which is particularly sensitive to interest rates. In most African countries, the macroeconomic environment today is much more favorable for agriculture than was the macroeconomic environment that existed in Brazil during the 1960s, when a highly overvalued exchange rate heavily taxed agriculture.

Improved Business Climate
Many African countries—including, to varying degrees, Mozambique, Nigeria, and Zambia—have launched programs to improve the business environment. Investments in basic infrastructure such as roads, electricity, water, and communications are being heavily prioritized. Institutional reforms are being implemented to reduce corruption, and Transparency International recently reported that Africa has made more progress in reducing corruption than any other region. Most African countries are committed to strengthening their education and health systems, with the goal of building human capital and boosting workplace productivity. Decentralization initiatives and the development of civil society have improved the ability of rural populations to participate in their own development and defend their interests. This in turn has started to open space for producer organizations of all kinds. A number of African countries have already reformed or are in the process of reforming their land laws, protecting customary rights while at the same time opening opportunities for security of tenure for investors.

Increased Incentives to Invest in Agriculture
Strong demand, better macro and sector policies, and an improved business climate will help boost the returns to agriculture in Africa. This should help to increase savings and investment rates of producers, processors, traders, and all others involved in agricultural value chains. It should lead also to repatriation of capital that has fled from Africa over the past decades in vast amounts, spurring further domestic investment in the sector. In addition, foreign capital, which is needed for investment in commercial agriculture and especially in related value chains, is beginning to

flow into African countries, as evidenced by recent Chinese acquisition of land leases in Tanzania and the Democratic Republic of Congo, rising interest on the part of European energy firms in securing land concessions for production of biofuels feedstock, and surging foreign investment in high-value African agricultural export enterprises.

New Technologies

New technologies offer agricultural entrepreneurs in Africa's Guinea Savannah advantages that their Thai and Brazilian counterparts have acquired over the past four decades. Techniques for managing Guinea Savannah soils to make them more productive and reduce environmental damage are much more advanced than a generation ago, although applied research is still needed to adapt technologies developed in other regions to African conditions. The biotechnology revolution offers the potential to tailor solutions more quickly to biological constraints limiting expansion of cash crops in Africa, but only if the African countries develop the regulatory and research capacity to exploit this potential (Eicher, Maredia, and Sithole-Niang 2006).

Technological change has started to make an impact not only at the farm level but also further down the value chain. For example, the cell phone revolution is helping to link African farmers and traders quickly and affordably to information about potential sources of demand and supply.

Constraints to Be Overcome

Although clear potential exists for commercial agriculture to take off in Africa's Guinea Savannah zones, five main factors constrain the ability of African entrepreneurs to replicate the successes of the Brazilian Cerrado and Northeast Region of Thailand.

Tougher International Competition

Compared with Brazilian and Thai producers during earlier decades, African producers today face a more competitive international environment, not only for agricultural commodities, but also for manufactured goods.[1] Product specification requirements have become more exacting than in the past, even for unprocessed bulk commodities, as evidenced by the recent tightening of regulations relating to levels of aflotoxin that may be present in grains and the percentage of genetically modified organisms that may be present in grains and oilseeds for some importers. OECD agricultural subsidies continue to reduce export and import substitution opportunities, although these have become less important as world commodity prices have risen.

Exogenous Shocks: HIV/AIDS and Global Climate Change

Despite the spread of antiretroviral drugs, the human immunodeficiency virus/acquired immunodeficiency syndrome (HIV/AIDS) epidemic continues to exact a heavy toll in Africa, eroding African capacity in agricultural research and extension among many other areas. Global climate change, which is likely to reduce the level of rainfall in Guinea Savannah zones and significantly increase rainfall variability, will create new challenges in many areas, including research, crop and land management, and financial intermediation. Finally, volatility of global agricultural markets is likely to remain high because of a number of factors, including climate change and the close link between agricultural and oil prices as a result of the growing influence of biofuels production on agricultural markets.

Weak National Commitment

In Mozambique, Nigeria, and Zambia, policy makers have made encouraging declarations regarding the importance of agricultural development, but these declarations generally have not been supported by sustained political commitment, policy reforms, and investments similar to those seen in Brazil and Thailand in earlier decades. Today, African governments invest only 4 percent of the value of agricultural GDP in the sector, relative to at least 10 percent in other regions, where agriculture is a much smaller share of the economy (World Bank 2007c). In Thailand and Brazil, development of "backward" regions such as the Cerrado and Northeast Region was made a political priority and backed up by high levels of sustained public investment. Even though development of these regions was not an end in itself, it was seen as instrumental to reaching broader national policy objectives (for example, development of the "empty interior" in Brazil and the need to combat communist influence in Thailand).

Weak Donor Commitment

The weak commitment to agriculture seen at the national level is also evident at the level of the donors. Like many African governments, most of the major donors have declared their strong support for agricultural development, and in recent years the level of support to agriculture has increased modestly from earlier extremely low levels. Yet as with the African governments, the donors' rhetoric in support of African agriculture has far exceeded their actual funding commitments. In contrast, the development of commercial agriculture in Brazil and especially Thailand both benefited from large-scale foreign assistance, particularly from the United States, directly through investments in agricultural development projects, and indirectly through investments in infrastructure, agricultural research and extension, and agricultural higher education.

Lack of Social Cohesion, Political Instability, and Weak Capacity

In many parts of Africa, emergence of a successful commercial agriculture is impeded by the lack of social cohesion, which reduces trust among and between market participants and raises transaction costs. Brazilian and Thai societies both are characterized by a common national language, a strong national identity, and a single dominant religion. Few African countries can claim these features. In quite a few African countries, including (for example) Nigeria among the CCAA case study countries, when business is being conducted, ethnic identity frequently trumps national identity. Lack of social cohesion raises transaction costs, not only when it comes to negotiating among individuals in the private sector and ensuring fair adjudication of any subsequent contract disputes but also when it comes to mobilizing investment in the public goods that are critical to agricultural growth, such as agricultural research, education, and infrastructure.

More generally, in many parts of Africa the development of commercial agriculture faces a chronic low-level threat of civil unrest. Thailand and Brazil also faced political instability during the period of rapid expansion of commercial agriculture, including a communist insurgency in Thailand and occasional bouts of armed conflict among large landholders, small landholders, and indigenous peoples in Brazil. However, the violence in these countries never reached the levels seen in some African countries, including the civil wars of Mozambique and Nigeria.

The capacity of African government bureaucracies to facilitate coordination among different actors in the value chain while maintaining a competitive environment remains underdeveloped. In Thailand and Brazil, even though governments changed during the 1960s and 1970s as a result of military coups, both countries continued to benefit from a stable and competent civil service, which contributed to steady implementation of development programs and an attractive environment for private sector development. In addition, despite the introduction in recent years of policies that are more friendly to the private sector, many African bureaucrats are still wary of the private sector. This is why Africa has seen fewer public-private partnerships than accompanied the growth of commercial agriculture in Brazil and Thailand.

Needed Interventions: Policies, Investments, and Institutional Development

With the help of well-designed macro and sectoral policies, appropriately targeted strategic investments, and successful institutional development, Brazil and Thailand were able to transform the comparative advantage of their Guinea Savannah zones, making these zones much more competitive in national and international markets. At the same time, the experiences of Brazil and Thailand provide lessons, both positive and negative, about how African countries can manage the social and environmental impacts of such a transformation.

The public and private sectors in Africa, civil society organizations, and the development partners will need to build upon the existing inherent comparative advantage of Africa's Guinea Savannah zones by undertaking key actions that will create new comparative advantages to enhance the competitiveness of these zones. The needed actions can be broadly classified into (a) broadening and deepening ongoing policy reforms, (b) massively scaling up public and private investment, and (c) developing the institutional base needed to make markets work efficiently and with socially desirable outcomes. All of these interventions are common to successful agricultural development in Africa more generally; those highlighted in this section are especially important for commercial agriculture.

Broadening and Deepening Ongoing Policy Reforms
Macro and sectoral policies. In recent years, marked progress has been achieved in improving the overall macroeconomic environments in Mozambique, Nigeria, and Zambia, as well as in many other African countries. Policy reforms throughout Africa have generally favored agricultural development. Agricultural exports in Africa are still being taxed at higher levels than in other developing regions, so governments need to continue to move domestic prices toward export prices by removing export taxes and replacing them with other less distortionary sources of taxation. Some countries such as Malawi, Senegal, and Uganda have succeeded in raising replacement revenues through simplified systems of excise and valued added taxes. Countries rich in natural resources will also need to manage exchange rates during commodity booms in ways that do not undermine export-oriented commercial agriculture. One

approach to exchange rate management has been pioneered by Chile, which has implemented a novel rule-based system to smooth the inflow of commodity revenues and build offshore reserves during periods of high prices for copper and other commodities.

Although the three African case study countries have already made many of the painful reforms needed at the macro and sectoral levels, the development of the regional markets that are so important to expansion of commercial agriculture remains weak. Regional integration is a core pillar of NEPAD initiatives, and all subregions have agreed to move toward common markets. However, many countries have been slow to implement needed reforms, including banning of arbitrary export restrictions, streamlining border logistics, and harmonizing standards and regulations that constitute major impediments to regional trade. Given that regional markets have been identified as the major channel for development of commercial agriculture, faster progress in implementing regional integration agreements is urgently needed.

Land policies and land administration arrangements. The contrasting experiences of Brazil and Thailand show that land policy and land administration arrangements, perhaps more than any other policy-related measures, influence the pattern and distributional impacts of agricultural growth. Providing secure and transferable land rights is critical to protecting the interests of indigenous populations while allowing entrepreneurial farmers to acquire unused land in regions of low population density. This allows land to change hands over time and to flow to those who can use it most productively, which in turn provides incentives to invest in increasing land productivity. The new Mozambican land policy and land law provide a state-of-the-art framework for balancing competing interests, and the legal frameworks of Madagascar and Zambia are similarly well designed.

Many African land laws do not provide for freehold tenure for land that is allocated for commercial farming, but instead provide long-term, renewable leases for periods ranging from 50 to 100 years. Such arrangements provide sufficient security of tenure for most agricultural investments. Pushing for freehold tenure in such countries is not necessary and can be counterproductive. The land policy of Malawi, for example, provides for 50-year leases for all classes of land, whether held by smallholders or by large investors.

Much progress has also been achieved in designing relatively low-cost mechanisms for the certification of land rights of communities and individuals. Ethiopia represents a good example: individual land certificates are being issued in Ethiopia at a cost of just above one U.S. dollar per certificate. Impact evaluation of the Ethiopian program shows that it has significantly reduced conflicts, improved women's rights and status, and increased agricultural productivity (Songwe and Deininger 2008). Such land certification schemes involve strong participation of the community in the delineation of the land rights, in conflict resolution, and in the subsequent registration of transfers. In Mozambique, the law provides for the certification of community land rights, and a recent study suggests that group certification could be implemented nationally at an affordable cost (World Bank 2005b).

The CCAA case studies make abundantly clear that good land policies and good land administration laws are only the starting point for ensuring desirable developmental and distributional outcomes from agricultural commercialization. To translate the legal provisions into practice, strong political commitment is needed to ensure the protection of customary rights, as well as strong implementation capacity. Where either of the two is lacking, powerful interests will succeed in thwarting the intentions of the best policy and legal frameworks. In several recent cases, land rushes have occurred even in the presence of good legislation; for example, in Mozambique, there were excessive allocations of provisional certificates for land, and in Tanzania, there was a rush to acquire land for biofuel production. Preventing such excesses can be achieved by introducing ceilings on land ownership and by imposing a land tax to reduce incentives to hold large amounts of land for speculative purposes.

Few countries in Africa have *both* good land laws and good land administration implementation capacity. For this reason, the risk that rapid commercialization will lead to adverse distributional outcomes remains high. Comprehensive land policy and land administration implementation packages therefore need to include the following:

- A legal framework for the allocation of land to smallholders, including women, and to national or international investors, combined with clearly spelled-out processes for community consultation, involvement, and/compensation
- Legal provisions that make land leases fully tradable and usable as collateral for credit and the capacity to register land transactions
- A land tax to discourage acquisition of land for speculative purposes
- Strong decentralized administrative capacity to implement the legal provisions, combined with the political will to do so
- Certification of communal land rights, on either a group or individual basis, using low-cost participatory methods

- Provisions that recognize and protect communal land rights and the land rights of women
- Capacity development for local governments and communities to manage and defend their land rights.

Scaling Up Investment

Development of competitive commercial agriculture in Mozambique, Nigeria, and Zambia, as in many other African countries, will not be possible without sharply increased levels of investment. Agricultural development cannot be done on the cheap, ignoring the fundamental pillars of productivity growth in the food system, as governments and donors have tried to do in Africa over the past 20 years. Evidence from a large number of studies suggests that the three top priorities for public investment include agricultural science and technology, human capital, and infrastructure (Fan 2008). Although public investment is critical, providing a suitable investment climate for private investment will be even more important over the longer term.

Priorities for public investment. **Science and technology.** Particularly damaging to the prospects of African agriculture has been the low level of investment in agricultural research, combined with the fragmentation of research capacity across many small and underfunded institutions. Agricultural productivity growth cannot be achieved and sustained without continuous technical change, which can be assured only through sustained investments in agricultural research over decades. Brazil's long-term commitment to developing EMBRAPA and the payoffs in developing the Cerrado from that investment are particularly striking. Indeed, EMBRAPA has continued to deepen investments, with announced plans to add 600 additional scientists in the period 2008–10.

The governments in Mozambique, Nigeria, and Zambia have committed to investing more in agricultural science and technology systems, but the promised increase in funding has yet to materialize. The problem is in fact widespread: about one-half of all African countries have experienced absolute declines in research investment during the past decade (Beintema and Stads 2006). Increased funding to agricultural science and technology requires increased overall allocation of public expenditures to agriculture, as envisaged in the NEPAD Maputo accord, as well as giving priority to research within agricultural budgets, where it is often crowded out by expenditures with short-run, more visible payoffs (for example, fertilizer subsidies). In addition, because of the relatively small size of most

African research systems, the potential to achieve rapid gains through regional cooperation is much larger than it was in the cases of Brazil and Thailand. The current interest in strengthening the capacity of subregional research organizations is a welcome step toward realizing this goal.

The international agricultural research system allocates about one-half of its budget to Africa. Yet impacts of international agricultural research have been smaller in Africa than in other developing regions. Furthermore, the impacts that have been realized in Africa have resulted from an extremely small number of successful initiatives, for example, the development of improved maize and cassava varieties, and the development of biological control mechanisms to combat cassava mealybug (Maredia and Raitzer 2006). Although promising new technologies are in the pipeline, including the NERICA rices and drought-tolerant maize varieties, the effectiveness of the international agricultural research system is threatened by stagnating budgets and its reorientation toward downstream development R&D activities that should be the domain of national or subregional systems. The recent agreement on revitalizing the Consultative Group for International Agricultural Research (CGIAR) should strengthen the international system's capacity to address Africa's priority research challenges.

Finally, tapping the potential of the Guinea Savannah will require a balance of improved varieties and improved soil and water management practices, again reflecting the successful experiences of Thailand and Brazil. Although many promising initiatives have been launched recently to promote the uptake of improved varieties, including the Alliance for a Green Revolution in Africa (AGRA), funded by the Bill and Melinda Gates Foundation and the Rockefeller Foundation, a concerted effort focusing on technologies for sustainable soil and water management must be the highest priority, including efforts to adapt conservation tillage approaches to African conditions.

Education and skills. Increased investment is also needed in the CCAA African case study countries to strengthen agricultural education at all levels, starting from the vocational level (where it is needed to instill in rural households the basic skills needed to access and master new production technologies) to the technical level (where it is needed to fill the demand for the well-trained technicians required for modernizing agriculture and value chains) to the postgraduate level (where it is needed to replenish Africa's graying agricultural research establishment). Development of commercial agriculture will also require farmers to develop new skills in business development, market intelligence, and quality standards. Perhaps one of the most daunting challenges is how to do this, given the extremely weak condition of most extension systems. Some skills may be imparted through technical assistance provided by private agents through contract farming, if this is the preferred mode of organization of value chains. However, other approaches will also be needed, including revamped services through strong producer organizations and increased capacity of public and nongovernmental extension providers.

Irrigation. Although the development of commercial agriculture in Africa likely will be driven by rainfed farming, there is an important role for small-scale and supplementary irrigation to extend the cropping season and ensure against climatic risks, especially in the drier parts of the Guinea Savannah. Recent successes with small-scale irrigation (for example, in Nigeria and Malawi) show that this can be done.

Infrastructure. In many parts of Africa, massive investment is needed to build the infrastructure base needed to launch and sustain internationally competitive commercial agriculture. Vast areas remain poorly served by infrastructure, with most households having limited access to transport services. Even where roads exist, transport costs remain significantly higher than in other parts of the developing world. It is not clear that stepped-up provision of road infrastructure will be sufficient to bring transport costs down to levels comparable to those in Asia. More competition in vehicle imports, greater competition in the trucking industry, and reductions in informal extractions by police and border posts are urgently needed. Improved road and rail links at the subregional level will be critical for exploiting the opportunities present in regional markets. This adds urgency to rapid implementation of the NEPAD-sponsored African Development Corridor Partnership, an agreement among public, private, and multilateral financial organizations to invest in infrastructure to develop 12 multicountry strategic trade and development corridors.

Logistics and energy services are deficient in all three CCAA African case study countries. High logistics costs threaten the ability of producers to compete effectively in export markets, especially export markets for low-value agricultural commodities. Unreliable energy supplies sharply increase agricultural processing costs because processors often have to provide their own generators rather than rely on electricity over the larger grids. The experiences of Brazil and Thailand show that investment in infrastructure at ports and other border crossings is critical to the achievement of competitiveness, along with policies to improve logistics. Although port and railroad investments and concession systems are advancing in many African countries, it is not clear that progress is fast and deep enough to reduce significantly the costs of shipping agricultural commodities or of acquiring agricultural inputs, especially fertilizer. Not all such investments need to be public, but a good part of them must be, particularly if African countries promote a smallholder-based approach to development of these zones.

Inducing private investment. Given the scope and complexity of the tasks needed to develop agriculture in Guinea Savannah zones, ranging from farm-level investments to international marketing, the private sector needs to take the lead in many of the critical investments and activities. The powerful incentives created by the search for profits encourage an efficient use of resources often missing in government bureaucracies. Yet the private sector can be productive and serve broader social objectives only if public policies are appropriately designed so that private incentives are consistent with public interests, implementation is consistent and perceived as fair, there are transparent means to resolve disputes, and political space is created for wealth creation and influence that are independent of the governing political elite.

Cumbersome business regulations and behind-the-border transaction costs still pose a major impediment to private investment in agriculture in many parts of Africa. Continuing efforts to improve the business climate are especially important for commercial agriculture and, if successful, will facilitate the entry of private seed and agriprocessing companies that have played an important role in Latin America and Asia.

Stronger associations of farmers and traders are needed to push reforms. The lack of power of these professional organizations helps explain the persistence of illegal taxes extorted at roadblocks, which pose a major impediment to regional trade, as well as the weak political commitment to promoting successful commercial agriculture. Creating such space and promoting vigorous private sector and civil-society organizations are vital, as the Thai experience vividly illustrates. There are hopeful signs, however. During the past decade, the number of effective farmer and trader organizations active in Africa has increased markedly.

Institutional Reforms to Make Markets Work Better
Almost by definition, successful commercialization of agriculture depends on well-functioning markets. The greatest challenge to commercial agriculture in Africa is to put in place the institutions to make markets more efficient and less risky. This will require concerted efforts on a range of fronts.

Commodity markets and risk management. Commodity markets in most African countries are plagued by incomplete or missing markets and high transaction costs. Price risks are also very high and will likely remain high for commercial export-oriented agriculture, given the increasing volatility of global markets. In these circumstances, the state will need to offer certain critical services that the private sector currently has few incentives to provide. The needed actions will vary by commodity, and experimentation is required to develop appropriate models, for example in the provision of market information and in developing and implementing additional tools for managing risks and uncertainty, which are likely to increase with growing commercialization. A key challenge is knowing when the state should step aside and give greater scope to the private sector as markets for these services mature, because it is easy for the state to overreach and crowd out private initiative.

There are certain basic prerequisites to improving market performance. Standardizing and enforcing grades and standards and improving flows of market information are two of the most important priorities. Development of commodity exchanges using modern electronic communication technology through a public-private partnership (as is being piloted in Ethiopia) is an important step toward more integrated national markets. Commodity exchanges can also help reduce price risks, and some could eventually be developed into full-fledged options and futures markets at the regional level, a role already played by the South African Futures Exchange for the countries of southern Africa. Commodity exchanges can also include warehouse receipt systems to reduce distress sales after harvest and encourage seasonal storage. Considerable initial support is needed to test such innovations and adapt them to local needs.

Input distribution systems. Modern commercial agriculture depends critically on ensured access to purchased inputs, especially seed of improved varieties, fertilizer, crop chemicals, and machinery. Given the poor record of state agencies and parastatals in importing inputs and delivering them to farmers, the priority must be to develop private sector–led input distribution systems. However, devising policies to stimulate the emergence of such systems has proven difficult. The instability of government policy in this domain leads to great uncertainty in the private sector, discouraging investments, and thus, ironically, confirming government views that the private sector is unresponsive.

The recent revival of input subsidies in the form of "market-smart" approaches needs to be carefully assessed as a basis for scaling up. Market-smart approaches are defined as those that encourage private sector participation (for example, through a voucher system) and that are targeted to farmers and regions that would not otherwise use the input, often poor farmers and those in remote regions. The theory is that once farmers have experience in using the input and volume grows enough to allow economies of scale, subsidies can be scaled back and eliminated. Yet the rapid scale-up of subsidy programs (as in Malawi) threatens to bring back the problems of previous subsidy programs, many of which became fiscally unsustainable and crowded out other key government investments in research, extension, and infrastructure (Dorward et al. 2008).

In any event, input subsidies need to be complemented by other measures to develop private input suppliers, such as training and financing for input dealers, regulation of input quality, and development of trade associations. The experiences of the Rockefeller Foundation and now AGRA in developing input dealer networks in several countries show considerable promise for wider scaling-up.

Financial systems. Access to finance is central to successful development of commercial agriculture. Yet there has been very little progress in Africa in creating self-sustaining rural financial systems with significant outreach to the farm population. In the absence of reliable rural finance systems, many alternatives have been tried, from group lending to interlinked markets to subsidized distribution of agricultural inputs. These alternatives have produced mixed results. For example, the contract farming model under which input distribution and credit recovery have been linked to output markets has sometimes been a key driver of export growth, especially in a tightly coordinated single marketing channel, such as some cotton systems. But this model is coming under pressure in Francophone countries in the face of mounting questions about financial sustainability and falling farm productivity. Policy makers must continue to seek ways to tie rural savings-and-loan associations more effectively to broader commercial banking systems to provide greater financial intermediation and diversification of risks. This is an area in which significant experimentation is still needed. Also, many African countries still have poorly performing state banks for agriculture. Will it be possible to replicate the Thai success through reform of these banks? With strong political support and effective champions, countries in other regions have done so (for example, Guatemala) (see World Bank [2007c]).

Management of Social Impacts

Commercial agriculture in Africa is unlikely to contribute effectively to national policy objectives of broad-based growth and poverty reduction unless care is taken to ensure that the wealth created by commercial agriculture is shared widely. The smallholder-led agricultural transformation that occurred in Thailand provides a better model for Africa than the transformation that occurred in Brazil, which was dominated by wealthy farmers who had the economic and political power to secure large tracts of land and to leverage the capital needed to invest in large-scale, highly mechanized production technologies.

Socially desirable outcomes will be achieved only if three critical challenges can be overcome.

The first critical challenge is how to reform customary land policies to allow equitable distribution of land and secure tenancy.

The second critical challenge is how to ensure that factor prices reflect opportunity costs and are not distorted by subsidies on credit and machinery that encourage premature mechanization.

The third critical challenge is how to ensure that agricultural services are developed in ways that level the playing field for small-scale farmers. Special efforts will be needed as well to ensure that women farmers are able to participate in opportunities to expand commercial agriculture.

Of course, broad-based social benefits need not derive from primary production alone. Experience in a number of countries (for example, Chile and Thailand) has shown that, with appropriate policies, a vibrant commercial agriculture can generate a large number of jobs in both upstream and downstream portions of the value chain. This consideration is particularly important in the many African countries in which it is questionable whether very small farms using currently available technology can provide farm households with an income high enough to escape poverty, especially if they focus entirely on production of staples. For these farmers, diversification of incomes or (in land-abundant areas) use of labor-saving technologies to expand farm size are potential pathways out of poverty.

Management of Environmental Impacts

Transforming the natural ecosystems found in the Guinea Savannah into vibrant commercial farming systems will not be possible without converting forest and pasture land to permanent cropping. This will inevitably bring some environmental costs. However, current strategies of low-input extensification of agriculture are incurring especially high environmental costs through deforestation and land degradation, loss of biodiversity, and release of sequestered carbon in soils and trees. A more intensive pattern of land use can reduce these costs by reducing land conversion and through the use of fertilizers and other soil amendments. Of course, more intensive strategies can also bring risks of pollution of water resources and negative health impacts from increased use of agrochemicals.

Experience from many parts of the world shows that the environmental costs associated with the development of commercial agriculture can be reduced and managed through use of appropriate technologies combined with vigilant monitoring of environmental impacts backed by effective enforcement of environmental rules and regulations. The development of conservation approaches to farming, including zero tillage, has been a major factor in sustaining and improving land quality and reducing water runoff in the Brazilian Cerrado, and similar approaches show considerable promise in the Guinea Savannah of Africa. In low-density population areas that characterize the Guinea Savannah, providing for sufficient allocation of land to ecological reserves to preserve biodiversity should be a first priority.

As with land policy, it is one thing to develop appropriate environmental rules and regulations, and quite another to enforce the rules to ensure favorable environmental outcomes. National-level enforcement capacity has to be complemented by greater involvement of communities in managing their natural resources. Payments for environmental services also show potential to reduce deforestation and land degradation, especially if these services are included in carbon-trading schemes in the follow-up to the Kyoto agreement on climate change, expected by 2010.

Public Sector Reform and Governance

The above list of reforms makes it clear that the state must play an important facilitating role in the development of a dynamic and equitable commercial agriculture. A major challenge is to develop governance structures and capacities for the state to assume these roles. Ministries of agriculture that grew up with state-led input supply and marketing schemes require sharply upgraded capacities and skills in areas such as marketing and business development services, as well as the ability to forge a variety of public-private-civil-society partnerships that characterize new roles of the state. Moreover, these skills must extend well beyond the ministries of agriculture to local governments with responsibility for newly decentralized agricultural services, and to a range of other ministries such as science and technology, land, environment, and commerce and trade that have important roles in commercial agriculture.

Not surprisingly, the major governance challenge to successful commercial agricultural development will be how to coordinate the services and investments of multiple ministries and levels of government and coordinate public and private investments. Here high-level political leadership is needed to ensure that agricultural development for specific regions is a priority, as seen in both the Brazil and Thai examples. The importance of this coordination role suggests that efforts to foster commercial agriculture should be spatially organized into priority development corridors, with the coordination role, or even a regional development authority, located in the office of the prime minister or president.

Final Thoughts

Perceptions similar to those that fueled agropessimism 30 years ago in Brazil and Thailand were until recently fueling agropessimism in many parts of Africa. Yet the success achieved in Brazil and Thailand suggests that the pessimism heard in Africa may be exaggerated. Based on a careful examination of the factors that contributed to the agricultural commercialization experiences seen in Brazil and Thailand, as well as comparative analysis of evidence obtained through detailed case studies of three African countries, this report has argued that opportunities exist for African agriculture to regain international competitiveness, provided that appropriate measures are taken. Indeed, the case studies highlight that significant successes have already been achieved in Africa in some regions and commodities (for example, cotton in Zambia, cassava and soybeans in Nigeria, and maize in Mozambique).

While there are good reasons to be optimistic about the future prospects for African agriculture, at the same time it is important to be clear-eyed about the challenges that lie ahead. The CCAA study has identified a set of constraints that will need to be overcome to support the emergence of competitive commercial agriculture in Africa. Although it would be easy to feel overwhelmed by the list of constraints, fortunately Brazil and Thailand provide important lessons about how these constraints can be overcome. Arguably the most important lesson of all relates to the role of the state. In Brazil and Thailand, successive governments played a vital role by establishing a conducive enabling environment characterized by favorable macroeconomic policies, adequate infrastructure, a strong human capital base, competent government administration, and political stability. This conducive enabling environment was a critical factor that allowed governments in both countries to mobilize effectively the creativity, drive, and resources of the private sector. Rather than relying solely on heavy state management and investment that were characteristic of the import substitution phase of development economics, the governments of Brazil and Thailand were able to engage effectively with private investors, farmers' organizations, rural communities, and civil-society organizations. It is encouraging to note that after decades of state domination, many initiatives currently under way in the African countries are using similar approaches. Prospects are good that these initiatives will allow the creation of the political space needed for public-private partnerships, private investments, and civil-society–led initiatives to succeed.

One advantage that African policy makers have today is the knowledge that there are multiple paths to successful agricultural commercialization. The Brazilian and Thai experiences show that modern commercial agriculture need not be synonymous with large, highly mechanized farms and that the distributional impacts of the commercialization process are likely to differ depending on the scale of the dominant production systems. This knowledge can help policy makers to guide the commercialization process so that it contributes most effectively to national policy objectives. Although the Brazilian and Thai experiences show that agricultural revolutions in the Guinea Savannah regions can be driven by either smallholders or large-scale commercial farmers, the results are generally more equitable and pro-poor if smallholders widely participate. Second-round employment and poverty-alleviation effects are likely to be much larger with the smallholder-led model because of the nature of the consumption linkages associated with growth in smallholder income, which tends to generate more demand for locally produced nontradables. Smallholders can compete in domestic and international markets, as amply shown by the Thai experience, the cassava revolution all over Africa, the cotton-food grain systems in Africa, and smallholder tea and coffee production. In the case of low-value staples, however, it is unlikely that land-constrained households farming 1–2 hectares or less will be able to earn sufficient income from food staples to exit poverty without expanding farm size through labor-saving technologies in areas with abundant land or diversifying income sources.

The encouraging news is that if the development of smallholder-based commercial agriculture begins solidly, the process can be self-reinforcing. As the Thai experience illustrates, those who initially gain in the process (commercial farmers, farmer organizations, and agribusiness firms) will be motivated to lobby for policies and investments that can sustain the commercialization process, while at the same time generating some of the needed financial resources. As commercialization broadens and deepens, larger private sector actors will have increasing incentives to invest in infrastructure and supporting services for value-chain coordination, thereby reducing the burden on government while generating expanded off-farm employment. At the same time, political leaders must continue to play an active role by providing the vision, strategy, consistent implementation, and long-term commitment needed to make the promise of agricultural transformation a reality.

Note

1. The competition in manufactured goods affects the potential of commercial agriculture, particularly small-scale commercial agriculture, to reduce poverty through consumption linkages. As incomes of small-scale farmers increase, as was the case in Thailand, they spend some proportion of their higher income on locally made nontradable goods, thereby inducing expanded local employment. With the spread of very low-cost Asian manufactured goods that compete with African nontradables (for example, Asian plastic sandals displace demand for locally made African sandals), one would expect that the second-round poverty alleviation effects of expanded commercial agriculture to be less in Sub-Saharan Africa than was the case in Asia in the 1960s.

List of CCAA Background Reports

In preparing this synthesis report, the authors drew heavily on a series of background reports that were specially commissioned for the CCAA study.

The background reports are available at http://go.worldbank.org/ XSRUM2ZXM0.

Value Chain Methodology

Description of Methodology and Presentation of Templates for Value Chain Analysis
John C. Keyser, Consultant

Synthesis of Quantitative Results
John C. Keyser, Consultant

Review of Agricultural Commercialization Experiences in Africa

Commercial Agriculture in Africa: Lessons from Success and Failure
Colin Poulton, Geoff Tyler, Peter Hazell, Andrew Dorward, Jonathan Kydd, and Mike Stockbridge, Centre for Development, Environment and Policy, School of Oriental and African Studies, University of London, United Kingdom

The Fall and Rise of the Colonial Development Corporation
Geoff Tyler, Consultant

Cotton Case Study
Colin Poulton, Centre for Development, Environment and Policy, School of Oriental and African Studies, University of London, United Kingdom

An African Success Story – The Development of a Competitive Tea Export Industry
Geoff Tyler, Consultant

The African Sugar Industry – A Frustrated Success Story
Geoff Tyler, Consultant

Critical Success Factors in the African High Value Horticulture Export Industry
Geoff Tyler, Consultant

Case Study on Malawi Tobacco
Colin Poulton, Jonathan Kydd, Dalitso Kabame, Centre for Development, Environment and Policy, School of Oriental and African Studies, University of London, United Kingdom

Case Study on Cashews
Colin Poulton, Centre for Development, Environment and Policy, School of Oriental and African Studies, University of London, United Kingdom

Case Study on Food Staples
Peter Hazell, Colin Poulton, Centre for Development, Environment and Policy, School of Oriental and African Studies, University of London, United Kingdom

Case Study on Livestock
Peter Hazell, Centre for Development, Environment and Policy, School of Oriental and African Studies, University of London, United Kingdom

Case Study on Oil Crops
Colin Poulton, Centre for Development, Environment and Policy, School of Oriental and African Studies, University of London, United Kingdom, and Geoff Tyler, Consultant

Environmental Impacts
Michael Stockbridge, Consultant

Social Impacts
Michael Stockbridge, Consultant

International Markets Overview

Cassava: International Market Profile
Adam Prakash, FAO

Cattle and Beef: International Commodity Profile
Nancy Morgan and Gregoire Tallard, FAO

Cotton: International Commodity Profile
Shangnan Shui, FAO

Maize: International Market Profile
Abdolreza Abbassian, FAO

Rice: International Commodity Profile
Concepción Calpe, FAO

Soybean: International Commodity Profile
Peter Thoenes, FAO

Sugar: International Market Profile
Jennifer Nyberg, FAO

Sugar-Based Ethanol: International Market Profile
Jennifer Nyberg, FAO

Competitiveness Country Case Studies

The Brazilian Cerrado Experience with Commercial Agriculture: A Critical Review
Geraldo Sant'Ana de Camargo Barros, Lucilio Rogério Aparecido Alves, Humberto Francisco Soplador, Mauro Osaka, Daniela Bacchi Bartholomeu, Andreia Cristina De Oliveira Adami, Simone Fioritti Silva, Guilherme Bellotti de Melo, and Matheus Henrique Scaglica P. de Almeida, Universidade de São Paulo

Competitive Commercial Agriculture in the Northeast of Thailand
Benchaphun Ekasingh, Chapika Sungkapitux, Jirawan Kitchaicharoen, and Pornsiri Suebpongsang, Chiang Mai University

Mozambique Case Study
John C. Keyser, Consultant

Nigeria Case Study
Aderibigbe S. Olomola, Nigerian Institute of Social and Economic Research (NISER)

Zambia Case Study
John C. Keyser, Consultant

Environmental and Social Impacts

Mozambique, Nigeria, and Zambia: Social and Environmental Impact Assessment
Pasquale De Muro, Riccardo Bocci, Sara Gorgoni, Lucia Lombardo, Elisabetta Martone, Laura Silici, and Lucia Russo, Università degli Studi Roma Tre

References

Abbott, P. C., and M. E. Brehdahl. 1994. "Competitiveness: Definitions, Useful Concepts, and Issues." In *Competiveness in International Food Markets*, ed. M. E. Brehdahl, P. C. Abbott, and M. Reed, 1–13. Boulder, CO: Westview Press.

Alfieri, A., C. Arndt, and X. Cirera. 2009. "Mozambique." In *Distortions to Agricultural Incentives in Africa*, ed. K. Anderson and W. A. Masters, 127–46. Washington, DC: World Bank.

Alston, J. M., C. Chan-Kang, M. C. Marra, P. G. Pardey, and T. J. Wyatt. 2000. "A Meta-Analysis of Rates of Return to Agricultural R&D: Ex Pede Herculem?" Research Report 113, IFPRI, Washington, DC.

Araújo, C., A. de Janvry, and E. Sadoulet. 2002. "Geography of Poverty, Territorial Growth, and Rural Development." Paper presented at Annual World Bank Conference on Developing Economies Economists' Forum, April 30. World Bank, Washington, DC.

ARD (Associates in Rural Development). 2002. "Nigeria Environmental Analysis Final Report." Unpublished, ARD, Burlington, VT. http://pdf.usaid.gov/pdf_docs/PNACP627.pdf.

Arua, E. O., and E. C. Okorji. 1997. "Multidimensional Analysis of Land Tenure Systems in Eastern Nigeria." *Land Reform, Land Settlement, and Cooperatives* 1997/2: 112–24.

Badiane, O., and D. Resnick. 2005. "Regional Trade Liberalization and Domestic Food Market Stabilization in African Countries." Paper presented to the workshop, "Managing Food Price Instability in Low-Income Countries," Washington, DC, Feb. 28 to March .

Beintema, N. M., and G. B. Ayoola. 2004. "Nigeria: Agricultural Science and Technology Indicators." ASTI Country Brief 10, IFPRI, Washington, DC. http://www.asti.cgiar.org/pdf/nigeria_cb10.pdf.

Beintema, N. M., and G.-J. Stads. 2006. "Agricultural R&D in Sub-Saharan Africa: An Era of Stagnation." Background report, Agricultural Science and Technology Indicators (ASTI) Initiative, IFPRI, Washington, DC. http://www.asti.cgiar.org/pdf/AfricaRpt_200608.pdf.

Bell, R. W., and V. Seng. 2004. "Rainfed Lowland Rice-Growing Soils of Cambodia, Laos, and North-East Thailand." In *Water in Agriculture*, ed. V. Seng, E. Craswell, S. Fukai, and K. Fischer, 161–73. Proceeding 116e, Australian Centre for International Agricultural Research (ACIAR), Canberra. http://www.environment.murdoch.edu.au/groups/aciar/images/Bell_SengWaterinAgriculture.pdf.

Bello, W., S. Cunningham, K. P. Li, and C. Nikhom. 1998. *A Siamese Tragedy: Development and Disintegration in Modern Thailand*. London: Zed Books.

Binswanger, H. P., K. Deininger, and G. Feder. 1995. "Power, Distortion, Revolt and Reform in Agricultural Land Relations." In *Handbook of Development Economics, Vol. IIIB*, ed. J. Behrman and T. N. Srinivasan. Amsterdam: Elsevier.

Binswanger, H. P., and J. McIntire. 1987. "Behavioural and Material Determinants of Production Relations in Land-Abundant Tropical Agriculture." *Economic Development and Cultural Change* 36 (1): 75–99.

Binswanger, H. P., and M. R. Rosenzweig. 1986. "Behavioral and Material Determinants of Production Relations in Agriculture." *The Journal of Development Studies* 22 (3): 503–39.

Boserup, E. 1993. *The Conditions of Agricultural Growth: The Economics of Agrarian Change under Population Pressure*. London: Earthscan.

Bromley, D. W. 1997. "Rethinking Markets." *American Journal of Agricultural Economics* 79 (5): 1383–93.

Burns, A. 2004. "Thailand's 20 Years Program to Title Rural Land." Background paper prepared for *World Development Report 2005*, World Bank, Washington, DC. http://siteresources.worldbank.org/INTWDR2005/Resources/burns_thailand_land_titling.pdf#search=%22Thailand%2020%20years%20program%20to%20title%20rural%20land%22.

Byerlee, D., X. Diao, and C. Jackson. 2005. "Agriculture, Rural Development, and Pro-Poor Growth: Country Experiences in the Post-Reform Era." Agriculture and Rural Development (ARD) Discussion Paper 21, World Bank, Washington, DC.

Byerlee, D., and C. K. Eicher. 1997. "Introduction: Africa's Food Crisis." In *Africa's Emerging Maize Revolution*, ed. D. Byerlee and C. K. Eicher. Boulder, CO: Lynne Rienner Publishers.

Byerlee, D., T. S. Jayne, and R. J. Meyers. 2006. "Managing Food Price Risks and Instability in a Liberalizing Market Environment: Overview and Policy Options." *Food Policy* 31(4): 275–87.

Carney, J. 1993. "Converting the Wetlands, Engendering the Environment: The Intersection of Gender with Agrarian Change in The Gambia." *Economic Geography* 69 (4): 329–48.

Chemonics International, Inc. 2008. "Mozambique Biodiversity and Tropical Forests 118/119 Assessment." Report produced for the United States Agency for International Development (USAID).

Christiaensen, L., and L. Demery. 2007. *Down to Earth: Agriculture and Poverty Reduction in Africa*. Directions in Development. Washington, DC: World Bank.

Collier, P. 2008a. "Food Shortages: Think Big." *Financial Times*. April 15.

———. 2008b. "The Politics of Hunger: How Illusion and Greed Fan the Food Crisis." *Foreign Affairs*. November/December.

Conservation International. 1995. "Estimativas de perda da área do cerrado brasileiro." http://72.14.209.104/search?q=cache:FCMjb69NFaEJ:cartamaior. uol.com.br/templates/materia.

Cotula, L., N. Dyer, and S. Vermeulen. 2008. "Fuelling Exclusion? The Biofuels Boom and Poor People's Access to Land." International Institute for Environment and Development (IIED) and FAO, London. www.iied. org/pubs/pdfs/12551IIED.pdf.

Cropper, M., C. Griffiths, and M. Mani. 1997. "Roads, Population Pressures, and Deforestation in Thailand, 1976–89." Environment, Infrastructure, and Agriculture Division, Policy Research Department, World Bank, Washington, DC.

Davison, J. 1988. "Who Owns What? Land Registration and Tensions in Gender Relations of Production in Kenya." In *Agriculture, Women, and Land: The African Experience*, ed. J. Davison. Boulder, CO: Westview Press.

Dawe, D. 2001. "How Far Down the Path to Free Trade? The Importance of Rice Price Stabilization in Developing Asia." *Food Policy* 26(2): 163–75.

Diao, X. S., and Y. Yanoma. 2007. "Exploring Regional Dynamics in Sub-Saharan African Agriculture." Development Strategy and Governance Division Discussion Paper, International Food Policy Research Institute (IFPRI), Washington, DC.

Dixon, J. A., A. Gulliver, and D. P. Gibbon. 2001. *Farming Systems and Poverty: Improving Farmers' Livelihoods in a Changing World*. Rome and Washington, DC: FAO and World Bank. See Summary at ftp://ftp.fao.org/docrep/fao/004/ AC349E/ac349e00.pdf.

Dolan, C. S. 2001. "The Good Wife: Struggles over Land and Labour in the Kenyan Horticultural Sector." *Journal of Development Studies* 27 (3): 39–70.

———Dolan. 2002. "Gender and Witchcraft in Agrarian Transition: The Case of Kenyan Horticulture." *Development and Change* 33(4): 659–81.

Dorward A., E. Chirwa, D. Boughton, E. Crawford, T. Jayne, R. Slater, V. Kelly, and M. Tsoka. 2008. "Towards 'Smart' Subsidies in Agriculture? Lessons from Recent Experience in Malawi." Natural Resource Perspectives 116, Overseas Development Institute (ODI), London. http://www.aec.msu.edu/fs2/inputs/documents/NRP_116.pdf.

Dorward, A., J. Kydd, and C. Poulton. 2005. "Beyond Liberalisation: Developmental Coordination Policies for African Smallholder Agriculture." *IDS Bulletin* 36 (2): 80–5.

Douthwaite, R., M. Chitalu, and C. Lungu. 2005. "Zambia National Environment Situational Analysis Report." Ministry of Tourism, Environment, and Natural Resources, Republic of Zambia.

Economic Commission for Africa. 2004. *Economic Report on Africa 2004: Unlocking Africa's Trade Potential.* Economic Commission for Africa: Addis Ababa.

Eicher, C. K. 2006. "The Evolution of Agricultural Education and Training: Global Insights of Relevance for Africa." World Bank, Washington, DC. http://www.fao.org/sd/erp/Documents2006/globalAETInsightsEicher.pdf.

Eicher, C. K., K. Maredia, and I. Sithole-Niang. 2006. "Crop Biotechnology and the African Farmer." *Food Policy* 31 (6): 504–27.

Ellis, F. 2000. *Rural Livelihoods and Diversity in Developing Countries.* Oxford: Oxford University Press.

Ekboir, J. M. 2003. "Research and Technology Policies in Innovation Systems: Zero Tillage in Brazil." *Research Policy* 32 (4): 573–86.

Fafchamps, M. 1992. "Cash Crop Production, Food Price Volatility, and Rural Market Integration in the Third World." *American Journal of Agricultural Economics* 74 (1): 90–9.

Fan, S. 2008. *Public Expenditures, Growth, and Poverty: Lessons from Developing Countries.* Washington, DC: International Food Policy Research Institute (IFPRI).

FAO (Food and Agriculture Organization). 2001. *Strategic Environmental Assessment: An Assessment of the Impact of Cassava Production and Processing on the Environment and Biodiversity, Vol. 5.* FAO, Rome. ftp://ftp.fao.org/docrep/fao/007/y2413e/y2413e00.pdf.

———. 2002. Gateway to Land and Water Information: Nigeria national report. FAO, Rome. http://www.fao.org/ag/aGL/swlwpnr/reports/y_sf/z_ng/ng.htm.

————. 2005. "Global Forest Resources Assessment 2005: Zambia Country Report." FRA2005/062, Forestry Department, FAO, Rome.

Francis, E. 1998. "Gender and Rural Livelihoods in Kenya." *Journal of Development Studies* 35: 72–95.

Gemo, H., C. K. Eicher, and S. Teclemariam. 2005. *Mozambique's Experience in Building a National Extension System*. East Lansing: Michigan State University Press.

Gittinger, J. P. 1982. *Economic Analysis of Agricultural Projects*. 2nd ed. EDI Series in Economic Development. Baltimore: The Johns Hopkins University Press.

Goetz, S. 1993. "Interlinked Markets and the Cash Crop–Food Crop Debate in Land Abundant Tropical Agriculture." *Economic Development and Cultural Change* 41 (2): 343–61.

Govereh, J., and T. Jayne. 2003. "Cash Cropping and Food Crop Productivity: Synergies or Trade-Offs?" *Agricultural Economics* 28: 39–50.

Grain Briefing. 2008. "Seized: The 2008 Land Grab for Food and Financial Security." (October). http://www.grain.org/briefings_files/landgrab-2008-en.pdf.

Grimm, M., and I. Günther. 2004. "How to Achieve Pro-Poor Growth in a Poor Economy. The Case of Burkina Faso." Report prepared for the "Operationalizing Pro-Poor-Growth" project sponsored by the World Bank, DFID, AFD, GTZ, and KFW. GTZ, Eschborn.

Hafner, J. A. 1990. "Forces and Policy Issues Affecting Forest Use in Northeast Thailand 1900–1985." In *Keepers of the Forest: Land Management Alternatives in Southeast Asia*, ed. M. Poffenberger, 69–93. West Hartford, CN: Kumarian Press.

Hassett, K. A., and R. J. Shapiro. 2003. "How Europe Sows Misery in Africa." On the Issues, American Enterprise Institute for Public Policy Research, AEI Online. http://www.aei.org/publications/pubID.17839/pub_detail.asp.

Hatton, J., S. Telford, and H. Krugmann. 2003. "Mozambique: Country Report on Environmental Assessment." Southern African Institute for Environment Assessment. http://www.saiea.com/SAIEA-Book/Mozam1.pdf.

Hazell, P., C. Poulton, S. Wiggins, and A. Dorward. 2007. "The Future of Small Farms for Poverty Reduction and Growth." 2020 Vision Discussion Paper No. 42, International Food Policy Research Institute (IFPRI), Washington, DC.

Hazell, P., G. Shields, and D. Shields. 2005. "The Nature and Extent of Domestic Sources of Food Price Instability and Risk." Paper prepared for World Bank–DFID workshop, "Managing Food Price Risks and Instability," Washington, DC, February 28 – March 1.

Heald, S. 1991. "Tobacco, Time and the Household Economy in Two Kenyan Societies: The Teso and the Kuria." *Comparative Studies in Society and History* 33 (1): 130–57.

Hershey, C., G. Henry, R. Best, K. Kawano, R. H. Howeler, and C. Iglesias. 2001. "Cassava in Asia: Expanding the Competitive Edge in Diversified Markets." In *A Review of Cassava in Asia with Country Case Studies on Thailand and Vietnam*. Proceedings of the Validation Forum on the Global Cassava Development Strategy, held in Rome, April 26–28, 2000, Vol. 3, 1–62. FAO/International Fund for Agricultural Development (IFAD), Rome.

Hine, J. L., and C. Rizet. 1991. "Halving Africa's Freight Transport Costs: Could It Be Done?" Paper presented at the Transport and Communications in Africa International Symposium, Brussels, Belgium, Nov. 27–29.

Ikdahl, I., A. Hellum, R. Kaarhus, T. A. Benjaminsen, and P. Kameri-Mbote. 2005. "Human Rights, Formalisation and Women's Land Rights in Southern and Eastern Africa." Studies in Women's Law 57, Institute of Women's Law, University of Oslo, Norway. http://www.ielrc.org/content/w0507.pdf.

IFC (International Finance Corporation). 2008. *Doing Business 2009. Comparing Regulation in 181 Economies*. Washington, DC: IFC.

Jayne, T. 1994. "Do High Food Marketing Costs Constrain Cash Crop Production? Evidence from Zimbabwe." *Economic Development and Cultural Change* 42 (2): 387–402.

Jayne, T. S., J. Govereh, Z. Xu, J. Ariga, and E. Mghenyi. 2006. "Factors Affecting Small Farmers' Use of Improved Maize Technologies: Evidence from Kenya and Zambia." Paper presented at Symposium on Seed-Fertilizer Technology, Cereal Productivity, and Pro-Poor Growth in Africa: Time for New Thinking? Held at the International Association of Agricultural Economists Tri-Annual Meetings, Gold Coast, Queensland, Australia, August 12–18. http://www.aec.msu.edu/fs2/inputs/power_points/iaae_maize_technology_adoption.pdf.

Kangasniemi, J. 2002. "Financing Agricultural Research by Producers' Organizations in Africa." In *Agricultural Research Policy in an Era of Privatization*, ed. D. Byerlee and R. G. Echeverria. Wallingford, Oxon, U.K.: CAB International.

Kennedy, E., and R. Oniang'o. 1990. "Health and Nutrition Effects of Sugar Cane Production in South-Western Kenya." *Food and Nutrition Bulletin* 12 (4): 261–7.

Keyser, J. C. 2006. "Definition of Methodology and Presentation of Templates for Value Chain Analysis, Competitive Commercial Agriculture in Africa (CCAA)." Environmental, Rural, and Social Development Unit, World Bank, Washington, DC.

———. 2007. "Zambia Case Study." Background report for Competitive Commercial Agriculture in Africa, World Bank, Washington, DC.

Krueger, A. O., M. Schiff, and A. Valdés. 1988. "Agricultural Incentives in Developing Countries: Measuring the Effect of Sectoral and Economy-wide Policies." *World Bank Economic Review* 2 (3): 255–72.

Leonard, R., and K. N. Ayutthaya. 2003. "Thailand's Land Titling Programme: Securing Land for the Poor?" Paper presented at "Politics of the Commons" International Conference, Regional Centre for Sustainable Development, Chiang Mai University, Thailand, July 11–14. http://dlc.dlib.indiana.edu/archive/00001150/00/Rebeca_Leonard.pdf.

Lopes, M. de R., I. Vidigal Lopes, M. Silva de Oliveira, F. Campos Barcelos, E. Jara, and P. Rangel Bogado. 2008. "Brazil." In *Distortions to Agricultural Incentives in Latin America*, ed. K. Anderson and M. Valdés, 87–118. Washington, DC: World Bank.

Mackenzie, F. 1993. "Exploring the Connections: Structural Adjustment, Gender and the Environment." *Geoforum* 24 (1): 71–87.

Maertens, M. 2008. "Horticulture Exports, Agro-Industrialization and Farm-Nonfarm Linkages with the Smallholder Farm Sector: Evidence from Senegal." LICOS Discussion Paper 214/2008, Katolieke Universiteit Leuven, Belgium.

Maertens, M., and J. Swinnen. 2006. "Trade, Standards, and Poverty: Evidence from Senegal." LICOS Discussion Paper 177/2006, Katolieke Universiteit Leuven, Belgium.

Mamman, A. B. 2004. "Transport Aspects of Livestock Marketing at the Achida and Sokoto Kara Markets." Paper prepared under a network supported by the UK Department of International Development (DFID), Sokoto.

Maredia, M. K., and D. A. Raitzer. 2006. *CGIAR and NARS Partner Research in Sub-Saharan Africa: Evidence of Impact to Date*. Rome: Science Council Secretariat, CGIAR.

McMillan, M., K. Horn, and D. Rodrik. 2002. "When Economic Reform Goes Wrong: Cashews in Mozambique." NBER Working Paper No. 9117, National Bureau of Economic Research, Cambridge, MA.

MENR (Ministry of Environment and Natural Resources). 2005. "National Biodiversity Strategy and Action Plan." Lusaka, Zambia.

Ndulu, B. 2007. *Challenges of African Growth: Opportunities, Constraints, and Strategic Directions*. Washington, DC: World Bank.

Neef, A., and R. Schwarzmeier. 2001. *Land Tenure and Rights in Trees and Forests: Interdependencies, Dynamics and the Role of Development Cooperation: Case Studies from Mainland Southeast Asia*. Eschborn, Germany: Deutsche Gesellschaft für Technische Zusammenarbeit (German Agency for Technical Cooperation; GTZ).

NESDB (National Economic and Social Development Board), Government of Thailand. 2006. "Poverty in Thailand." Knowledge Management and Poverty Reduction Policy Unit, Community Economic Development and Income Distribution Office, Bangkok.

Nijhoff, J. J., D. Tschirley, T. Jayne, G. Tembo, P. Arlindo, B. Mwiinga, J. Shaffer, M. Weber, C. Donovan, and D. Boughton. 2003. "Coordination for Long-Term Food Security by Government, Private Sector and Donors: Issues and Challenges." Policy Synthesis No. 65, Michigan State University, East Lansing, Michigan.

Nobel, A. D., and S. Suzuki. 2005. "Improving the Productivity of Degraded Cropping Systems in Northeast Thailand: Improving Farmer Practices with Innovative Approaches." Proceedings of the International Conference on Research Highlights and Vanguard Technology on Environmental Engineering in Agricultural Systems, Kanazawa, Japan, September 12–15, 371–80.

North, D. C. 1990. *Institutions, Institutional Change, and Economic Performance.* Cambridge: Cambridge University Press.

Nweke, F. 2004. "New Challenges in the Cassava Transformation in Nigeria and Ghana." EPTD Discussion Paper 118, IFPRI, Washington, DC. http://www.ifpri.org/divs/eptd/dp/papers/eptdp118.pdf.

Nweke, F., D. S. C. Spencer, and J. K. Lynam, eds. 2002. *The Cassava Transformation: Africa's Best Kept Secret.* East Lansing: Michigan State University Press.

OAE (Office of Agricultural Economics), Government of Thailand. 1973–2005. *Agricultural Statistics of Thailand.* Bangkok.

———. 1981. *Selected Economic Indicators Relating to Agriculture* 84 (5): 65. Bangkok. (in Thai)

———. 1985. "Facts about Thai Agriculture." Agricultural Economic Report 56, Ministry of Agriculture and Cooperatives, Bangkok. (in Thai)

———. 2001. "Agricultural Statistics of Thailand Crop Year 2000/2001." Agricultural Statistics 9/2001, 142–43, Ministry of Agriculture and Cooperatives, Bangkok.

———. 2006. "Commodity Profile." Bangkok. http://www.oae.go.th/OAE-WEB-SITE/profile/commodityPRo/index.html.

OECD and FAO. 2008. *Agricultural Outlook 2008–2017.* Paris and Rome: OECD and FAO.

OEPP (Office of Environmental Policy and Planning), Government of Thailand. 2002. "National Report on the Implementation of Convention on Biological Diversity: Thailand." Ministry of Science, Technology and Environment. Bangkok.

Ongile G. 1999. "Gender and Agricultural Supply Responses to Structural Adjustment Programmes. A Case Study of Smallholder Tea Producers in Kericho, Kenya." Research Report No 109, Nordik African Institute, Uppsala.

Oniang'o, R. 1999. "Trends in Women's Contributions to Agricultural Productivity: Lessons from Africa." Paper prepared for the Conference on the Roles, Constraints and Potentials of Women in Agricultural Development, Centre for Social Development, Bonn, Germany, Aug. 26–27.

Pandey, S., N. Khiem, H. Waibel, and T. Thien. 2006. "Upland Rice, Household Food Security and Commercialization of Upland Agriculture in Vietnam." International Rice Research Institute, Los Banos, Philippines.

Panyakul, V. 2001. "Organic Agriculture in Thailand." A national report prepared for ESCAP. In *Exploring the Potential of Organic Farming for Rural Employment and Income Generation in Asia*. Thailand: Earth Net Foundation.

Pardey, P. G., J. James, J. Alston, S. Wood, B. Koo, E. Binenbaum, T. Hurley, and P. lewwe. 2007. "Science, Technology and Skills." Background paper for *WDR 2008*, International Science and Technology Practice and Policy (InSTePP) Center, University of Minnesota, St. Paul, MN; and CGIAR, Science Council Secretariat, Rome. http://www.instepp.umn.edu/documents/Pardey%20et%20al%202007%20—%20Science%20Technology%20&%20Skills.pdf.

Peters, P., and M. G. Herrera. 1994. "Tobacco Cultivation, Food Production, and Nutrition among Smallholders in Malawi." In *Agricultural Commercialization, Economic Development, and Nutrition*, ed. J. von Braun and E. Kennedy. Baltimore: Johns Hopkins University Press.

Pingali, P. L., Y. Bigot, and H. Binswanger. 1992. *Agricultural Mechanization and the Evolution of Farming Systems in Sub-Saharan Africa*. Baltimore: Johns Hopkins University Press.

Pinthong, J. ed. 1992. *Evolution of Forest Occupancy for Farming*. 2nd ed. Bangkok: Institute of Local Community Development. (in Thai)

Platteau, J-P., and Y. Hayami. 1996. "Resource Endowments and Agricultural Development: Africa vs. Asia." In *The Institutional Foundation of East Asian Economic Development: Proceeding of the International Economic Association Conference, Tokyo*, ed. Y. Yayami and M. Aoki. New York: Macmillan.

Porter, M. E. 1998. *The Competitive Advantage of Nations*. New York: Free Press.

Poulton, C. 1998. "Cotton Production and Marketing in Northern Ghana: The Dynamics of Competition in a System of Interlocking Transactions." In *Smallholder Cash Crop Production Under Market Liberalisation: A New Institutional Economics Perspective*, ed. A. Dorward, J. Kydd and C. Poulton, 113–76. Wallingford: CAB International.

Ratanawaraha, C., N. Senanarong, and P. Suriyaphan. 2000. "Status of Cassava in Thailand: Implications for Future Research and Development." In *A Review of Cassava in Asia with Country Case Studies on Thailand and Vietnam*. Proceedings of the Validation Forum on the Global Cassava Development Strategy, Rome, April 26–28, Vol. 3, 1–62. Rome: FAO/International Fund for Agricultural Development.

Ribemboim, J. 1997. "Meio Ambiente e Competitividade Global: os casos do camarão e das florestas brasileiras." Textos para Discussão n 405, Universidade Federal de Pernambuco, Departamento de Economia, dez, Recife.

Ricardo, D. 1821. *On the Principles of Political Economy and Taxation*. 3rd ed. London: John Murray.

Robinson, P., J. Govereh, and D. Ndlela. 2009. "Zambia." In *Distortions to Agricultural Incentives in Africa*, ed. K. Anderson and W. A. Masters, 175–204. Washington, DC: World Bank.

Rodrik, D., ed. 2003. *In Search of Prosperity: Analytical Narratives on Economic Growth*. Princeton, NJ: Princeton University Press.

Rosegrant, M. W., J. Huang, A. Sinha, H. Ahammad, C. Ringler, T. Zhu, T. B. Sulser, S. Msangi, and M. Batka. 2008. "Exploring Alternative Futures for Agricultural Knowledge, Science and Technology (AKST)." ACIAR Project Report ADP/2004/045, IFPRI, Washington, DC.

Rubin, D. S. 1990. *Women's Work and Children's Nutrition in South-Western Kenya*. New York: United Nations University Press.

Schiff, M., and A. Valdés. 1998. "The Plundering of Agriculture in Developing Countries." In *International Agricultural Development*, 3rd ed., ed. C. K. Eicher and J. M. Staatz, 226–33. Baltimore, MD: Johns Hopkins University Press.

Schuh, G. E. 1976. "The New Macroeconomics of Agriculture." *American Journal of Agricultural Economics* 58: 802–11.

Singer, P. 2002. *One World: The Ethics of Globalization*. The Terry Lectures. New Haven, CN/London: Yale University Press.

Songwe, V., and K. Deininger. 2008. "Foreign Investment in Agricultural Production: Opportunities and Challenges." Photocopy, World Bank, Washington, DC.

Sorensen, A., and D. von Bulow. 1990. "Gender and Contract Farming in Kericho, Kenya." Project Paper 90.4, Centre for Development Research, Copenhagen.

Sumner, D. A. 2003. "A Quantitative Simulation Analysis of the Impacts of U.S. Cotton Subsidies on Cotton Prices and Quantities." Paper presented to the WTO Cotton Panel (DS267), October 26, Rome.

Tefft, J., J. Staatz, and J. Dioné. 1997. "Impact of the CFA Devaluation on Sustainable Growth for Poverty Alleviation: Preliminary Results." Bamako, Mali: INSAH/PRISAS.

Tefft, J., and V. Kelly. 2004. "Understanding and Reducing Child Malnutrition in Mali: Interim Research Findings for the Project on Linkages between Child Nutrition and Agricultural Growth (LICNAG)." Agricultural Economics Staff Paper 2004-27, Michigan State University, East Lansing.

Temple, J., and L. Wößmann. 2006. "Dualism and Cross-Country Growth Regressions." *Journal of Economic Growth* 11 (3): 187–228.

Tyler, G. 2008a. "The African Sugar Industry–A Frustrated Success Story." Background paper prepared for the Competitive Commercial Agriculture in Africa (CCAA) study, World Bank, Washington, DC.

———. 2008b. "Critical Success Factors in the African High Value Horticulture Export Industry." Background paper prepared for the Competitive Commercial Agriculture in Africa (CCAA) study, World Bank, Washington, DC.

Unger, R. M. 2007. *Free Trade Reimagined: The World Division of Labor and the Method of Economics*. Princeton, NJ: Princeton University.

Vityakon, P. 2007. "Degradation and Restoration of Sandy Soils under Different Agricultural Land Uses in Northeast Thailand: A Review." *Land Degradation & Development* 18 (5): 567–77.

Vityakon, P., S. Subhadhira, V. Limpinuntana, S. Srila, V. Tre-loges, V. Sriboonlue. 2004. "From Forest to Farm Fields: Changes in Land Use in Undulating Terrain of Northeast Thailand at Different Scales during the Past Century." *Southeast Asian Studies* 41(4): 444–72. http://nels.nii.ac.jp/els/110000281317.pdf;jsessionid=7C494BB5D9F11FD27571A98E57D73131?id=ART0000718691&type=pdf&lang=en&host=cinii&order_no=&ppv_type=0&lang_sw=&no=1237994870&cp=.

von Braun, J., and E. Kennedy, eds. 1994. *Agricultural Commercialization, Economic Development, and Nutrition*. Baltimore: Johns Hopkins University Press.

Walkenhorst, P. 2009. "Nigeria." In *Distortions to Agricultural Incentives in Africa*, ed. K. Anderson and W. A. Masters, 441–62. Washington, DC: World Bank.

Williamson, D. R., A. J. Peck, J. V. Turner, and S. Arunin. 1989. "Groundwater Hydrology and Salinity in a Valley in Northeast Thailand." In *Groundwater Contamination*, International Association of Hydrological Sciences (IAHS) Publication 185, 147–54.

World Bank and NESDB, Government of Thailand. 2005. *Thailand: Northeast Economic Development Report*. Washington, DC: World Bank; and Bangkok: NESDB. http://siteresources.worldbank.org/INTTHAILAND/Resources/333200-1097667766090/need_report-2005-eng.pdf.

World Bank. 2004. Transport sector data, Sub-Saharan Africa Transport Policy Program. http://go.worldbank.org/TEBRX0FYT0.

———. 2005a. "Food Safety and Agricultural Health Standards and Developing Country Exports: Re-Thinking the Impacts and the Policy Agenda." World Bank, Washington, DC.

———. 2005b. "Mozambique – Country Economic Memorandum: Sustaining Growth and Reducing Poverty." Report No. 32615-MZ, World Bank, Washington, DC.

———. 2007a. "Cultivating Knowledge and Skills to Grow African Agriculture: A Synthesis of an Institutional, Regional, and International Review." Agricultural and Rural Development Department, World Bank, Washington, DC. http://go.worldbank.org/VO99X3ZUA0.

———. 2007b. "Investment in Agricultural Water for Poverty Reduction and Economic Growth in Sub-Saharan Africa." A collaborative programme of ADB, FAO, IFAD, IWMI, and World Bank. Synthesis Report, World Bank, Washington, DC. http://siteresources.worldbank.org/RPDLPROGRAM/Resources/459596-1170984095733/synthesisreport.pdf.

————. 2007c. *World Development Report 2008: Agriculture for Development.* Washington, DC: World Bank. http://go.worldbank.org/LBJZD6HWZ0.

————. 2009. *Global Economic Prospects 2009: Commodities at the Crossroads.* World Bank, Washington, DC.

World Economic Forum. 2007. *Global Competitiveness Report 2007–2008.* Davos: World Economic Forum.

Yee, P. H., and M. Paludetto. 2005. "Nigeria: Value and Supply Chain Study." Final Report prepared for the World Bank, Consilium International Inc. Seattle, Washington.

Zeddies, J., R. P. Schaab, P. Neuenschwander, and H. R. Herren. 2001. "Economics of Biological Control of Cassava Mealybug in Africa." *Agricultural Economics* 24 (2): 209–19.

Index